Life in the Age of Exploration

Published by

The Reader's Digest Association Limited

London New York Sydney Montreal

JOURNEYS INTO THE PAST

LIFE IN THE AGE OF EXPLORATION

Life in the Age of Exploration
Edited and designed by Toucan Books Limited
Sole author: Christopher Falkus

First edition copyright © 1994
The Reader's Digest Association Limited,
11 Westferry Circus, Canary Wharf,
London E14 4HE
www.readersdigest.co.uk

Reprinted with amendments 2001

Printing and binding:
Printer Industria Gráfica S.A, Barcelona
Paper: Perigord-Condat, France

ISBN 0 276 42125 6

A Wider World A picture of life in the Far East, a place of exotic sights regarded with wonder by European visitors.

Front Cover (clockwise from top left): Vasco da Gama; Spanish coins; Indian brought to Europe by Columbus; fish market in Antwerp; Peruvian figure of Inca period; Columbus's ship, the *Santa Maria.*

Back Cover: Sea monster; astrolabe; market scene in Venice; wooden bowls used at sea; Indian with cacao utensils; map of Caribbean.

Page 1: An engraving of a ship sailing through unknown seas by the prolific artist Theodore de Bry.

Pages 2-3: A 16th-century sailing ship is seen through the window in this portrayal of Penelope refusing her suitors.

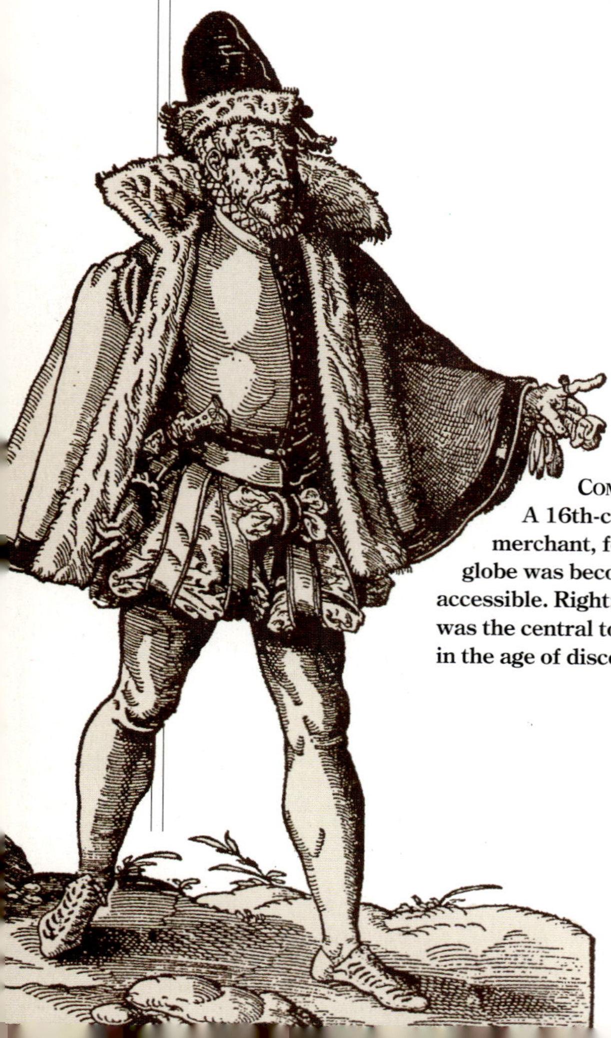

Commerce Rules A 16th-century merchant, for whom the globe was becoming ever more accessible. Right: The compass was the central tool of navigation in the age of discovery.

Contents

New Horizons 1492-1620 6

Ships and Seamen 13
Life in Port and Harbour 14
Ships and Supplies 23
Captain and Crew 32

Fortune Seekers in the New World 41
Pioneers of a New Age 42
Land of the Conquistadores 48
Along the Coast of Brazil 60

Settlers in North America 69
Seamen in Atlantic Waters 70
New France in the North 76
The English Colonists 85

Lands of Silks and Spices 95
Travellers in the East 96
The Portuguese Colonists 104
Life in China and Japan 118

Dark Continent and Southern Seas 125
Across Unknown Oceans 126
A Life of Slavery 133
People of the Pacific 143

Time Chart 150

Index 156

Acknowledgments 160

Triumph of the European
A Spaniard, supported by local allies, draws his sword against Mexican adversaries. The native inhabitants of America proved powerless against the horses and weaponry of the Old World.

NEW HORIZONS 1492–1620

The great age of European discovery started with Columbus's voyage to the New World. The era it created culminated in the settlement of the Pilgrim Fathers on the American continent.

THE DAILY LIFE of the maritime explorers was bound to the fortunes of their ships. Their households were the vessels they sailed in; their bedrooms and dining rooms were normally the crowded deck; and their neighbours were their shipmates. The day could consist of the hard monotony of shipboard routine; or perhaps a series of enchantments, landfalls on hitherto unknown islands, and encounters with welcoming natives; or perhaps sudden attacks, storms and shipwreck. But whatever the everyday pleasures or privations, these voyages were to transform our knowledge of the globe from one of ignorance and assumption into something recognisably modern in little more than a century.

The sheer hardiness of these European ocean voyagers was amazing. The discoverers had to

FEARS, IMAGINED AND REAL **A medieval view of outlandish creatures that were thought to inhabit far-off places. Below: *The Storm,* painted by Pieter Bruegel the Elder in 1568, vividly portrays every sailor's nightmare.**

CENTURIES OF IGNORANCE A view of the globe that lasted from the days of the ancient Greeks until the age of the discoverers.

overcome extremes of weather, from the ice-bound waters of the Arctic to the insufferable heat of the tropical sun. Shipboard illness was a constant threat and even on a successful voyage a quarter of the crew, or more, could be dead before the ship reached its destination. The illnesses were horrible – scurvy through want of fresh food, or any one of a number of contagious diseases such as smallpox and cholera.

If these were not frightening enough, there were fears born of ignorance: legends of sea monsters, for example, or unnavigable currents that swept all ships to their doom. Navigation itself was a hazard: instruments such as the quadrant and astrolabe were useful, yet no one could calculate longitude with any exactness throughout the age of exploration. This meant that the scale of the globe was a mystery, and that the sizes of the Atlantic and the Pacific Ocean, or the landmass that proved to be America, were far greater than anyone realised at the time. As late as the American War of Independence in the 1770s, Virginia claimed territorial rights stretching to the Pacific, believing that this consisted of a hinterland of 300 miles (480 km) at most.

Some of the pioneers were motivated partly by curiosity, others by thoughts of fabled wealth in far-off lands. For the 16th century abounded in stories of rich but mythical kingdoms: the gold of El Dorado or of the Seven Cities of Cibola; the lands of a 'lost' Christian

THE SAILOR'S PRAYER Sailors from Catholic Europe prayed to the Virgin Mary as they sought to spread their faith across the world.

heathen. After all, the Bible taught them that Christ's Second Coming would follow the Word of God once it had spread to all parts of the world – a powerful incentive in an age of faith.

The age of exploration – from Columbus's discovery of the New World to the settlement of the Pilgrim Fathers in New Plymouth – was an astonishing episode in the history of fortitude, faith and force of arms. The Atlantic yielded the secret of the American continent; the Pacific Ocean was discovered and navigated for the second time – the Polynesians having done this many centuries earlier; the route to the East, via the Cape of Good Hope, established a passage that was followed by voyagers until the opening of the Suez Canal in 1869; and global colonisation began its relentless spread. It was the start of what became known as the 'triumph of the West'.

king called Prester John; the treasures of the Island of Hy-Brasil; and the Fountains of Eternal Youth believed, at the time, to lie in Florida. Other motives included the ambitions of the European powers themselves, who were anxious to lay claim to overseas possessions and, above all, to the trade in spices and precious metals. But, in many ways, it was the missionaries, particularly the Jesuits, who were the 'professional colonists' of the age, learning native languages, building churches and converting the

DID YOU KNOW?

Visits to Chinese officials were formal affairs centring on the 'kow-tow', an act of submission whereby the 'barbarian', or tribute-bearer, knelt three times and bowed his head to the ground nine times before the high official who received him. Europeans who found this humiliating did not realise that it was part of court etiquette, and that the emperor performed the kow-tow to the images of his ancestors in heaven.

A World Full of Indians

The West's 'triumph' was, naturally, one that reflected the European point of view – a perspective reinforced by the very words we sometimes use today to describe inhabitants of many parts of the globe. The Europeans (initially the Portuguese or Spanish, and subsequently the French, Dutch and English) were looking for 'the Indies' – that land of Asian wealth known to them only from such trade as passed through Arab hands in the Eastern Mediterranean or from the *Travels of Marco Polo*. And so, because captains and governments are reluctant to admit mistakes, we now find the world full of 'Indians'. There are the Indians of North America; Central American Indians; South American Indians; the Indians of India; the inhabitants of the East Indies where the Dutch established themselves in Indonesia; and the West Indians of the Caribbean.

NEW WAYS A Spanish priest gives Holy Communion to Mexican Indian converts. The 'new religion' is still dominant in Latin America today. Below: An Indian drawing of the *encomienda* system, a method of land appropriation and forced labour that the European settlers initiated.

With hindsight, the European 'triumph' may appear inevitable, but the positions could easily have been reversed. Muslim ships that plied the Indian Ocean as far as Madagascar, and Chinese junks that ranged over the same ocean, could easily have reached the Cape from the East.

But the period between Columbus's voyage in the *Santa Maria* to the colony established by the passengers of the *Mayflower* was not just one of geographical discovery. It was an age of expansion in a wider sense. For example, the Portuguese travelling round the Cape and up the east coast of Africa found well-established Muslim trading posts busily exchanging goods across the Indian Ocean with India and the Spice Islands. They found a world new to them, but one that had existed for centuries for the Arabs. The 16th century was also the first age of global empire, as colonists followed in the wake of the discoverers to found settlements and to create distinctive colonial lifestyles in Mexico, Peru, Brazil

EUROPE'S IMPACT A depopulated African village, ravaged by the combined effects of slave-trading, disease and exploitation.

and North America, and in India, South-east Asia and the Far East. Alongside the seafarers went other travellers, who made spectacular overland journeys to the East via the Asian deserts, or perhaps to the unexplored inland areas of North America.

The spread of the Europeans was one side of the coin; their impact on native cultures was the other. Lifestyles as rich as those of the Aztecs in Mexico, as diverse as the societies of the American Indians, and as simple as those of the Eskimos of the far north or the Polynesians of the South Seas, were changed permanently when the first Europeans arrived. Sometimes they vanished altogether. Nobody knows, for example, exactly how many people lived in Hispaniola when Columbus landed; half a century later they had been wiped out. In South and Central America millions more died, falling before the weapons, the forced-labour schemes and, above all, the diseases brought by the Europeans. To replace the vulnerable Indians of the New World and to dig the mines, black slaves were transported in ever-increasing numbers from Africa. As a result, the everyday lives of countless numbers of native peoples, with centuries of tradition behind them, were transformed with brutal suddenness. Yet in some places it was the Europeans who had to adjust. In the confident and highly sophisticated civilisation of China, it was the visitors who had to conform to

FASHION FROM CHINA Items such as these porcelain plates, dishes and jars set a style for Europeans to adopt.

the customs of their hosts, often in ways that to them seemed humiliating.

The age of exploration had an impact everywhere. In Europe, ports such as Lisbon flourished as never before, becoming centres of trade in spices and other commodities from all over the world. Gold and silver from America played havoc with the finances of Europe. Tobacco addiction spread from its New World home, while alcohol went the other way. African servants in Brazil wore European styles of fashion, while in the Far East wealthy Europeans were carried about in elaborate local sedan chairs by native bearers. European languages, particularly English, Portuguese and Spanish, spread around the globe to places where they are still spoken today. The horse transformed the lives of Latin American farmers and the Plains Indians, while the introduction of cattle, sheep and sugar cane to the New World had an equally fundamental impact. And the Cross – in the form of Christian monuments, churches and mission huts – followed the traders throughout the world.

Missionary activity, though, was not always one-sided. The Jesuits in Asia sometimes 'went native', wearing Buddhist or Brahmin robes and adopting many of the rituals of the 'heathen' creeds; their colleagues were critical, questioning exactly who was converting whom. As well as meeting resistance of an instinctive kind because people wanted to cling on to ancient traditions and customs, the missionaries also met with more reasoned opposition. One American Indian leader, threatened by the Spanish authorities because he refused to be converted, asked if there were likely to be any Spaniards in Heaven. When told there certainly were, he refused conversion on the grounds that he had already met enough in this world and had no wish for further encounters in the next. In the same way, Huron Indians sometimes rejected French efforts, telling the priests that they had no wish to go to Heaven which, from their accounts, was likely to be overrun with Frenchmen.

A Changing World

The discoveries may have had little immediate effect on the peasants of Europe, many of whom still lived as serfs, or indeed on the inhabitants of untouched islands and unvisited interiors. But for the explorers themselves, and for millions of indigenous peoples all over the world, everyday life changed with bewildering speed. It was the beginning of a process which, by the 20th century, would have left no one on the planet unaffected.

One of the most revolutionary changes was colonialism, and the imposition of a 'Western' culture across the globe. The age of exploration led to the expansion of Europe and to the spread of resources and technologies from great European areas of settlement such as the United States of America, Asia

High Life The Spanish in Peru displayed their wealth in ostentatious imitation of Europe's nobility.

and Australia. Thus the languages, laws and institutions of the 'mother countries' spread throughout the world. The rest of the world became possessions or spheres of influence under the domination of the European powers: the British in India, for example, the Dutch in South Africa, the French in Indochina, and the Iberians in South America. Lives across the world would become subject to decisions taken in the capitals of Europe.

RED HOT Cayenne pepper comes from a plant native to South and Central America.

Europe's needs became the engine of development overseas. Such developments included the vast meat industries of South America, rubber plantations in Malaya, tea plantations in India, and cotton and tobacco supplies from the New World. The exploitation of these seemingly unlimited supplies of raw materials in the 16th century eventually turned the wheels of Europe's Industrial Revolution in the 18th and 19th centuries.

Colonialism also provided opportunities for many who would never have succeeded at home. Those who sought a new life overseas were, on the whole, drawn from the less privileged classes in society, or from families whose fortunes had collapsed. The nobles and financial grandees took little part directly in overseas expansion, though they participated in some of it as business ventures. Thus the conquistadores were not great noblemen, or even professional soldiers; many of the British in North America were not drawn from the landowning classes; and many of the settlers in Asia and Africa were without prospects at home (some of them had been transported as undesirables or convicts). For these people, a life overseas generally entailed hard work for generation after generation.

In one spectacular instance, the colonial lifestyle led to a direct challenge to the mother country and to the creation of the world's greatest democracy. It was no accident that the hard-earned sense of freedom enjoyed by the British settlers of North America proved strong enough to turn the tables on one of the great European powers. In turn, it was the words and deeds, from across the Atlantic, of George Washington and Benjamin Franklin that helped to inspire the French Revolution and the beginning of a new era of liberty. Such dramatic changes in the lives of millions stemmed directly from the age of exploration, and the opportunities it created for people to develop away from the oppressive restrictions of the previous centuries.

OLD AND NEW A Spanish-style gateway cut into the old walls of the Inca city of Cuzco symbolises the imposition of Spanish rule on the indigenous culture.

SHIPS AND SEAMEN

Wind and current alone propelled the ships of the age of exploration, when the crews of fragile-seeming sailing vessels made epic voyages into uncharted seas. They faced extremes of climate and dangerous coastlines. The achievements of the explorers and of the ships they sailed redrew the maps of the world, and led Europeans to settle in colonies across the globe.

LIFE IN PORT AND HARBOUR

Ports great and small studded Europe's coastline, and were crucial to their nations' trading fortunes and defences. They were the centres of shipbuilding skills that made the age of exploration possible.

ALREADY, BEFORE DAYBREAK, farmers and their sleepy-eyed families were arriving in carts from the surrounding countryside. They were going to market, the port's daily fair, with freshly laid eggs, oven-baked bread and new-made cheeses, hoping for a good price. At dawn – for life in the port, as elsewhere, was dictated by daylight hours – the cries of seagulls mixed with shouts from the market place and streets: 'Fresh herrings, fresh mackerel.' From the halls of the great merchants' houses, servants hurried out to make their purchases. Their masters and mistresses, however, would be staying at home for a while yet.

VAGABONDS The dreaded 'sturdy rogues'. Below: The rural life.

The rest of the port was already wide awake. Shopkeepers were unbolting their doors; other townspeople were beginning to crowd the streets and squares. Here and there stragglers could be seen, swaying after night-long vigils in cheap taverns. Some were sailors making the most of brief spells ashore before sailing with the morning tide.

The noise swelled with the din from the market-place: the growing clatter of foot, hoof and wheel along cobbled stones; the babble of the street, some of it in foreign tongues as befitted a port. The sound of grinding and clanging came from the shipyards, mingling with the yells of urchins at play or at their task of chasing the horses to collect saleable manure. Smells, too, were everywhere: that of hay coming from hundreds of stables – which were as common then as garages are today; the smells of bread, fruit, vegetables and meat; salt smells from the sea and harbour, and the smells of fish and tar – known only to the people of the coasts.

Europe during the age of exploration was still overwhelmingly rural. The bulk of the population was bound to the land, through either the ties of feudal serfdom, which prevailed across central and eastern Europe, or those of subsistence farming in the more advanced countries such as England. In

England, some four-fifths of the people worked on the land, and even those who lived in towns often had access to fields or small plots where they kept goats and chickens and grew fruit and vegetables.

Tied to the Land

Rural society was static. Most people lived and died in the same county, seldom travelling more than a few miles from their home village. Travel was difficult and hazardous, and there were other restrictions on mobility, including wages that were never enough to live on and kept people tied to the village lands where they could cultivate the food they needed. In Elizabethan England, wages stood at around three pence a day with meals, or seven pence a day without, for an ordinary labourer.

In many countries, too, laws restricted people's freedom to move around and seek work. According to the English Statute of Artificers of 1563, local Justices of the Peace had to make sure that anyone not trained as a craftsman, or not worth 40s or more a year, was set to work as an agricultural labourer, with hours of 5 am to 8 pm in summer, or dawn to dusk in winter.

Governments everywhere had a horror of mobility, and passed numerous acts against 'Egyptians' (meaning gypsies), itinerant beggars and other such 'sturdy rogues and vagabonds'. In part, this fear was due to local authorities lacking the means to keep proper law and order, but it was also because supporting the poor imposed burdens on the parishes harbouring them.

This life was very different from that of the seaports, whose very existence depended on mobility. Here, some men earned their living by fishing in coastal waters, while others embarked on trading voyages that lasted a year or more and took them to the lands skirting the Indian Ocean or across the Atlantic to the New World of the Americas opened up in the wake of

Trade and Defence **The port of Naples, like many large ports, had a dual role. Right: The growing fishing industry needed new waters.**

HIGH AND LOW A merchant receives payment. Below: The coopers make storage barrels.

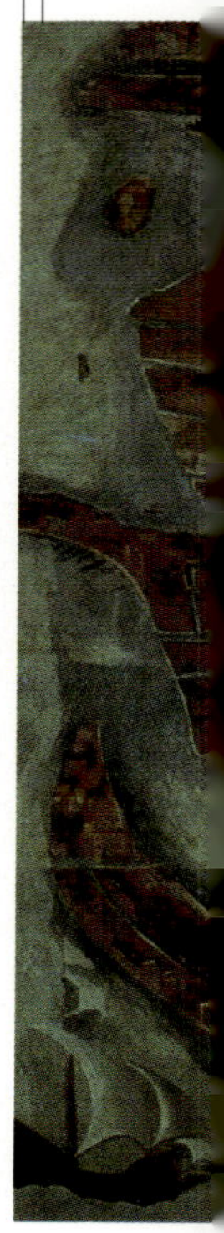

Columbus. One effect of the long trading missions was that large sections of the ports' male populations were away for much of the year, leading women to form close communities of their own. Women played more visible roles in the working life of ports – as market traders, shopkeepers and even financiers – than anywhere else.

The hazards of the sea could never be forgotten. The best fishing was in such inhospitable waters as those of the North Sea and Iceland; the age of exploration also opened up Newfoundland's Grand Banks, whose waters were filled with icebergs, fogs and reefs as well as fish. Cod fishing off Newfoundland started within a few years of John Cabot's voyage in 1497, and fleets were soon sailing regularly from France, Portugal and England. The fishermen of Brittany, Normandy and Gascony were particularly active. Thousands of tons were brought back to ports such as Dieppe and La Rochelle; in 1542, 60 vessels left La Rochelle for Newfoundland on the same day.

The crews of these ships did not receive wages. Normally, they would share one-third of the profits of the catch, the rest going to the owner. When the fleets arrived, the ports filled with 'factors', or middlemen, who made their purchases and arranged shipment onwards to other destinations – perhaps London, itself a great river port, or Paris.

Onward shipment, of many imported and exported goods, was a crucial element in the life of any port. Sizable ports, such as Bristol with about 10 000 inhabitants in 1500, had a substantial merchant elite dominating the trade, who built themselves splendid houses, and were benefactors of schools and churches and, as likely as not, were shipowners and financial investors, too. They were the dominant class, jealously preserving their many privileges.

Other occupations reflected the different aspects of the life of the sea. Probably the least popular people were the government officials. They were voices of authority, regulating traffic, licensing cargoes and manning the customs houses sited near the jetties. They checked travel documents, estimated the value of the cargoes, looked out for ships carrying illicit goods, and tried to ensure that holds were not overladen. They had a practised eye and made rough-and-ready calculations of ships' tonnages, which were the basis on which they levied government duties. The cargoes, meanwhile, would be loaded by porters, with supplies for a voyage bought from ships' chandlers, biscuit makers, brewers, rope makers, sail makers, instrument makers, map makers, coopers and so on. Ports also employed the artisans, craftsmen and traders found in other towns of comparable size: clothiers, shoemakers, stone masons, toolmakers, grocers, bakers, blacksmiths, silversmiths and pawnbrokers.

Like most towns, ports were still largely confined within their medieval walls. They also varied considerably in size. At the grand end of the scale were places such as London, one of Europe's largest cities, with a population at the end of the 16th century that some scholars estimate at 250 000 people – about the size of present-day Plymouth in England or Tampa in Florida. There were also the powerful north German ports such as Lübeck and Hamburg, which formed the Hanseatic League and dominated the trade of the Baltic. The great Italian seaports included Venice and Genoa, and there were other ports whose growth reflected the power of national governments, such as Antwerp (then in the Netherlands), the river port of Seville in Spain and Lisbon in Portugal. At the other end of the spectrum were smaller places that still had their days of fame. Columbus, for example, sailed from the small Spanish port of Palos; Jacques Cartier, the discoverer of the St Lawrence River in Canada, set out from St Malo in Brittany; some of Magellan's ships were built by the master shipbuilders of Bilbao, home of the Basques; and the Elizabethan sea dogs made the Devon port of Plymouth a name to be feared from Cadiz to Panama.

DID YOU KNOW?

When sailors' coats and hats wore out they made new ones from old sailcloth, called tarpaulin because it was treated with tar to make it waterproof. Clothes made of tarpaulin became standard uniform in heavy weather, and their wearers became known as 'tars'.

Sovereign over the Adriatic

In all this diversity, one port outshone all the others – Venice, Queen of the Adriatic. The driving force behind the early journeys of exploration was the desire to find new routes to the 'Indies', the eastern lands of gold, spices and silks. It was this trade that Venice monopolised by its domination of the eastern Mediterranean, through which most of the goods of the Orient reached Europe, via the Muslim traders of the Levant. Venice, in 1500, was a city-state of 120 000

East Meets West Luxuries from the East were imported into Venice for sale to the rest of Europe.

CROSSROADS AT LISBON

Portugal's explorers gave her an empire embracing all the known continents of the world.

LISBON PROSPERED during the age of exploration to become one of Europe's largest and richest cities. In 1490, its population stood at 40 000 people. By the end of the 16th century, it had quadrupled to 165 000 people. Wealthy merchants built great town houses and commissioned ocean-going fleets, while much of the revenue taken by the Portuguese Crown from the city's trade went towards fine churches, public buildings, wide streets and imposing squares. Little remains today of Renaissance Lisbon – as a result of the great earthquake that devastated the city on All Saints' Day in 1755 – but the Church of the Jeronimos, built to celebrate Vasco da Gama's voyage round the Cape of Good Hope in 1497-8, stands as a testament to its former glory.

That success was founded on trade in luxuries, notably slaves and spices. From the middle of the 15th century to the middle of the 16th, Portuguese traders established themselves right across the globe: from West Africa to Brazil; from East Africa to India; from Sri Lanka and Indonesia to China and Japan. Lisbon became the gateway between the Old World and the New.

The city's impact on the lives of people across all the continents was immense. It helped to meet insatiable demand in Europe for spices, perfumes, silks and lacquers from the East, at a time when Venice was no longer the dominant force it had been. At the same time, it was Lisbon that provided much of the slave labour on which the New World depended for its wealth from its deposits of precious metals and crops such as sugar and tobacco.

Its position at the centre of this worldwide network was achieved at royal command. The Crown kept monopolies of the most valuable commodities and employed many thousands of government officials in Lisbon who presided over, regulated and profited from its trade. Much of this trade was conducted at a vast emporium established in the beginning of the 16th century, the House of India. Goods passed through the House of India, and then those destined for Europe were directed through another government establishment, the House of Mines. These were two of the commercial hubs of Lisbon life, where fortunes were forged and lost, arrangements made for new ventures, and old accounts settled. Another, of course, was the great harbour where ships unloaded their cargoes and took on new ones.

The departure, every spring, of a fleet of up to 14 ships bound for India was a great event. Its *naos* and great carracks, some of 1000 tons, set off for an 18 month round trip accompanied by blaring trumpets and booming guns. On their return, the wharves, quaysides and warehouses would be filled with produce from all over the known world. Something of the flavour of mid-16th-century Lisbon can be recaptured from the lists of goods unloaded.

First there were the slaves, most of them from Africa's west coast, sullen, bewildered, manacled. By the end of the 16th century many thousands were being shipped each year for work in Brazil and other Iberian territories in America. European countries, especially those of the Mediterranean, bought slaves for household service.

Then there were the other cargoes, such as those of sugar and the much-prized red brazilwood from Brazil. Ivory, red and black peppers, musk and gold, as well as exotic animals like monkeys and parrots, came from West Africa; ebony, more gold and ivory, ambergris (a waxy substance secreted by sperm whales and used as a fixative in perfumes), ginger, indigo, coconut oil, diamonds and rubies, perfumes and precious woods came from East Africa, India and South-east Asia. Cinnamon, cloves, nutmeg, mace and the full panoply of luxuries from aromatic woods (such as sandalwood) to fragrant gum, resin, saffron and lacquer came from Sri Lanka and the Spice Islands; silks, porcelain and medicinal plants came from China and Japan.

Lisbon also traded within Europe in less exotic goods: wheat, cloth and manufactures of iron and bronze. But it was from its position at the crossroads of the world, importing and re-exporting across the globe, that its impact on daily life in the age of exploration was felt everywhere.

HER FINEST HOUR Portugal's empire in Asia, Africa and the New World brought Lisbon to a dazzling peak of activity and prosperity in the age of exploration.

BUYING AND SELLING The harbour at Venice, a major city, was a marketplace for over 100 000 citizens.

people, an important colonial power, the greatest city in Italy and a seaport of legendary wealth.

Its supremacy stemmed from its position on the Adriatic which enabled it to look both east and west, and hence to trade with Muslim and Christian alike. It was maintained by a republican government dedicated solely to the development and defence of her commercial prosperity. Here the rulers of the state were the merchants themselves, unlike Spain, for example, whose nobility was far too grand for commerce. Venice was in business at all levels of her society.

Thus life in Venice was geared to the customer: from the rich for whose palaces it manufactured the famous Venetian glass ornaments, to pilgrims making their way to the Holy Land and eager to buy the trinkets that were another Venetian speciality. By the standards of the time Venice was tolerant, too. Arabs, Jews and Christians all did business together, and that took precedence over religious or ideological considerations.

In all things, the Venetians were consummate professionals. One example was the running of a formidable state-owned navy which numbered 146 galleys in 1581 and, if mobilised in full, would have required a complement of 30 000 men. Naval activity centred on the Arsenal, the state dockyard. It was a complex of docks, slipways – some of them covered – and shipyards with every conceivable facility for fitting and rigging ships, using materials imported from many parts of Europe, as far east as the Black Sea. A galley could be towed down a channel past a series of warehouses and loaded with weapons and supplies from the windows as she passed. She would then be ready to sail.

It was assembly-line activity. The Arsenal, employing up to 3000 people, was the largest single industrial enterprise in Europe. Foreshadowing the Industrial Revolution, workers were clocked in after the ringing of a bell and, at the end of the day, clocked out.

DID YOU KNOW?

The phrase 'not enough room to swing a cat' refers to any confined space. It comes from the cat-o'-nine-tails used for flogging by almost all navies in the age of sail. The victim was lashed on his bare back, and if the space did not allow a full swing it lacked room to 'swing a cat'.

SERVICE AND DISCIPLINE

Discipline at work was severe, not least in Venice's great slave houses, where rigid controls dictated everything that happened. Venice's slaves came mainly from North Africa; some were sold as household servants, others were used as oarsmen in the galleys. If allowed out, they went in pairs, manacled and under guard. Food was closely regulated. In Genoa, which had a similar system, a slave's rations were laid down in 1552 as a daily biscuit, soup twice a month,

meat twice a year and wine after a hard row. In Venice, the slaves had bean soup every day, not for humanitarian reasons, but to keep up their strength for rowing.

Some aspects of life were common to most ports. In time of war, for example, port life everywhere was disrupted. Ships and crews were requisitioned; soldiers camped outside the towns waiting to embark. In dark alleyways, press gangs operated a

SEA MONSTER A carrack carried huge volumes of cargo, soldiers and guns. Above: An Arab trader offers the favours of his female associates to Oriental merchants.

form of legalised kidnapping to make up for shortfalls in the ships' crews.

Populations were cosmopolitan. Many ports had clearly defined quarters, called 'colonies', for foreign communities. They included an Italian colony in La Rochelle, an Irish one in Bristol, a Genoese in Seville. Crews, too, were multinational. Spaniards, Genoese, Sicilians, Portuguese, French, Flemings and one Englishman all served together in the fleet of the Portuguese explorer Ferdinand Magellan when he set off on the first circumnavigation of the world.

Ports were also well served by inns, some of them able to cater for 100 or more travellers, and had an

even greater supply of alehouses and taverns. The traveller could hire a horse for short journeys inland: in England the price was about three pence a mile. Carriers operated from the main ports to transport people's heavier luggage by road – too generous a word for the muddy tracks that linked even the largest cities. Rather than use roads, travellers preferred to use rivers and waterways, which were comfortable and safe compared with the roads.

PERILS AT SEA Navigational help was almost non-existent. Above: The bustle of river life.

The sea itself was the most dangerous element of all. Entrances to harbours were often treacherous, and channels were not marked. Nor were there any lighthouses in the modern sense. Crude beacons were erected on some headlands and at harbour entrances, and the burghers of Dieppe put up a coal-fired construction outside their harbour. Usually, however, the pilots had to make their way in without such assistance.

Daily life for the seaman, whether threatened by storms far out at sea or navigating offshore banks and reefs close to a home port, held permanent dangers, with constant reminders of the closeness of death. Probably because of this, coastal communities were conspicuously devout. Congregations prayed for the safety of the men at sea, and for many voyagers, like Christopher Columbus and his crew, their first act on landing was to hold a service to give thanks to God for their safety.

Ships and Supplies

The shipwrights of the age of exploration built for performance, not comfort. For the crews, conditions on board were cramped, and their food, water and other provisions quickly went foul.

To the casual observer a shipyard was a scene of chaos, but to the more tutored eye it was a scene of order and precision, with a multitude of different jobs expertly dovetailed. The food of the yard was its timber, which lay around in numerous stacks and piles. Some were of rough wood, others of wood that had already been cut and shaped; there were gigantic logs of oak, and pieces no more than a few inches long. At the yard's centre were the sawpits, domain of powerful sawyers and their assistants. They wielded their big two-handled instrument in pairs, often at the sawhorse which let the sawyer straddle the log from above while his assistant heaved and pushed from below.

Most of the men in the yard were carpenters, who brought their own equipment: saws, axes, adzes, chisels, mauls, augers, gauges, files, planes, hammers, levers. Carts trundled through

Square and Triangular European ships mixed their own square-rigged styles with those of the Arab shipbuilders. They adopted the triangular, or lateen, sail used by Arab ships in the Mediterranean for their caravels. Below: An early 16th-century illustration of a square-rigged *nao* and a lateen-rigged caravel.

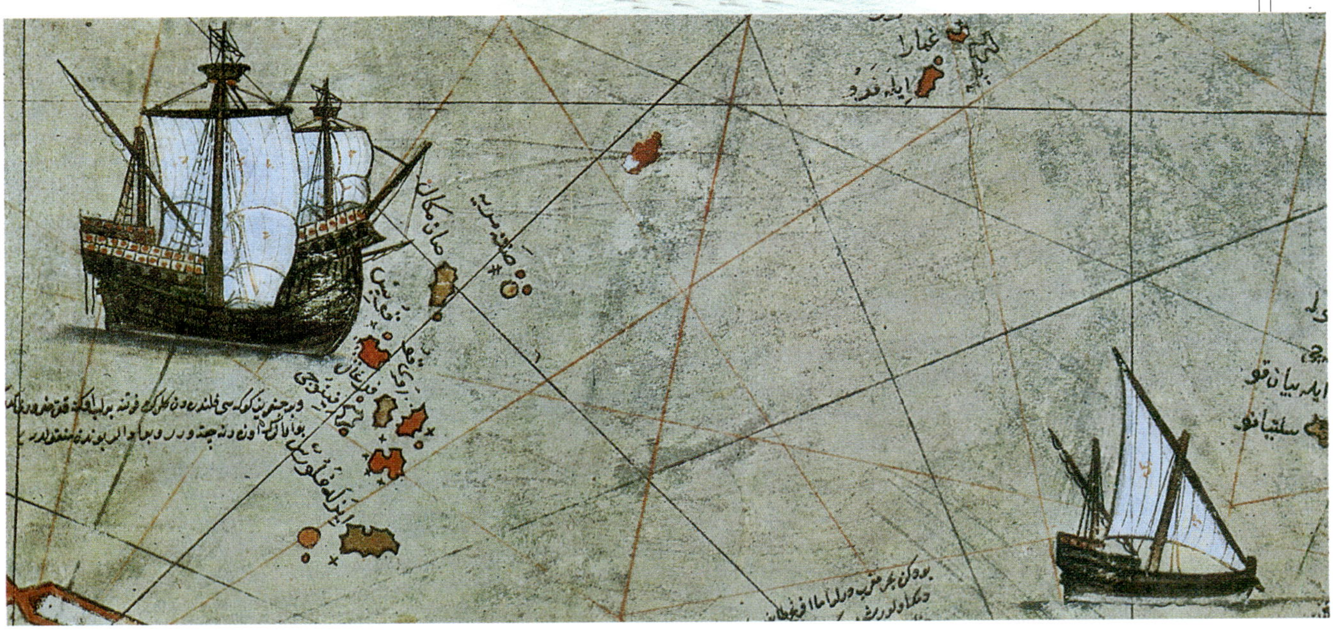

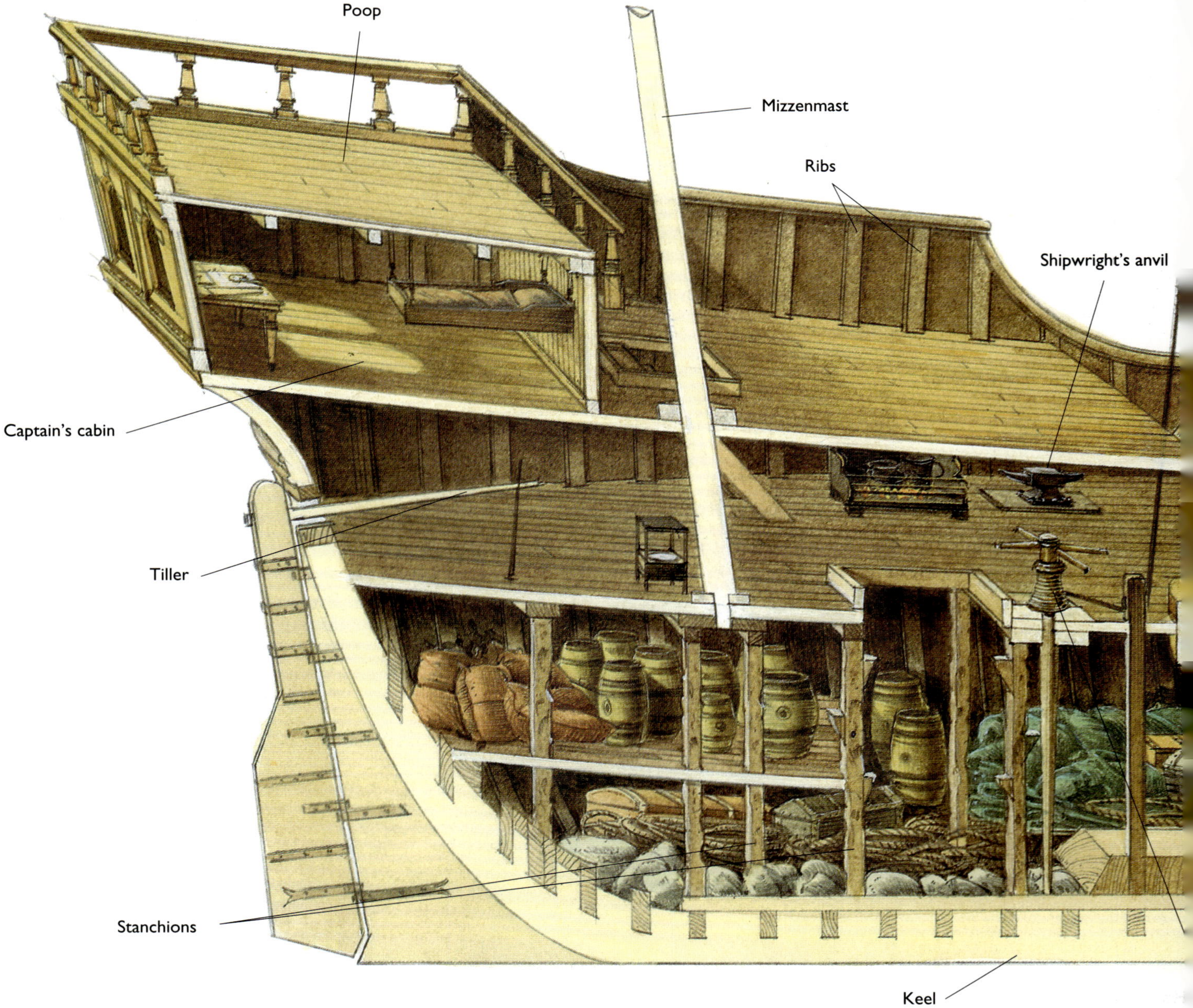

the gangs of workmen, moving logs from one stack to the next, one shed to another, or across to the jetty. In one corner of the yard stood the smithy and smiths: blackened, grimy men who worked with forge and bellows, hammer and anvil, fashioning clasps, rivets, bolts and other metal fittings. Theirs was fierce labour, carried out amid belches of smoke and searing heat. Elsewhere stood the stove, boiling pitch for the caulking teams. They carried the pitch in containers down to the slipways, and used it to make the hulls as watertight as possible; when they arrived, it was a sure sign that the hull was nearly ready for launching.

Somewhere in the yard, the captain himself might be casting an anxious eye around him, while his mind wandered to images of people and places as yet unseen. There, the work he saw now would prove itself in fortune or disaster for himself, his ship and his crew.

Small Ships in High Seas

Ships in the age of exploration were never large. In his first voyage to the New World, in 1492, Columbus had three ships: two caravels and his flagship, the *Santa Maria*, known as a *nao*. Caravels and *naos* were just two of the different types of ocean-going vessel

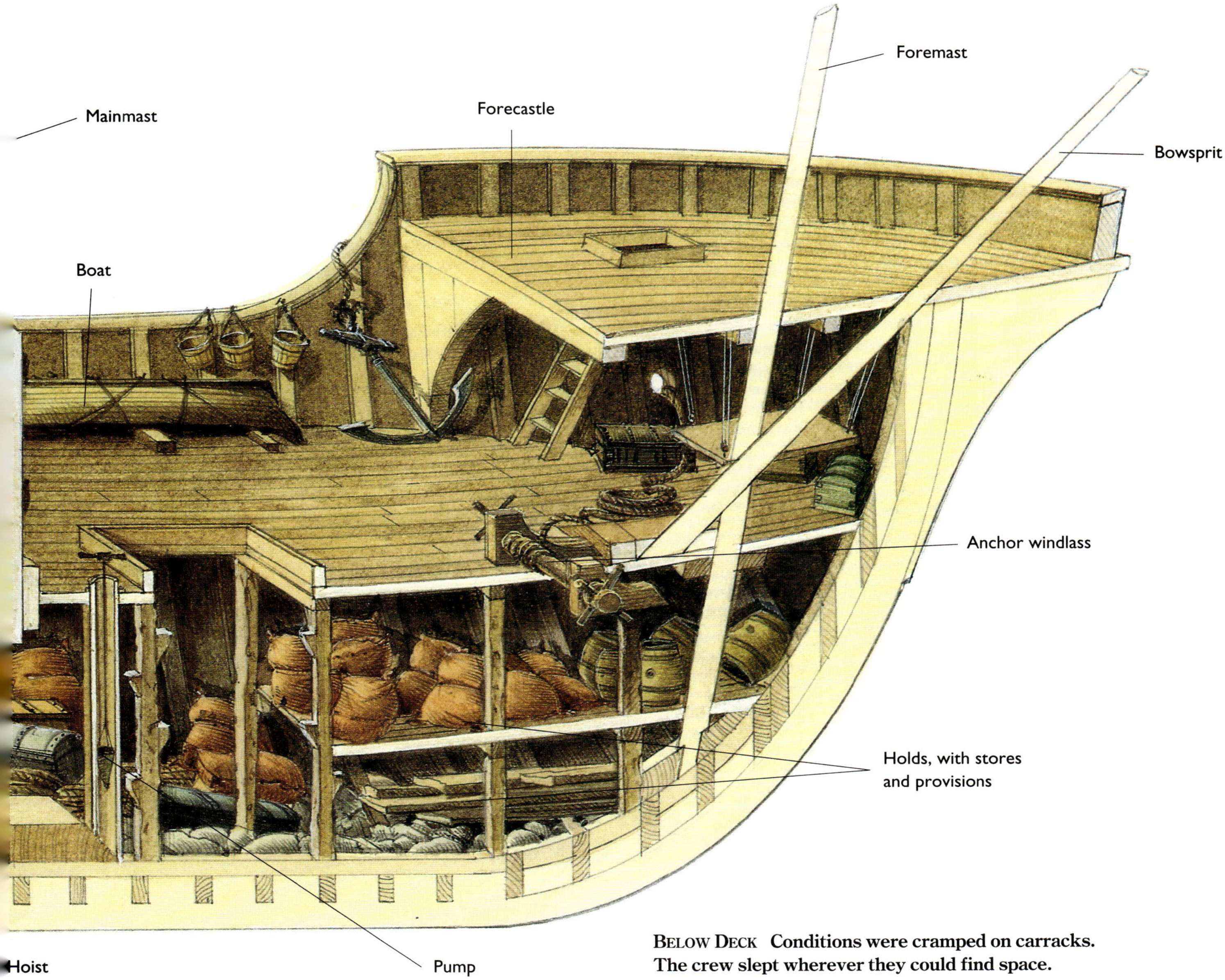

BELOW DECK Conditions were cramped on carracks. The crew slept wherever they could find space.

favoured by the European explorers. A caravel might be 50 to 60 tons (a term defining the ship's cargo-carrying capacity, rather than the weight of water displaced, as today). It measured between 55 and 70 ft (17 and 21 m) from stem to stern, and 19 to 25 ft (6 to 8 m) across – making it both narrower and shorter than a modern tennis court.

But for all their small size, the ships were sturdy, and in some ways – in speed across the Atlantic, for example – their performances would scarcely be excelled until as late as the 20th century. This was because later improvements generally emphasised comfort rather than speed, whereas the explorers' ships were, above all, functional.

Both the caravel and the *nao* usually had three masts: the main mast which carried the mainsail; the foremast ahead of it; and the mizzen mast behind. The earliest caravels had lateen – that is, triangular – sails which made them more manoeuvrable when they had to change course rapidly while tacking into a headwind. Lateen sails were less effective, however, when sailing before a steady wind, and this led more and more mariners to adopt square rigging (rectangular sails) for the foremast and main mast, leaving a lateen

MAESTRO **The shipwright makes precise calculations of the size and shape of every component of the ship.**

sail for the mizzen alone. A caravel of this size would carry between 22 and 27 men.

The *nao* was larger: about 100 tons, 90 ft (27 m) long and over 30 ft (9 m) in the beam. It could carry livestock, either to provide extra food for the crew or, more likely, to be shipped across the ocean for the early colonists of the New World. It might have a crew of about 40 men, and was always square-rigged.

The caravel was especially fast and agile. Being light, it also drew little water and could navigate shallows, which made it a favourite for negotiating entrances to strange harbours and inlets. As the age progressed, ocean-going ships tended to increase in size, so that some *naos* reached 500 or 600 tons and other ships 1500 or even 2000 tons. Some, such as galleys, were powered by banks of oars; others, such as the great galleons, were powered by sail; galleasses were a mixture of both, with oars to back up sail power when necessary.

BOOSTING THE FISH TRADE

Most Protestants regarded the Catholic tradition of having fish, rather than meat, on Friday – in memory of the day on which Christ was crucified – as no more than popish flummery. But some found the tradition useful. In Elizabethan England Wednesdays became another day for eating fish – in an attempt to encourage the fishing industry, rather than to foster piety.

THE MASTER SHIPWRIGHT

Shipbuilding was a specialised skill, and a master shipwright a man of substance. In Spain he was known as the *maestro* – an appropriate term since his role was like that of the conductor of an orchestra, with numerous individual activities to be coordinated. The *maestro* had to be designer, mathematician and builder.

It was no accident, of course, that major shipyards grew up where there were good supplies of wood and labour, and ready access to important sea-trading routes. Also vital were shipbuilding traditions, often built up over generations and sometimes associated with individual families of shipwrights. As in all areas of maritime life, particular regions acquired a reputation for particular skills. Just as people traditionally sought navigators from Portugal and gunners from Flanders, so ships built in Lagos, Seville, Le Havre, Bristol and, above all, Bilbao in the Basque region were particularly popular with the explorers.

The right kind of wood usually meant oak for strength and pine for planking. Much of Europe was still densely forested, which was just as well since as many as 80 mature oak trees went into a single 100 ton *nao*. The master shipwright supervised the tree felling and the first cutting of logs. It was an elaborate exercise, with gangs of axemen, sawyers, carriers and other helpers. They felled the trees soon after the last leaves fell in autumn, when the sap was low, an important consideration in the seasoning of timber.

Even before tree felling, there were tasks to be done. The builders drew up a design for the ship, and when they had made all the necessary calculations they fashioned templates, or exact models, of the key structures out of light wood. Carefully labelled, these templates were carted to the forest and matched as closely as possible to the trees felled; thus the convenient angles at which oak trees branched would be carefully preserved when they were suitable for the various knee-shaped joints required for reinforcing parts of the hull and decks.

Once 'live' work, as it was called, began, the shipyard operated at full throttle. Teams of carpenters and sawyers cut, honed and shaped the wood, and the pieces were repeatedly matched against the templates, with the master determining any necessary adjustments. Pine was cut into planks for the ship's sides and decks. Here they needed smooth surfaces, so that the water which constantly drenched the crew at sea would run off as quickly as possible.

Gradually, the ship's components were assembled: keel, long straight masts, sternpost, stempost and yards; curved beams for the hull; canvas and rope for

IN THE SHIPYARD Two sawyers cut a log into shape, while behind them lies the hull, nearing completion.

the sail and rigging; heavy iron anchors; planks for the sides and decks; powerful timbers to receive the rudder; and large cut stones (taking two men to carry them), which would be laid at the ship's bottom as fixed ballast.

Building the Hull

The hull's outline took shape on the shore, rather than at the yard – to prevent too much cumbersome material accumulating there. This 'skeleton' was a frame-first construction, built on wooden blocks and positioned so that it sloped gently towards the water.

The long, straight keel was always the first piece to be laid. It had to withstand the stresses of the whole structure and, in the middle, provide the point where the mainmast was fixed ('stepped'), secured by a series of reinforced wedges. This was the crucial meeting point for the strains of a rolling, plunging ship lashed by heavy seas and swept by fierce gales.

The keel dictated the size of the ship and, to a large extent, its behaviour at sea. If the keel was too short, the ship would ride high in the water and be vulnerable to winds coming from the side. If it was too long, the ship would sit low and be sluggish when rapid manoeuvres were required. The relation between the size of the keel and the rest of the ship varied, but the Portuguese had a simple rule of thumb for the *nao*: *As, dos, tres*; ace (one), two, three. This was a ratio for the breadth, length of the keel and length of the ship. A *nao* measuring 30 ft (9 m) across at its broadest point would have a keel 60 ft (18 m) long and would be 90 ft (27 m) or so from stem to stern. Caravels had longer keels than *naos* in relation to their size.

The timber cut for the sternpost (at the back) and the stempost (at the front) was also brought to the shore. The sternpost had to take the rudder – another point of stress – and be substantial enough for an

Hive of Activity **A team of shipwrights work on the frame of a caravel. Left: The final touches are added.**

NO LEAKS! Caulking – filling gaps between the planks with hemp and pitch – is one of the final stages before the launch.

opening for the tiller. At sea, this opening was the wettest place on the ship. While the hatches could be battened down and made watertight, nothing could be done about the gap in the sternpost, so that helmsmen must have been permanently soaked.

When the skeleton was finished, the builders added planking for the decks and sides and made the final preparations. These included the all-important job of caulking – that is, crushing shredded pieces of hemp (known as oakum) into the narrow gaps between the planks and finishing off with pitch. No wooden sailing ship was watertight, but it was the caulker's task to see that the ship at least started the voyage as impregnable as possible. Tallow (a kind of wax made from beef and mutton suet) was applied below the waterline, and even lead sheathing, too, to fend off the many highly destructive sea organisms, such as *teredo* shipworms which could turn a fine hull into shredded timber.

Eventually the hull was ready to be floated. The wooden blocks on which it was built were converted into greased slipways, and men on board pulled on ropes attached to the ship's anchor which was wedged firmly in the seabed out in the harbour. Launching was the moment, too, for a religious ceremony; in Catholic countries, everybody sang a traditional hymn, *Salve Regina,* as the hull went afloat.

The final preparations included putting up masts, rigging and sails; bringing on board equipment and provisions; and fitting the 'castles' fore and aft. The castles grew in size over the period. As the highest and driest part of the ship, the sterncastle in particular was used to provide extra accommodation. The masts were partially rigged before the backbreaking job of lifting them by crane and pulley began. Although the mainmast was secured through the deck to the keel, the others were simply attached to the deck. Shrouds of rigging fastened them to the hull, and doubled as rope ladders for climbing aloft.

The sailmaker, meanwhile, prepared cloth to fit the long poles, known as 'yards', that carried the sails. The mainyard was roughly the length of the ship and the sail canvas correspondingly vast. As the 16th century progressed, however, the mainsail area was reduced and topsails were added to both mainmast and foremast. Other additions were a square

OAR MAKER Ships carried rowing boats for ferrying men and supplies.

THE ARSENAL Carpenters at work in Venice's 'assembly belt', which built, supplied and launched ships.

spritsail (hanging from the bowsprit at the front), and a sail at the stern behind the lateen mizzen, known as the 'bonaventure' – possibly because *bonaventure* ('good fortune') was a common ship's name. Furthermore, rectangular 'bonnet' sails were fitted at the bottom of the main and foresails. This multiplication of sails made them much more flexible. The topsail, for example, could be furled, unfurled or removed without any of the labours involved in shortening or extending the mainsail.

With the hull equipped with masts, sail and rigging, the rest of the equipment was taken on board: rowing boats; stone and pebbles for extra ballast; pitch and tar for caulking; glass beads and bells for trading; tools, pumps, spare planking, canvas and rope, navigating instruments, anchors . . . and so on. Most important to the men, of course, were the supplies of food and drink.

FOOD AND DRINK

A good captain would choose and order these supplies himself. Columbus gave his views in a letter to Ferdinand and Isabella, the joint sovereigns of Spain, in about 1500:

'Victualling them should be done in this manner:

EYEWITNESS

THE CAVALRY IN THE NEW WORLD

UNTIL THEY WERE introduced from Europe in the age of exploration, horses were unknown in America. Their appearance caused panic among the inhabitants, giving European mounted soldiers an overwhelming advantage. This account of the seizure of Atahualpa, the Inca chief, by Governor Pizarro is by Pizarro's secretary, Francisco de Jeréz:

❛. . . he came to the litter where [Atahualpa] was, and fearlessly seized him by the arm . . . Then the guns were fired off, the trumpets were sounded, and the troops, both on horse and foot, sallied forth.

On seeing the horses charge, many of the Indians who were in the open space fled, and such was the force with which they ran that they broke down part of the wall surrounding it, and many fell over each other. The horsemen rode them down, killing and wounding, and following in pursuit . . .

So great was the terror of the Indians at seeing the Governor force his way through them . . . and beholding the charging of the horses, a thing never before heard of, that they thought more of flying to save their lives than of fighting.❜

CHARGERS Cortés's cavalry in Mexico.

the third part of the breadstuff to be good biscuit, well seasoned and not old, or the major portion will be wasted; a third part salted flour, salted at the time of milling [salt was an all-purpose preservative, used in most foods] ; and a third part of wheat. Further there will be wanted wine, salt meat, oil, vinegar, cheese, chick peas, lentils, beans, salt fish and fishing tackle, honey, rice, almonds and raisins.'

This was a good, varied diet by the standards of the time, but even if all of it was available there were still plenty of hazards. One was the water, which rapidly became algae-infested and undrinkable; as a result, it was rarely drunk while wine was available or, on English and Dutch ships, beer. The rations for a ship captained by the Elizabethan explorer Martin Frobisher into the Canadian Arctic, in 1578, included eight pints of beer per man per day.

The most obvious problem was keeping food and drink in reasonable condition and protecting them from worms and maggots. The iron-hard ship's biscuit, known to sailors through the ages as 'hardtack', was as vulnerable as anything else. Describing one of his father's voyages, Ferdinand Columbus wrote: 'What with the heat and dampness our ship's biscuit had become so wormy that, God help us, I saw many who waited for darkness to eat the porridge made of it, that they might not see the maggots; and others were so used to eating them that they did not even trouble to pitch them out because they might lose their supper had they been so nice [fussy] .'

Nevertheless, supplies on the relatively short transatlantic crossings – lasting weeks, rather than the months taken around the Cape of Good Hope to India – usually proved adequate. A Spanish record of the 1530s orders a daily ration of $1^{1}/_{2}$ lb (675 g) of bread, 2 pints (1.15 litres) of drinking water, 1 pint (570 ml) of bathing water and 2 pints of wine per man per day, in addition to a list of salt fish, salt meat, chick peas and cheese, all provided while supplies lasted. Frobisher stipulated – apart from the generous beer allowance – 1 lb (450 g) of biscuit per day, 1 lb of salt beef or pork per man on 'flesh' days and one dried codfish between four men on 'fish' days, which included Fridays when people abstained from meat in memory of Christ's death.

TREADMILL Heavy barrels could be lifted by cranes. This remarkable crane, worked by three men on a treadmill, was in Bruges, the rich port of Flanders.

CAPTAIN AND CREW

Every sailor had his job, from the captain-general of the fleet to the ship's boy who swept the decks. Each job was vital, and punishments for poor work were instant and harsh.

SEAFARING COMMUNITIES considered themselves a breed apart, and that was how others, too, saw them. It was not normally a compliment, for landsmen tended to look down on the rough ways of the sailor. The Englishman Richard Braithwait gave one view of the typical sailor of the age – as he was seen by most landlubbers – in a book entitled *Whimzies, or New Cast of Characters* (1631): 'He was never acquainted much with civilitie, the Sea has taught him other Rhetoricke. Hee is most constant to his shirt, and other his seldome wash'd linnen. Hee has been so long acquainted with the surges of the Sea, as too long a calme distempers him. He cannot speake low, the Sea talks so loud . . . Death hee has seene in so many shapes, as it cannot amaze him.'

Ships' crews were composed, in the main, of such hardened seamen. At their head, in a fleet of exploration, stood the captain-general, who was ultimately responsible for everything that happened on the voyage – its success or failure, and the fate of the crew. It was he who organised the financing of the expedition; lobbied the Crown or other investors; arranged terms with the officers and men; negotiated with the shipowner and shipbuilder; and plotted the course of the journey. He was also responsible for telling the

DAILY CHORES Repairing the sails was skilled work carried out by able seamen.

NOT FLAT! This early 16th-century drawing shows that most people knew the earth was round.

crew what the destination was: it was not unusual to break the news when the expedition was safely at sea, partly for reasons of secrecy, but also to prevent immediate desertion.

GIANTS AND MONSTERS

There were plenty of hazards, imaginary as well as real, to alarm even the most experienced sailors. Few people believed any more that the earth was flat. Seamen were familiar with the appearance or disappearance of the masts of a ship, or a headland, over the horizon and they knew the reason for it. But they did believe in devils, in giants on land and monsters at sea, and they could not be sure that stories about the terrors of the deep were untrue if nobody came back to tell the tale. In any event, few liked the idea of uncharted waters.

THE UNKNOWN Maps were decorated with sea monsters. Right: Spanish coins dating from the reign of Ferdinand and Isabella of Spain (1474–1504).

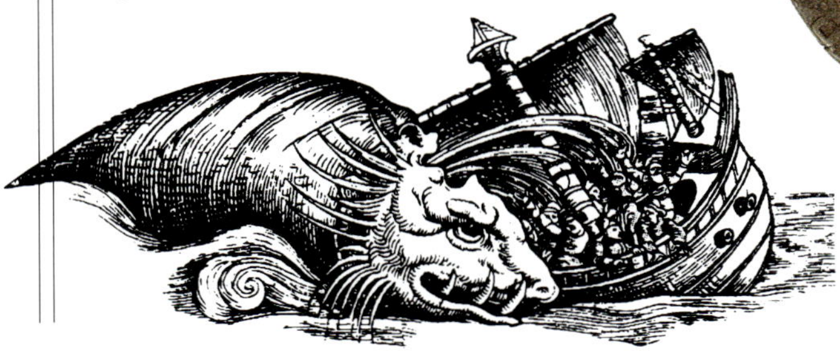

Moreover, not everyone, even on the ships of the explorers, was an experienced mariner. There were often a few specialised gunners (not necessarily used to the sea), and there might also be 'gentlemen travellers' – court favourites or relatives of the owners – who rarely pulled their weight. Distrustful nobles deliberately placed men of this type in high positions on Magellan's great voyage to find a westerly route to the Spice Islands. These 'travellers' intrigued against Magellan and fostered mutiny from the beginning. Sometimes there was 'forced labour', too, consisting perhaps of the victims of press gangs, or of convicts released by the Crown to complete a crew, or to provide men and women to help to settle new colonies.

Volunteers, however, manned most of the explorers' ships, hired for wages that were roughly comparable to those paid on land to skilled and unskilled labourers. In the Royal Navy of the English king, Henry VII, for example, a common seaman got 1s 3d per week, which was similar to the rate laid down for agricultural labourers at that time. Officers, meanwhile, usually settled for a share in the profits made during the voyage, rather than fixed wages, just as the rewards for fishermen in the fishing fleets depended on a division of the proceeds of the catch.

Europe was dominated by 'class', and that applied on board ship as well. The officers had special privileges, and ate at the captain's table. The petty officers, too, had their table, but the rest of the crew ate where they could.

Ranking next to the captain-general of the fleet came the captains commanding each of the ships. Under each captain came the master, who was directly responsible for the performance of the crew, for all sailing operations and for overall organisation on board. He had to see to it that equipment was properly stored, that supplies and cargo were in the right place,

Dog Watch and Graveyard Watch: The Mariners' Day

Except during emergencies, ritual and regulation ruled all aspects of shipboard life – thus helping to co-ordinate its myriad tasks. Most regular of all tasks was the turning of the sand glass, which happened every half hour. It was the only way to know that it was time to eat, sleep or change the watch. The ceremony was usually marked with a short song, or ditty, sung by one of the ship's boys.

A change of watch normally came at the eighth turn of the glass, that is, at four, eight and twelve o'clock. The crew below the rank of officer divided into two watches, each under the direction of an officer, who was in virtual command of the ship during his period on duty. Lookouts, placed fore and aft, and the helmsman were changed every hour, and the afternoon was 'dogged' into two two-hour stints – midday to 2 pm, and 2 pm to 4 pm – so that the sequence of watches would be maintained by different crews on alternate days and nights. This was welcome, since no one wanted the 'graveyard watch' – midnight to 4 am – every night.

After the graveyard watch came the dawn watch. This was the time for washing and scrubbing the decks with salt water; at the seventh glass of the watch a ship's boy would sing out something like:

Good is that which passeth,
Better is that which cometh,
Seven is past and eight floweth.

At 8 am there was a much more vigorous summons – perhaps:

On deck, on deck, Mr Mariners.
On deck for it's already time.
Shake a leg!

On English ships the mariners would snatch a quick breakfast. As the captain of the new watch took up his duties, he received the course from the relieved helmsman, instructed the men of his own watch and had a quick word with his navigator and chief petty officer about progress during the night, weather prospects and the day's objectives.

The crew ate the main meal of the day during the noon watch, with rations dispensed by the steward. At noon the time was checked against the position of the sun's shadow on the north point of the compass, the ship's speed calculated and its position plotted by the navigator.

All hands came on deck before the first night watch at eight. On Protestant ships psalms were sung, on Catholic ones the ancient chant *Salve Regina*. At the last turn of the glass the night watch started as a ship's boy sang out:

The watch is called, the glass
floweth.
We shall made a good voyage
If God willeth.

At Prayer Religious ceremonies were part of shipboard life, with the captain often leading the services.

COMPASS BEARINGS The navigator relied on the compass, kept in the sterncastle of the ship, for direction.

and that sails which had been hauled down were safely stacked: in short, that everything was 'shipshape'. It was he, too, who decided when the ship was ready to sail. He needed not only to be experienced but also to be thoroughly familiar with the idiosyncracies of the particular ship and, preferably, its crew; for this reason, the owner sometimes acted as master.

SKILLS OF THE NAVIGATOR

The pilot or navigator usually ranked below the master – though on some ships he might even rank above him. He was one of the ship's professionals, who in many cases had followed a three-year course of study, as well as gaining practical experience. Studies included astronomy, mathematics, latitude reading and what would now be called oceanography – that is, the study of the oceans and their characteristics. In Spain, from 1508 onwards, a school in Seville turned out specially trained royal navigators who had studied under a Pilot Major. Once a voyage was completed, these Spanish navigators had to return to the school to hand over records of the ship's routes and to describe any discoveries they had made. All new information was then incorporated into future maps and charts. It followed that the navigator had to be literate and educated; usually, he was the most educated man on board.

The navigator's principal jobs were to plot and keep the ship's course, to cope with the unexpected and to guide the ship home. To help him, he had only very rudimentary equipment, the most important being the compass. This was kept safe in the binnacle, a square wooden box in the sterncastle, fitted with sliding doors and a lamp. The compass itself consisted of a magnetic needle, suspended over a card which was divided into 32 points from north back to north again. From his position by the binnacle, the navigator could shout instructions to the helmsman through a hatch.

His other equipment included wooden, or sometimes metal-covered, quadrants and an astrolabe. These were for calculating the height of stars in relation to the horizon, though in fact only one star was used by most navigators of the time: the North Star, Polaris. The altitude of the North Star above the horizon gave the navigator his latitude above the Equator.

Most navigators relied on 'dead reckoning' rather than celestial navigation to plot the ship's course. This involved the calculation of three elements: direction, time and speed. Direction was noted from regular compass readings. Time was taken from sand-

SANDS OF TIME The glass was turned each half-hour by a ship's boy. Left: The astrolabe measured the sun's height at noon, giving the navigator his latitude.

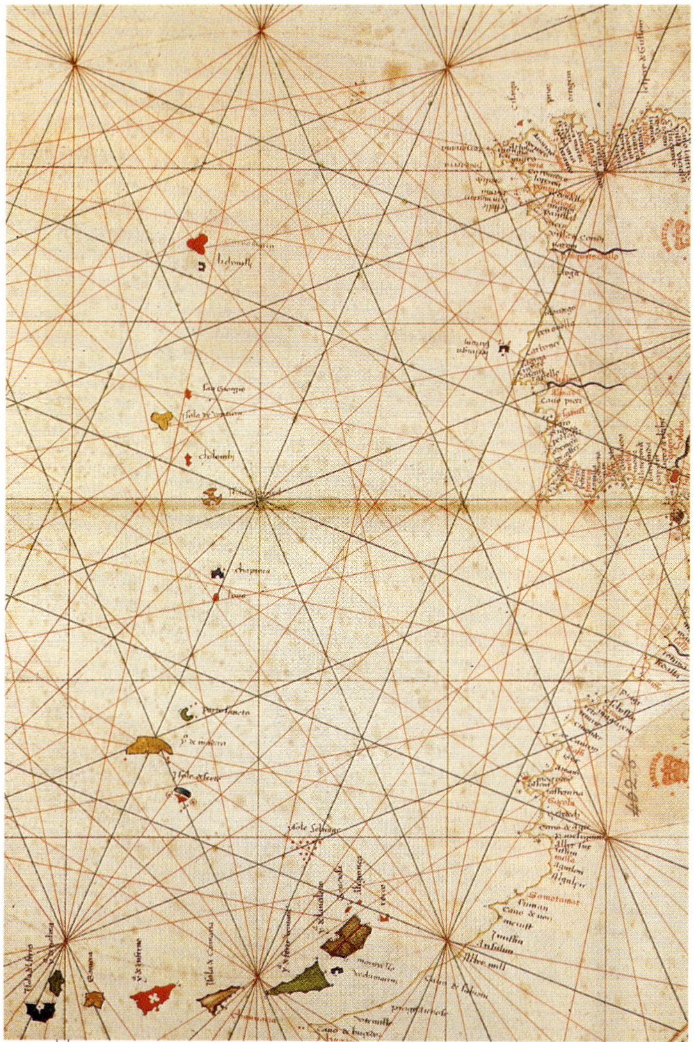

glasses, the only timepieces on board; the sand emptied from one half of the hourglass-shaped vessel to the other every half-hour, after which it was turned over. Eight turns meant four hours, at which point crew members on watch would be relieved by the next team on duty. In time a ship's bell was introduced to mark each turn of the glass and, as a result, 'eight bells' came to mean a change of watch.

The glass not only told the time but also helped to give the ship's speed. Distance travelled was measured by a log, a plank of wood attached to a rope and dropped into the water from the stern. The rope had knots tied in it every 42 ft (just under 13 m), and the number of knots that passed through a sailor's hands in a certain time gave the speed in 'knots', or nautical miles per hour. Knowing direction, time and speed, the navigator could plot the ship's latitude on a carefully designed chart – a method that enabled Columbus to discover a new world.

Quartermaster, Steward and Carpenter

The make-up of ships' crews varied according to the size of the ship and purpose of the voyage. On some voyages there were specialist officers, such as a Crown representative, who took careful note of all bullion and precious metals taken on board. He also kept the 'King's Fifth' (the Crown's share of discovered treasure)

Guidelines
The Portolan chart was covered with lines, used by navigators to plot their courses. Below and right: The nocturnal measured the time at night by means of the stars.

Discipline on the High Seas

Maintaining discipline was always a problem on ships whose crew might come from different nationalities, and where life was often stressful. Some ships carried a marshal, whose job was to enforce discipline. Ultimately, however, responsibility belonged to the captain. There were punishments for slack work as well as for shipboard crimes such as fighting, striking an officer, theft, insubordination, immorality, blasphemy and gambling.

Keelhaul The victim was tied to ropes from both ends of a yardarm, thrown overboard, and pulled under the ship and up the other side.

The punishments varied. Flogging was common, with the offender stripped to the waist, secured to the mainmast and lashed in full view of the ship's company. Another common punishment was to shut the offender up in the hold in chains for a few days – or for the rest of the voyage for such serious offences as incitement to mutiny. The most dreaded of all was 'keelhauling', in which the culprit was lowered into the water on one side of the ship, passed right underneath it and pulled up, half drowned and often badly cut by barnacles, on the other side.

Captains did not usually have the authority to order the loss of a limb or the death sentence. Yet there were instances when they felt they had no alternative. Magellan had the mutineer Luis de Mendoza executed. Another celebrated execution was of Thomas Doughty, a 'gentleman traveller' with Francis Drake on his voyage round the world. He was accused of planning mutiny, and found guilty at a court martial. When offered a choice of execution, marooning, or return to England to answer the charges, he chose the first. After a farewell dinner of mutual forgiveness with his captain, and shared Communion, Doughty was beheaded – the 'gentleman's death'.

in a locked chest. Sometimes there was a priest, and on Columbus's first voyage there was an interpreter.

Below officer rank came the petty officers, notably the quartermaster, who was also the boatswain. He had to record details of the loading and unloading of cargoes and supplies, and make sure that dirty jobs, such as cleaning the bilge and shifting the ballast, were done.

In fact, all roles on board these ships were vital. The steward, for example, was responsible for checking provisions and handing out the daily rations of food, wine and water. He carried keys to the storeroom and kept a constant lookout for telltale signs of theft. The great French explorer Samuel de Champlain – who founded the first settlement on the site of present-day Quebec – wrote of the importance of having a 'good and faithful steward, not a drunkard but a good manager; for a careful man in this office is above all price'.

Other petty officers included the carpenter, in charge of repairs, maintenance and replacements, and the caulker, who made daily rounds of inspection, equipped with supplies of pitch, tallow, leather and whatever else could be used to block spaces between the planks where water might pour in. Then there was the cooper, who looked after the various barrels, casks and buckets on board. Also essential was the barber-surgeon, who trimmed hair, cut beards, pulled teeth and kept supplies of simple medicines.

Among the common seamen, those

Provisions The steward checks the ship's supplies.

'Hail, O Queen' **The great hymn to the Virgin Mary, *Salve Regina*, was sung at dusk on board Catholic ships.**

ranked as able seamen were the most experienced. Most had been in and out of ships since childhood. They hoisted and lowered sails, knew every detail of the ship's rigging and how to repair it, and could read the compass when on duty at the helm. Below them were the 'gromets', apprentice seamen who worked the pumps, swarmed up and down the rigging, and coped with the arduous work of weighing anchor.

Finally came the ship's boys, who were cleaners and sweepers as well as servants at table for the officers and petty officers. Another of their jobs was to turn the glass every half-hour, and good singing voices were helpful, since they had to sing the various hymns, psalms and prayers traditionally chanted at different times through the day. They sang sea shanties as well, partly to entertain the crew, but also to announce meal times, the turning of the glass or changes of watch. Shanties also provided a rhythmical accompaniment to such tasks as hauling in the anchor.

SHAKE A LEG

When sailors were denied shore leave, wives and prostitutes came to the ships. Officers doing the morning rounds shouted 'shake a leg' at sleeping figures. If the leg was hairy it belonged to a man, who had to get up; if not, to a girl, who could sleep on.

Meals from the Cookbox

Ships' meals were cooked in a cookbox, built at the front where it was protected by the forecastle. The box was simplicity itself. A layer of bricks along the bottom provided a base for the fire. From this smelly, smoke-filled 'kitchen' the sailors transferred their rations to wooden bowls, and ate the food with their fingers wherever they found space.

A ship's cat was another vital member of the crew. Its job was to keep down rats and other vermin. This was less to protect sailors from disease than to prevent the constant gnawing damage done to rope and canvas by the rodents.

Generally, hygiene was non-existent, and the ships became so smelly that they often had to be 'rummaged' before the final run into home waters. That meant spring-cleaning them, removing the bilge water and washing the ballast to make them presentable in harbour.

Accommodation, too, was basic. The captain would have a cabin in the sterncastle and other officers might have their own bunks in the same area. But the ordinary seamen slept out on the open deck, on blankets or on hides.

Sleeping arrangements did, however, improve after Columbus's discovery of the hammock. He first saw hammocks in use in

MEALTIMES Wooden bowls, plates and spoons recovered from Henry VIII's ship, the *Mary Rose*. Below: Entertainment was part of shipboard life, and musical instruments were taken on board. Sailors were famous for their jigs, and ship's boys sang regularly to entertain the crew.

the New World, and they were later adopted at sea. For storing possessions, men had to rely on the hold, which would probably be no more than about 5 ft (1.5 m) high and had to provide space for the ship's supplies as well as the men's possessions. These included the seamen's chests, which were carefully controlled in number.

Yet life at sea was not all grim. There were various diversions, such as dances and shanties, dice, cards and fishing: Magellan's fleet took five drums and 20 tambourine-like instruments for shipboard entertainment. There was also the consolation of religion. For if a sailor's language and behaviour were ungodly, it would be wrong to doubt the part that prayer and belief played in the lives of those who confronted death more often than most.

Health and Hygiene on Board

Ships in the age of exploration were overcrowded, smelly and insanitary. The common sailor never changed his trousers during a voyage, never washed, and always slept exposed to the elements. At the bottom of the ship, bilge water slopped about in rat-infested darkness, containing not just putrid seawater but also vomit, urine and faeces. There were no 'conveniences': instead, men relieved themselves over the sides of the ship, or into the bilge, or just occasionally made use of the seats placed fore and aft which they called 'the garden'.

Food and drink both deteriorated quickly on long voyages. Food could not be kept fresh, and had to be shared with the ship's inevitable complement of rodents, maggots, cockroaches and weevils. It is hardly surprising that famine was common and the disease scurvy (caused by a deficiency of vitamin C) even more so. Mortality rates on crossings to the Americas or the East may have been 25 per cent, and on slave ships the average was nearer 50 per cent. Burial at sea was a normal event – the dead seaman was lowered overboard, wrapped in his mat or blanket, after a short service conducted by the captain or a priest.

The health of those on board was the responsibility of the barber-surgeon, who seldom performed any surgery and was unlikely to be qualified in medical matters. However, the various laxatives, purgatives and painkillers – including perhaps rhubarb, prunes, quince juice, rum, lily root, arsenic, honey and opium – that he handed out doubtless gave him some credibility.

The Spanish Dominican friar Tomás de la Torre left an account of conditions on a transatlantic voyage in 1544: 'One could not imagine a dirtier hospital, or one that resounded with more lamentations, than ours. Some men went below deck, where they were cooked alive; others roasted in the sun on deck where they lay about trampled on, humiliated and indescribably filthy. . . . The heat, the stuffiness, and the sense of confinement are sometimes overpowering. . . . Add to this the general nausea and poor health; most passengers go about as if out of their minds and in great torment. . . . There is very little desire to eat, but an incredible thirst, sharpened by a diet of hardtack and salt beef. . . . There are an infinite number of lice, which eat men alive, and you cannot wash clothing because the sea water shrinks it. There is an evil stink, especially below deck. . . . The most disturbing thing of all is to have death constantly staring you in the face; you are separated from it by only the thickness of one board joined to another with pitch.'

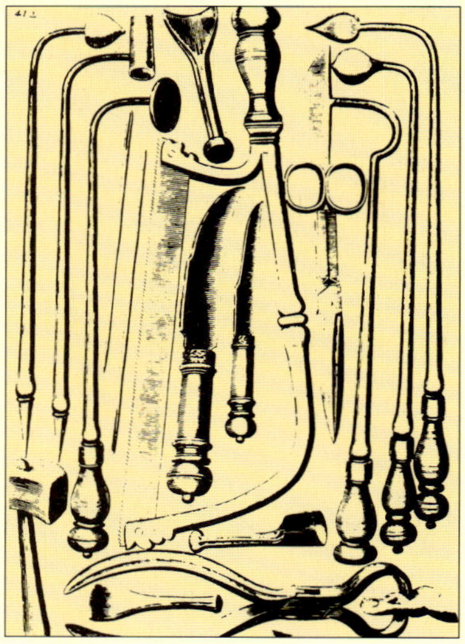

Torture A variety of instruments were used by barber-surgeons.

Ship's Oven Food was cooked in a cookbox.

FORTUNE SEEKERS IN THE NEW WORLD

Christopher Columbus had hoped to find the wealth of the Indies.
In his wake came those who found, instead, the treasures of the New World.
Gold and silver flooded back to Europe, and the American
continent acquired new masters. But, for its native inhabitants,
the arrival of the Europeans brought about a terrible transformation
of patterns of living that had developed over countless generations.

Pioneers of a New Age

The explorers found a massive continent between them and the peoples of the 'Indies' they so eagerly sought. The landmass stretched from the Arctic seas to the Antarctic. It was the New World of the Americas.

SAMUEL ELIOT MORISON, the 20th-century historian of the sea, heralded October 12, 1492, the date of Christopher Columbus's landfall in the New World, with the following words: 'His ships run on, pitching, rolling and throwing spray, white foam at their bows and end wakes reflecting the moon. *Pinta* is perhaps half a mile in the lead, *Santa Maria* at her port quarter, *Niña* on the other side. Now one, now another, forge ahead. With the fourth glass of the night watch, the last sands are running out on an era that began with the dawn of history. Not since the birth of Christ has there been a night so full of meaning for the human race.'

Columbus, born in Genoa but sailing on behalf of Ferdinand and Isabella, the joint sovereigns of Spain, stepped ashore on one of the islands of the Bahamas. He fell to his knees, kissed the ground, thanked God for safe deliverance, and, not knowing that he was in the Bahamas, named the island San Salvador, Holy Saviour. His mission had been to find Asia by sailing west and, believing he had done so, he imagined the new island chain to be off China or Japan. His mistake – that he had found a route to 'The Indies' – has outlived him in names such as West Indies.

That first voyage, lasting from August 1492 to March 1493, was a triumph. If Columbus discovered no rivers running with gold, he and his men were at least the first Europeans to set eyes on scores of islands, including Cuba and Hispaniola (Haiti and the Dominican Republic). On Hispaniola, he found that the natives 'believe, very firmly, that I, with these ships and people come from the sky'. Before sailing

home, he left a small colony of some 20 volunteers at a site on Hispaniola called Navidad (Nativity) and took six 'Indians' and enough crude gold ornaments and exotic plants to convince Ferdinand and Isabella that he had found the westward route to Asia.

Columbus made three more voyages to his new world, but each was progressively less happy. His fame as Admiral of the Ocean Sea ensured that there was no shortage of volunteers for his second voyage, a large-scale expedition of 17 ships carrying 1500 sailors and prospective colonists, as well as tools, seeds, livestock and building materials. On reaching Hispaniola he found that Navidad had vanished, destroyed by the Indians in revenge for atrocities committed by the Spaniards. Columbus founded a new settlement called Isabella and adopted a forced-labour system to compel the inhabitants to work for and feed the colonists. By the time of his third voyage, there was so much dissatisfaction with his regime on Hispaniola that word was passed to the Court in Spain; Columbus was relieved of his duties and returned home in chains. His fourth voyage was tragic – dominated by his own ill-health, storms and wrecks. He returned to Spain in 1504, broken in spirit, and died two years later.

IMMORTAL NAME Amerigo Vespucci, after whom the Americas were named, and the book that made his reputation.

NEW WORLD The ships of Columbus's first expedition: *Santa Maria*, *Pinta* and *Niña*. Left: Christopher Columbus.

Inevitably others followed Columbus to the New World. In 1500, the Portuguese Pedro Cabral, blown off course from the West African coastal route, made the accidental discovery of Brazil. And there was Vasco de Balboa, who explored the Isthmus of Panama and, in 1513, became the first European to set eyes on the Pacific Ocean.

Shortly after Cabral, Amerigo Vespucci voyaged down the coast of Brazil, Uruguay and Argentina. His reactions were enthusiastic: 'The land is very pleasant and full of an infinity of trees. At times the sweet scent of the grass and flowers and the taste of the fruits and roots is so wondrous that I could think myself close to paradise on earth . . . ' Vespucci's reports were translated into several languages, becoming bestsellers, and his Christian name was given by cartographers to the New World continents.

JOURNEYS OF THE CONQUISTADORES

Few martial epics have aroused the imagination more than that of Hernán Cortés, an official sent from Cuba by its governor, Diego Velasquez, on an expedition that resulted in the conquest of Mexico. Cortés set out on his adventures with about 500 soldiers and 16 horses. His marches were punctuated by continual battles in which Indian armies fell before the Spaniards with their heavy metal swords, cannon and mounted soldiers. The warlike Tabascan tribe was crushed and a princess, named Doña Marina by the Spaniards, captured. She became Cortés's mistress, interpreter and spy.

The formidable Tlaxcalan tribe was also overwhelmed. Resentful of the heavy tributes demanded by the Aztecs, they became Cortés's allies. They warned of Montezuma's capacity to put 150 000 warriors into battle, but Cortés pressed on until he reached the capital, Tenochtitlán – whose site is now engulfed by Mexico City. The lakeside city offered an impressive spectacle: 'We saw so many cities and villages built in the water and other great towns on dry land, and that straight and level causeway going to Mexico, we were amazed . . . and some of the soldiers even asked whether the things we saw were not a dream.'

Montezuma received Cortés and his men in the capital on November 8, 1519. The emperor's erratic behaviour, alternating between threats and warmth, was partly due to an ancient legend that told of a white-skinned god, Quetzalcoatl, who would return to triumph over his enemies. Perhaps he thought Cortés was Quetzalcoatl. In any event, it did not take long for Cortés to realise that he was potentially in a trap, inside a city with no escape. So, in a bold move, he seized the emperor, holding him hostage. He dealt with a rival Spanish force of about 800 men under Pánfilo de Narváez, sent to deal with the upstart conqueror, and on returning to Tenochtitlán faced an Aztec revolt. In the fighting, Montezuma was injured by a stone: 'The men with Montezuma pleaded with him to have his wounds tended and to eat, and though they spoke kindly to him he refused. Then to our surprise, those who had been with him reported that he was dead. Cortés, his captains, and his soldiers wept for him.'

LOVING COUPLE Hernán Cortés with Doña Marina. Left: A detail of a portrait of Cortés.

On August 13, 1521, after a 75-day siege, the capital surrendered and on its ruins Cortés ordered Mexico City to be built. He himself ruled as governor until 1534. Unusually among the leading conquistadores, Cortés died peacefully in Spain in 1547.

By the time of his death another, even richer, prize had fallen to Spanish arms. Francisco Pizarro and his companion Diego de Almagro had emigrated to Panama. After some years of initial reconnaissance, they set out in 1531 with a force of about 180 men and 27 horses to conquer the great Inca civilisation of Peru.

The Incas controlled a vast empire, though it was weakened by civil war. Rival claimants had fought for the succession to the throne, and by the time Pizarro reached northern Peru, one of them, Atahualpa, had defeated his enemy Huascar. Under a promise of safe conduct – to the Inca promises were sacred – Atahualpa was lured to the town of Cajamarca, whereupon he was seized, in the Cortés tradition, and his hundreds of attendants murdered. The emperor

SURRENDER The Aztecs try to flee as their capital, Tenochtitlán, falls to the Spaniards.

tried to buy his life. He undertook to fill a room 22 ft (6.5 m) long by 12 ft (3.7 m) wide with gold and silver if he was spared. Pizarro agreed, and gold and silver ornaments, religious objects and jewellery were collected from all over the empire. It took two months to fill the room, and then Pizarro – not wanting a focus of opposition – had Atahualpa executed. But the new Spanish rulers were no more united than their predecessors; warring factions broke out among the conquerors. Pizarro had Almagro murdered, and he himself was assassinated by rivals in 1541.

Southern States and Along the Amazon

Other conquistadores were less successful. In searching for the lost 'Kingdom of the Seven Cities', Pánfilo Narváez, Cortés' old enemy, landed at Tampa Bay in Florida in 1527 with 460 men and 42 horses. By now native Indians had learned to fear the white man, and as Narváez moved through the region's marshes and swamps he and his men found themselves constantly under attack. They were forced to abandon their quest, but discovered that the fleet they had left had vanished. They made new boats, but in the end only four men – Alvar Núñez Cabeza de Vaca and three companions – made it back, by way of Texas, the Rio Grande and the Gulf of California, to the safety of Spanish Mexico.

Spanish Atrocities
Pizarro promises Atahualpa safety, but later has him killed. Left: De Soto, enraged that no Indians can lead him to gold, has them tortured.

Cabeza de Vaca was followed by an expedition under Francisco de Coronado that explored the Rio Grande region, the Southern Rockies and the Great Plains. De Coronado returned in 1542. Another expedition, under Hernando de Soto, a profiteer of the Peruvian conquest, had reached Tampa Bay in May 1539. No one exceeded de Soto in brutality; he had captive Indians thrown to his dogs to be torn to pieces. His bloody path took him to Georgia, the Carolinas, Tennessee, Alabama and across the Mississippi into Arkansas and Louisiana. It was an awesome feat of endurance, though de Soto died of fever in the Lower Mississippi Valley in 1542.

At the same time, far to the south, Francisco de Orellana, sent by Pizarro's brother Gonzalo to seek supplies along the Napo River, found himself swept the entire length – some 3900 miles (6275 km) – of a great river that split the continent from the Andes to the Atlantic. Orellana's expedition came across, it seemed, a tribe of warrior women who 'fought so courageously that the Indian men did not dare to turn their backs . . . These women are very white and tall and have hair very long and braided and . . . are very robust.' Ancient Greek legends had told of such women and named them Amazons. From them – in fact, they were probably women fighting rather more conspicuously than usual alongside the men – came the river's name: the Amazon.

Routes are plotted according to the best estimates of modern scholarship. In some cases, however, accurate information is available only for parts of a voyage.

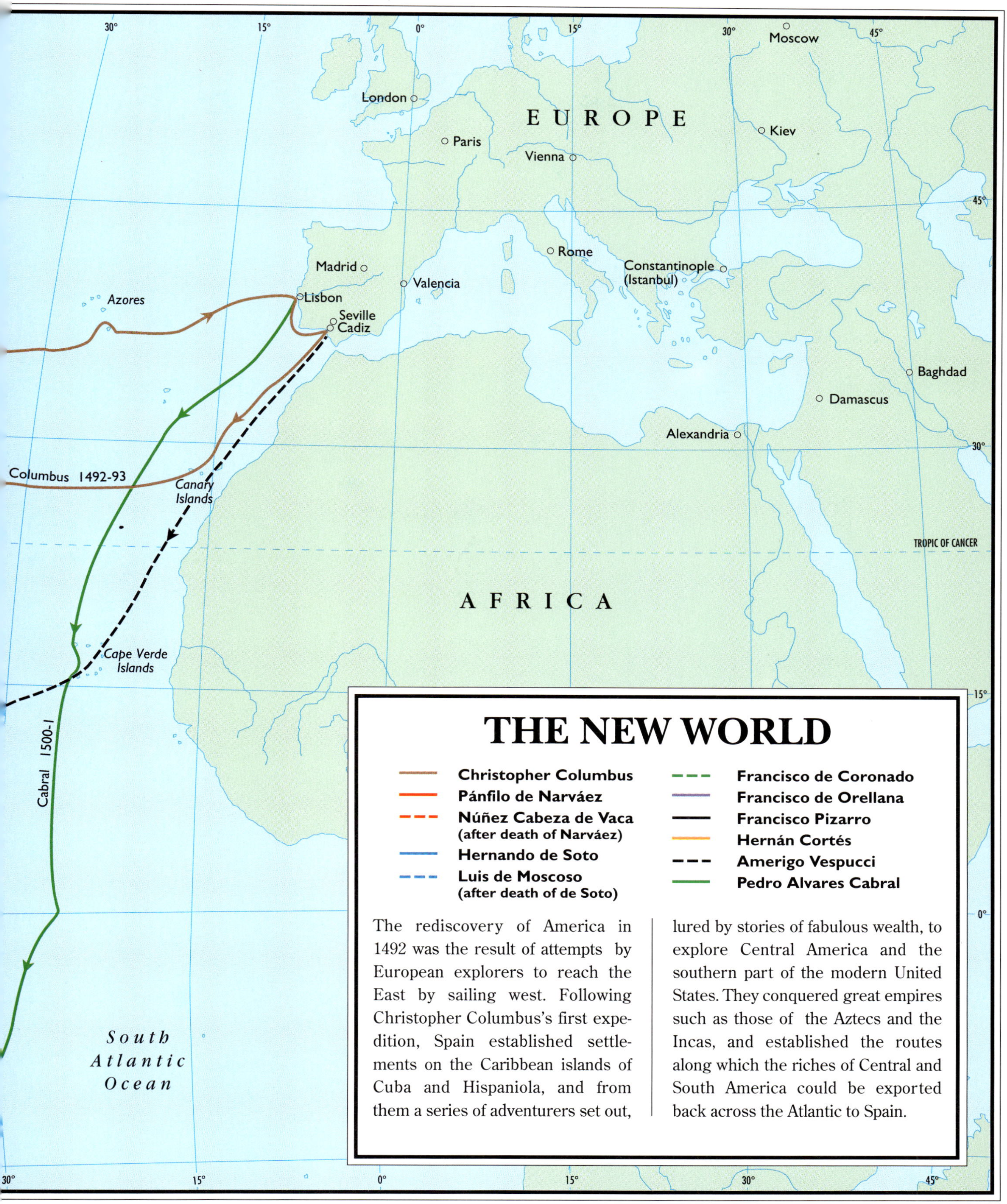

THE NEW WORLD

- Christopher Columbus
- Pánfilo de Narváez
- Núñez Cabeza de Vaca (after death of Narváez)
- Hernando de Soto
- Luis de Moscoso (after death of de Soto)
- Francisco de Coronado
- Francisco de Orellana
- Francisco Pizarro
- Hernán Cortés
- Amerigo Vespucci
- Pedro Alvares Cabral

The rediscovery of America in 1492 was the result of attempts by European explorers to reach the East by sailing west. Following Christopher Columbus's first expedition, Spain established settlements on the Caribbean islands of Cuba and Hispaniola, and from them a series of adventurers set out, lured by stories of fabulous wealth, to explore Central America and the southern part of the modern United States. They conquered great empires such as those of the Aztecs and the Incas, and established the routes along which the riches of Central and South America could be exported back across the Atlantic to Spain.

LAND OF THE CONQUISTADORES

Hungry for fame and wealth, Spanish soldiers of fortune arrived in South America. Their onslaughts destroyed ancient civilisations as they built an empire larger and richer than any since the days of Rome.

COLUMBUS'S HISPANIOLA was Spain's first colony in the New World, and the fate of its people, the Tainos, was later repeated in the stories of all those among whom the Spaniards settled. The Tainos were Stone Age farmers who lived in household units of several families – perhaps 100 or more living together. They cultivated root crops, particularly cassava, and grew maize and a few other seed crops. Their villages of 1000 or more inhabitants were ruled in an informal way by a chief or *cacique*; he and his 'nobles' had their produce grown for them by the villagers. The Tainos had no iron or other hard metals, and no cattle, sheep, goats or pigs. Possibly the most startling thing about them, to us, was their numbers. No one knows exactly how many there were, but recent estimates give a figure of 7 to 8 million.

Within 50 years of the Europeans' arrival, there were no Tainos left. A few hundred Spaniards, eager for gold and slave workers, introduced forced labour, which disrupted the family units and separated the men from the women for most of the year. Combined with the devastation caused by Old World diseases such as smallpox, cholera and influenza, this

FIRST COLONY On the map of Hispaniola above, Spanish settlements are indicated by churches.

WOMAN'S WORK Tainos women make bread from cassava or maize, their staple diet.

destroyed the population. With their native workers dying rapidly, the Spaniards began importing slaves from elsewhere: at first from neighbouring islands and then from Africa. Using slave labour, the Spaniards on Hispaniola developed a 'colonial' lifestyle based on prosperous cattle ranches and sugar plantations whose revenues supported the type of city life that the Spaniards always preferred. Thus a pattern that would revolutionise lives in New and Old Worlds alike had been established.

Hispaniola was not colonised by conquest, but the conquistadores who followed Columbus to his new world proceeded, in an astonishingly short space of time, to build by force the most extensive empire the world had known since the Romans. They came mostly from the Spanish classes known as *hidalgos* and *caballeros*. Though often poorly educated – even illiterate – these 'lesser nobles' had a place in a rigid Spanish caste system far above that of the common labourer and peasant. They were too grand for manual labour, fiercely proud, contemptuous of their inferiors, and ambitious for military glory and personal wealth. It was from their ranks that many of the new warlords came, most famously Hernán Cortés and Francisco Pizarro.

Cortés and Pizarro were the archetypal conquistadores. Their enduring fame rests not on their daring and cruelty, for that was matched by others. Rather, it

MASKED GOD
This mask of Quetzalcoatl, the Aztec god of learning, was placed over the god's effigy at religious festivals. Below: A map of the Aztec capital, Tenochtitlán, prepared under Cortés's supervision.

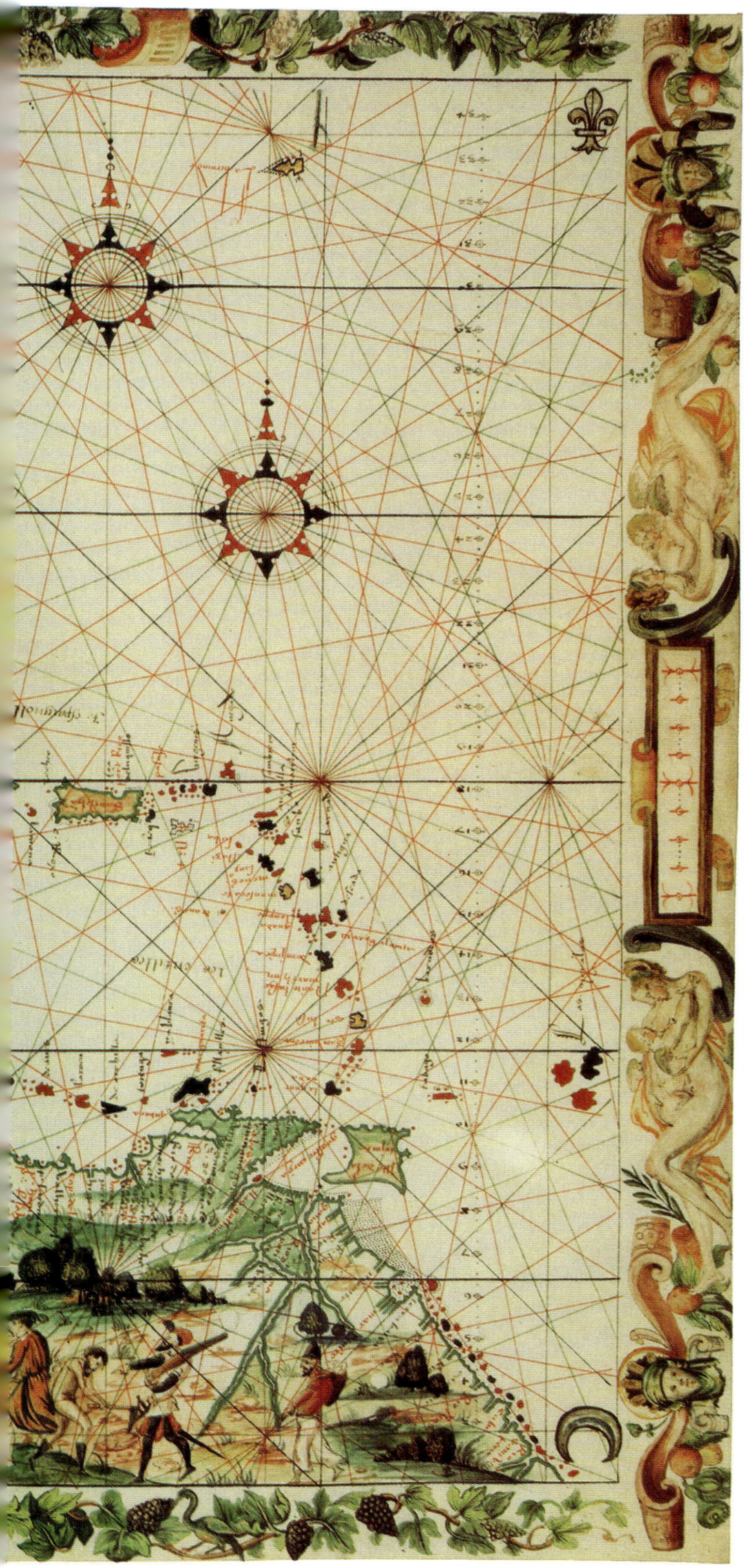

rests on the importance Mexico and Peru were to assume to Spain and the world; on the scale of Spanish settlement there, which duplicated many facets of European society; and on the fact that the conquests involved the overthrow of highly sophisticated existing civilisations.

Aztecs and Incas

The Aztec capital, Tenochtitlán, was larger than any contemporary city on the continent of Europe. Its causeways, wide streets, great houses of red brick covered with white stucco, and towers and temples astonished the Spaniards who first set eyes on it. The inhabitants were elegant, with cotton cloaks for the men and robes reaching to the ground for women. Both sexes painted their faces with coloured oils, stained their teeth with cochineal and wore rings through their noses. Their craftsmanship was of a high order: their tapestries depicted parrots, pheasants and hummingbirds; their pictographs were vivid and descriptive. Furniture was simple, with stools to sit on and low tables to eat from. And typical foods included a cake made from maize; spicy dishes such as frogspawn and stewed ants cooked with chilli sauce; and chocolate to drink.

Much of Aztec life seemed very backward to the Europeans. The door had not been invented, and neither had the wheel. There was no cash currency, and no European-style shops. On market days food, cloth,

HUMAN SACRIFICE Thousands died each year as human sacrifices to the Aztec gods. Left: A chart of 1540 shows the Caribbean and the Gulf of Mexico. Many of the islands were taken by the Spanish.

Ripe and Ready An Indian carries a basket of fruit. Most fruits associated with tropical America were introduced by Europeans.

ornaments, mats and other goods were bartered. The market also provided a barber, for washing hair and for shaving heads.

One aspect of society would have been familiar to the Europeans: the Aztec hierarchy that stretched from the emperor at the top through his nobles and priests down to lesser nobles, peasants and slaves. Yet any apparent similarities were overshadowed by differences. Most obvious was the lifestyle of Tenochtitlán itself, a city whose role was not primarily an economic or even administrative one, but mainly ceremonial, priestly and religious. The Aztecs worshipped many gods: there was the fire god, for whom a morsel of food would be thrown into a lighted brazier as an offering before each meal; there was a rain god too; but most formidable of all, there was a sun god, Huitzilopochtli, whose appetite demanded the sacrifice of thousands of humans every year. Aztec warriors went on endless raiding parties to capture their sacrificial victims. The sacrifices were a daily ritual, in which the victims would have their still-beating hearts torn out by a priest before their skulls were erected on walls sited near the temple.

Placating the gods was the business of Tenochtitlán, and it was supported by tribute gathered from the tribes of peasants and local chieftains, who lived in villages where they grew maize and cotton without the help of horse, ox, cart or plough. They were kept in reluctant vassalage by their Aztec rulers – the Aztecs were a military power and were now confronted with the Spaniards, before whom they would prove powerless.

Far to the south, in Peru, another great city was nearing the end of its dominion. High in the Andes was Cuzco, capital of the Incas, the rulers of an empire that stretched as far south as Central Chile and north into Ecuador. The people of this empire, like those of the Aztecs, consisted largely of farming tribes. There were significant differences, however. The farmers of Peru grew root crops, mainly potatoes, rather than grain. They obtained wool from the llama and alpaca; and their rulers tried to run their lives with a wide range of laws. For example, there were rules which regulated the tributes to be paid, the style of housing

Mountain Native The llama has a long fleece that was of great value and provided wool for the Incas.

EYEWITNESS

Chocolate, a New Drink, Comes from Mexico

CHOCOLATE is a Mexican food and drink from the cacao plant that grows in the hot and humid country along the coast of Mexico. The seed pods are allowed to rot and the almond-sized seeds to ferment, giving the chocolate drink an effervescent quality.

Although known in Europe from about 1520, chocolate did not become popular there until the end of the 17th century. This description of its use in Mexico is by the Jesuit Joseph de Acosta, writing in 1590:

❛ The chief use of this cacao is to make a drink that they call chocolate, which they greatly cherish in that country. But those who have not formed a taste for it dislike it, for it has a froth at the top and an effervescence like that formed in wine by dregs, so that one must really have great faith in it to tolerate it. In fine, it is the favourite drink of Indians and Spaniards alike, and they regale visitors to their country with it; the Spanish women of that land are particularly fond of the dark chocolate. They prepare it in various ways: hot, cold and lukewarm. They usually put spices and much chilli in it; they also make a paste of it, and they say that it is good for the chest and the stomach, and also for colds. Be that as it may, those who have not formed a taste for it do not like it. ❜

LUXURY The Indians valued cacao.

appropriate to each class and rank, and the style of headdresses and ornamentation that could be worn.

Despite the absence here, too, of the wheel and of hard metal tools, the Incas produced imposing buildings and remarkable feats of engineering. They had an elaborate network of roads, not confined to the cities, that tunnelled through hills and crossed fast-flowing rivers on floating or rope bridges. They also had a postal service, which would broadcast news at speeds of up to 125 miles (200 km) per day: someone with a message from the court would go and shout it (for the Incas had no writing) to a messenger waiting at a staging post; he would then sprint to the next staging post and deliver the message, which would be passed on in the same way until it reached its destination.

CARAVAN Llamas were used for transport in the difficult terrain of the Andes.

Changing Lifestyles

After they were conquered, the lands of Mexico were styled New Spain and those of Peru became New Castile. The names were appropriate, for the cities that arose were to some extent transplants, largely European both in design and lifestyle. Both Mexico and Peru proved rich in precious metals, and it was this wealth that built the cities and filled the treasure fleets that started to pour gold and silver into Spain. It also created unimaginable wealth for those conquistadores fortunate enough to live to enjoy it.

In the last decade of the 16th

century, the Italian merchant Francisco Carletti visited Lima and was overwhelmed by the luxury he encountered. Every Spaniard was attended by black slaves, male and female. The slaves themselves dressed magnificently on festival days, 'the women in silks, wearing pearls'. Silver was everywhere: 'There is no cobbler who does not eat off it.' The cost of living was high and even local produce such as fish, melons, grapes and figs were expensive. Yet nothing was wanting, and the Spaniards could afford the prices. Carletti found himself enjoying a 'comfortable, pleasant and delectable' Lent.

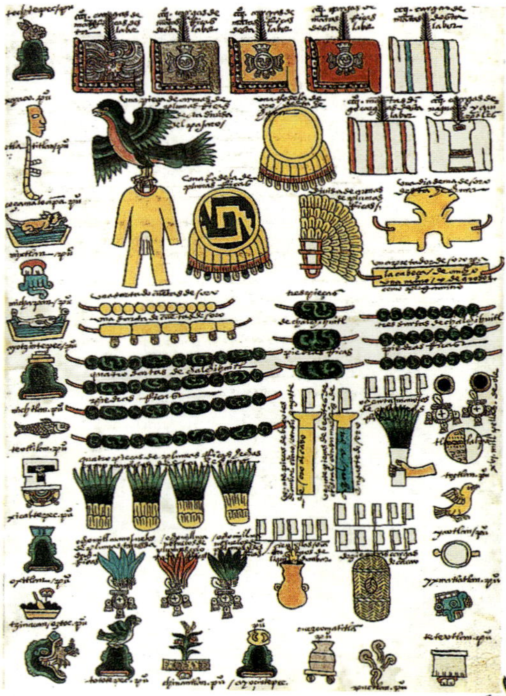

News of the riches brought new settlers: from Spain, and also from among existing colonists in the Caribbean, Panama, the Venezuelan coast and elsewhere. Hardly surprisingly, the cities became island-preserves for the Spanish settlers, surrounded by a sea of Indian village communities.

The countryside was drastically affected by the immediate adoption of the *encomienda* system: a method of rewarding the conquerors by 'commending' an Indian village or number of villages to each of them. The villages

TAX Cities had to provide tribute of various items to the emperor (left column). Left: Spanish and Indian styles mixed to produce ornate façades. Right: The Aztec god Quetzalcoatl.

paid tribute, normally in the form of labour, in return for protection and conversion to Christianity. It was, theoretically, a limited arrangement, but in practice it gave feudal rights to the *encomendero* and subjected the Indians to conditions of serfdom. And the scale was staggering. In the Valley of Mexico alone, 180 000 Indians were parcelled out between 30 *encomenderos*.

Some Indians adapted to the new ways, in particular the chiefs and nobles who became, in effect, collaborators. They were essential links in running forced-labour systems and in collecting tribute from the countryside; they soon took to Spanish dress, riding horses, gambling and city life. Humbler Indians

EYEWITNESS

Splendour and Ostentation in Mexico City

Not long after its foundation Mexico City was astonishing visitors with its grandeur, size and ostentatious wealth. In 1625, the Englishman Thomas Gage wrote a superb description of life in the city that had replaced Tenochtitlán:

❛ It is a byword that at Mexico there are four things fair, that is to say, the women, the apparel, the horses, and the streets. But to this I may add the beauty of some of the coaches of the gentry, which do exceed in cost the best of the Court of Madrid and other parts of Christendom; for there they spare no silver, nor gold, nor precious stones, nor cloth of gold, nor the best silks from China to enrich them....

To the by-word touching the beauty of the women I must add the liberty they enjoy for gaming . . . nay gaming is so common to them that they invite gentlemen to their houses for no other end....

Both men and women are excessive in their apparel, using more silks than stuffs and cloth. Precious stones and pearls further much their vain ostentation and a hat-band of pearls is ordinary in a tradesman; nay a blackamoor or tawny young maid and slave will make hard shift but she will be in fashion with her neck chain and bracelets of pearls....

The gallants of this city shew themselves daily, some on horseback, and most in coaches, about four of the clock in the afternoon in a pleasant shady field called *la Alameda* . . . where do meet . . . about two thousand coaches, full of gallants, ladies and citizens, to see and to be seen, to court and be courted. ❜

Mexican Capital A grand and opulent new capital developed as its inhabitants enjoyed their new-found wealth.

THE TREASURE FLEETS

GOLD AND SILVER were the lifeblood of the early Spanish Empire, paying for the great cities of the New World to be built, providing the Crown's share of profits, and enabling Old-World luxuries to be paid for by the surpluses of Mexico and Peru. As a result, ships carrying treasure were constantly on the move, and they were vulnerable to storms, shipwreck and raids from French, English and Dutch pirates. Desperate efforts were made to intercept enemy ships, though these were hard to find in hidden creeks, isolated harbours or in the open sea.

Two fleets left Spain each year, one in spring, the other in summer. More and more, they had to sail in large convoys with heavily armed escorts. When the ships reached the Caribbean, they made their way across to the Isthmus of Panama and Vera Cruz in Mexico, trading much of their cargo *en route* in towns such as Santo Domingo and Havana. Meanwhile, treasure from Peru was shipped up the Pacific coast to Panama. It was then taken by 'treasure train' – on the backs of mules and slaves – across the Isthmus to the Caribbean coast. Here, by the end of the 16th century, the few weeks of the 'Fair at Portobello' saw a wet, unhealthy and usually deserted town fill rapidly as the fleet anchored and the treasure began to arrive, a scene captured in this vivid account:

TREASURE SEEKERS The great fleet of Columbus's second voyage of 1493, bound for discovery, settlement and gold.

'The concourse of people, on this occasion, is such, as to raise the rent of lodging to an excessive degree; a middling chamber, with a closet, lets, during the fair, for a thousand crowns . . . the land is covered with droves of mules from Panama, each drove consisting of above a hundred, loaded with chests of gold and silver, on account of the merchants of Peru . . .

'The purchases and sales, as likewise the exchanges of money, are transacted by brokers, both from Spain and Peru. After this everyone begins to dispose of his goods; the Spanish brokers embarking their chests of money, and those of Peru sending away the goods they have purchased.'

changed less willingly, but change they did – not least through the introduction of a Christian hierarchy and the imposition of new codes of morality, marriage services and ceremonial. The first parishes were based exactly on the size of an *encomienda*, where the parish priest was usually more under the control of the *encomendero* than of his own bishop in the city. The priest did not see his job as one of conversion, but rather that of instruction in Christian behaviour. New words, many of them with religious significance, began to infiltrate the Nahuatl language of Mexico. There were also new words relating to such things as weights and measures, transport and tools. The effect of 'Hispanisation' on daily life also covered record-keeping, which had to conform to the Spanish system, and the seven-day week, which meant that festivals and markets had to be adjusted to an alien timetable.

HORSE POWER The Spanish horses revolutionised life in the New World.

The years after the conquests were golden ones for the conquistadores and their successors, with ample riches and free labour there for the taking. Yet their lifestyles were parasitic, built on the exploitation of natives and natural resources. These included the gold they seized or mined; cochineal which, at the end of the 16th century, ranked second only to silver in value as an export from Mexico; pearls from the Caribbean; and, most famously, silver from Potosi, a 'silver mountain' in New Castile that opened in 1545.

By the end of the age of exploration, Potosi had become one of the largest cities in Christendom, with brothels, dance halls, gambling saloons and all the characteristics of boom towns belonging to a later age. And in another way, too, Potosi's mines anticipated the future. Despite rota systems introduced for Indian workers, and the ever-increasing importation of black slaves, there was always a shortage of labour. So these capitalist mining enterprises began to pay wages and to develop an embryonic wage economy in an attempt, admittedly largely unsuccessful, to change the lifestyles of the surrounding tribal communities.

With the exception of Potosi, the years of direct exploitation had largely passed by mid-century. For one thing, many of the natural resources had been used up. For another, from the 1540s the government of Spain made a determined effort to take control of colonial affairs, sending armies of bureaucrats to begin the reversion of *encomienda* grants to the Crown. But above all was the stark fact of depopulation. The numbers directly slaughtered by the Spaniards were relatively few, but nothing could prevent the ravages of Old World diseases on people with no basic immunity. There was also the disruption of tribal and family life through the spread of cattle, horses and pigs, which ruined arable land and destroyed crops. The forcible removal of menfolk for months at a time to work far from their home villages was compounded by the separation of women from their children, for women, too, were in demand as labourers and servants. And in lands without native milk-producing domestic animals, children were not

GOLD DIGGERS Slaves mine for gold in Mexico, while a Spanish overseer keeps account. Gold poured into Europe, and was used to create rich decorations, such as at Seville Cathedral (right).

EYEWITNESS

Mining at Potosi - the Hardest of Labours

Silver from Potosi led to the growth of a heavily populated city: a vast industrial enterprise of extraction plants, dams and artificial lakes; deep mines; and, for a time, of unparalleled wealth. Producing this wealth were the miners, and their conditions of work are described in stark detail in an account dating from the late 16th century:

❛ They labour there in perpetual darkness, not knowing day from night: and since the sun never penetrates these places, they are not only always dark but very cold and the air is very thick and alien to the nature of men . . . The silver ore is generally of a flinty hardness, and they break it up with bars. Then they carry the ore on their backs up ladders made from three cords of twisted cowhide, joined by pieces of wood that serve as rungs, so that one man can climb up and another come down at the same time . . . Each man usually carries on his back two *arrobas* [one *arroba* is about 25 lb (11 kg)] of silver ore tied in a cloth . . . The one who goes first carries a candle tied to his thumb, because they receive no light from above. Thus, holding with both hands, they climb up that great distance, often more than 150 *estados* – a fearful thing, the mere thought of which inspires dread. ❜

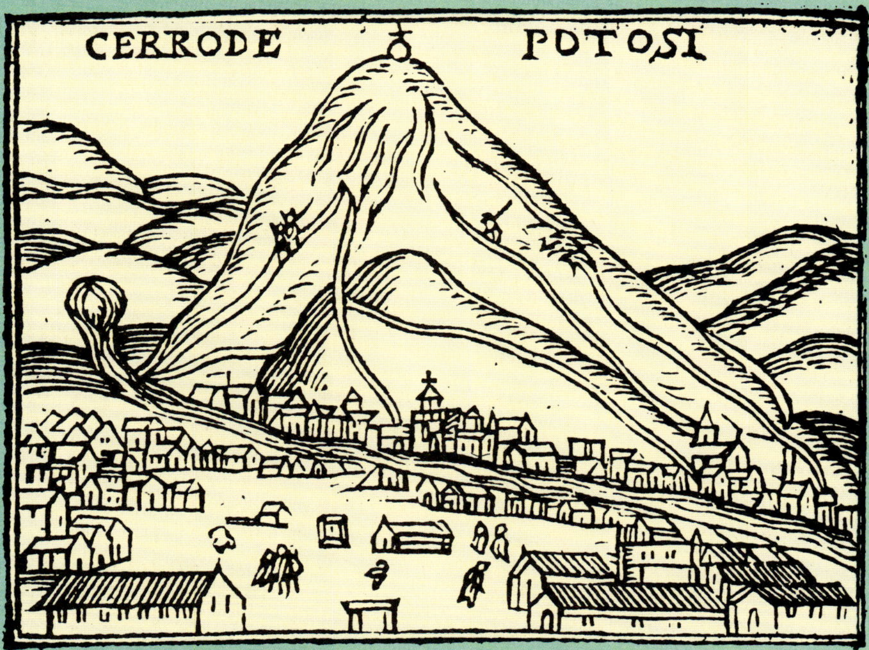

Silver Mountain Silver ore being crushed at Potosi.

weaned until the age of about three or four: separated from their mothers, they died. Finally, there were suicides, recorded often enough in reports and illustrations to reflect an overall collapse of morale.

Ranchers and Plantation Owners

The European settlers, on the other hand, adjusted to a different pattern of life, and for the richer ones a very good life it was too. They became mostly absentee ranchers and plantation owners, still living in the cities and presiding over colossal estates based on horses, cattle and the cultivation of sugar. Their enormous estates, or *haciendas*, became new centres of society. Cattle and horses multiplied so rapidly in the lush grasslands that they ceased to be fenced in; the cattle gave poor meat, so it was fed to Indians or to black slaves, and the hide and tallow were removed for export.

Fortunes were

DID YOU KNOW?

The flesh-eating piranha fish of the Amazon can devour large animals and people who fall into the rivers they inhabit in minutes, and this helped to delay European settlement.

Peruvian Craft Ceramic figurines with painted clothes.

also made from wool. Antonio de Mendoza, appointed the first Viceroy of New Spain in 1535, introduced the merino sheep, and such was its success that, within a few decades, a cloth industry had developed in Spanish America that seemed to threaten the industry in Spain itself. As with the Potosi mines, the Spanish American cloth industry was in part a capitalist, wage-paying enterprise, and the locked compounds of up to 700 workers, working long hours in shocking conditions, again anticipated features of the industrial revolution.

The wealth of the new economies, created on the backs of forced labour for the benefit of privileged Europeans, provided increasing opportunities for the great cities of Mexico and Peru. Here the elite wanted, and could afford, the most fashionable clothes and latest books from Spain, and also spices from the Moluccas and silks from China. For Spanish America's prosperity had produced a new trade route, centred on Manila, by which bullion from America paid for luxuries coming from China and the Spice Islands by way of the Pacific. There was plenty of inter-colonial trade too, such as the shipment of mules from Mexico to Peru, where they revolutionised transport in a country of high mountains and difficult passes.

If the lifestyle of the great cities became increasingly European, the racial mix developed characteristics of its own. At the top, of course, were Spanish or Creole aristocrats with their fine ladies and magnificent homes. (Creoles were full Europeans, born in Spanish America, who on visiting Spain for the first time were shocked to see whites working, something they had never seen before.) But there was also an increasing number of half-breeds, at best signs of inter-racial mixing, or at worst signs of a growing underclass. Mestizos were the offspring of whites and Indians; mulattos of whites and blacks; and zambos of Indians and blacks. Then there were the free blacks, the slave blacks, and inevitably the 'poor white' drifters who formed a subversive class of their own alongside many discontented free or escaped blacks. In other words, although the population mix differed, a true European pattern of lifestyles, ranging from the highly privileged to the chronically poor, had been created many thousands of miles from the Old World.

PRIME TARGETS Heavily laden treasure ships, which travelled in large convoys for safety, return to Spain.

BARBARISM EXPOSED Records of Spanish atrocities prompted protests on behalf of the native Indians, but laws were ineffective in protecting them.

ALONG THE COAST OF BRAZIL

Discovered by accident, Brazil was held to be the home of the Noble Savage in all his splendid innocence. Less romantically, it became the home of the vast slave-based sugar industry.

WHEN Pedro Cabral made his unexpected landing in Brazil in 1500, the most startling sight to greet him was the nakedness of the native Indians. Two of their warriors visited him on board his flagship, and he received them in his finest clothes, flanked by his officers. Presumably he was expecting dignitaries from China or Japan. But they came aboard 'naked and without any covering; they pay no more attention to concealing or exposing their private parts than to showing their faces'. And, making no sign of deference to the admiral, they 'finally lay on their backs on the carpet to sleep'.

These Indians belonged to one of the Tupi-speaking tribes who had spread all down the coastal regions from near the mouth of the Amazon in the north to the site of modern Rio de Janeiro in the south – roughly the limits of colonial settlement in the age of exploration. Their warmth, generosity and hospitality delighted the Portuguese. One sailor crossed a river to join a native dance and 'took with him one of our bagpipe players with his bagpipes and began to dance among them, taking them by the hands. They were very happy and laughed and accompanied him very well to the sound of the pipe.' Tupi men were only too pleased to offer their daughters for the pleasure of the sailors, though they expected their wives to remain faithful; and they willingly felled trees, cut logs and loaded ships with the brazilwood – a valuable source of red dye, in great demand for Europe's textiles, which gave the country its name.

The accounts of the discovery of a simple, unspoilt tribe of Brazilian Indians entranced European readers. Subsequent travellers brought back some Indians and these, together with exotic animals from the Brazilian jungles, became the sensations of the time.

KEEPING TO THE COAST A 16th-century chart of South America; European settlements were confined to the coast.

NOBLE SAVAGES Brazilian Indians stage mock battles with naked French sailors in front of an idyllic setting in the Rouen Pageant. Another side of native life is portrayed (right) in an early woodcut of cannibalism in Brazil.

When the French city of Rouen entertained Henry II and Catherine de Medici in 1550 it put on an elaborate display, creating a tropical-style jungle beside the Seine as a backdrop to performances by the Indians.

However over-enthusiastic the early accounts may have been, there is no doubt that these 'noble savages' had many qualities that quarrelsome, discontented and materialistic Europeans envied. The Indians had no concept of personal possessions and therefore no need to covet anyone else's. 'In every home they all live in harmony with no distinctions between them. They are so friendly to one another that what belongs to one belongs to all. When one has something to eat, no matter how small, the others share it.' In these homes there was no privacy; each long hut contained perhaps 200 to 300 people. Married couples lay together, but with no screen or other device to separate them from the others.

The Tupi were strong, healthy and long-lived. They were obsessed with washing and cleanliness, which bewildered the Europeans, and both sexes constantly combed their hair. The males shaved the tops of their heads like a monk's tonsure, and pierced their lower lips to accommodate a sea shell when they were boys and a jadeite stone when they reached puberty. It was considered a particularly rude gesture to remove the stone and stick the tongue out through the hole. Men and women were elaborately painted, pictures of birds being favourites, and men wore a proud scar to mark each enemy warrior they had killed in battle.

The first visitors thought the Indians had no religion or spiritual beliefs. In fact, many hundreds of tribes had quasi-religious rituals that marked every important aspect of their lives – rain cycles, crop cycles, life cycles, hunting and warfare. Each tribe

The Human Prize at Court

Many of the earlier discoverers returned with exotic human prizes, which they proudly displayed to their sovereigns to prove that their expedition had indeed been where it claimed and introduce his or her Majesty to new subjects ripe for conversion to Christianity.

Columbus returned from his first voyage in 1493 with six 'Indians', who were presented to Ferdinand and Isabella and baptised. At the baptism, the king and queen acted as godparents; one native took the name Ferdinand of Aragon, another Don Juan of Castile, and a third Don Diego. When the others returned, Don Diego remained with the royal household, living as a minor courtier and major curiosity until his death two years later.

Brazilian Indians, 'noble savages', were favourites everywhere. In 1513 three were presented to King Manuel I of Portugal in their full regalia of feathered headdresses, rings and paint. Seventeen years later a Brazilian chief was introduced by William Hawkins to Henry VIII at Whitehall. They talked through an interpreter, and the chief spent a year in England. The novelty of exotic arrivals did not last, however. Africans, Indians and even Chinese were to become familiar sights in the slave markets.

Mexican Arrivals One of the Indians who were brought to Spain by Cortés in 1529, causing a sensation.

Among the most celebrated arrivals in Europe was the wily Indian Huron chief Donnaconna. He had spun a series of tall stories to the French explorer Jacques Cartier, in particular claiming to have visited the fabled Sanguenay, a kingdom rich in gold. Cartier kidnapped the chief and took him back to France, where Francis I was captivated by his stories. Donnaconna spent four years in a blaze of publicity, promoting Sanguenay and inventing other wonderful lands, such as a place inhabited by a tribe of one-legged pygmies. He was baptised and given a royal pension, and when he died he received a Christian burial.

One of Queen Elizabeth I's more improbable visitors was an Eskimo, brought back by Martin Frobisher, whose voyages were financed by the queen. Frobisher brought his unusual passenger to London in October 1576, after his first voyage. There he and his men were 'joyfully received with the great admiration of the people, bringing with them their strange man and his bote, which was a wonder onto the whole city and to the rest of the realm that heard of yt'.

had its shaman, a powerful figure who combined the roles of medicine man, witch doctor and prophet, and who sometimes became the village chief. Village organisation was simple; the chief had few trappings of authority, except in time of battle, when he took undisputed command. At other times, he was merely the most prominent among a council of elders who gathered each evening to discuss tribal matters.

The Tupi were largely hunter-gatherers. They had few cereal crops, and no domestic animals of any kind or metal tools; they were fascinated by European dress and knives. The tribespeople lived in harmony with the rainforest, building long-timbered thatched huts in clearings created by 'slash and burn' – the trees were felled, but allowed to grow again when the village was abandoned for a new one after a few years. Since the poor soils that support gigantic trees will not normally allow settled agriculture, the tribes were often on the move, their lives dictated by the needs of the day.

These needs, naturally, included food, and the men hunted and fished with bow and arrow. The arrows, of bamboo or reed, had two half-feathers tied in a spiral at the tail to make the arrow spin. The head of the arrow might be hardened by fire, reinforced by bone, cut to a point, tipped with the tail of a stingray,

FLORA AND FAUNA An early 16th-century map shows the animals and timber that interested Europeans.

serrated with barbs or finished with a rounded knob. Different arrows were made for nearly every kind of bird, fish or mammal, and the power, speed and accuracy of the Indian bowman were compared favourably with the performance of Europeans. 'They draw and shoot them so fast that, with due respect to the good English bowmen, our savages, holding the supply of arrows with the hand with which they hold the bow, would have fired a dozen while [the English] would have released six.'

Apart from hunting, and fighting in time of war, the men were conspicuously idle. There was some farming, but it was women's work. After making the initial clearing, the men retired to their hammocks, or engaged in hunting, or worked on their feathered headdresses. Few crops were grown: there were manioc, maize, gourd, pumpkin, broad bean and peanut for food, and cotton for hammocks. The women prepared the food, too: home-grown vegetables, fish and game, bird's and turtle's eggs, wild honey, nuts, fruits, berries and edible insects, notably ants. With the exception of the root crops that each couple grew on a private patch of ground, providing food was an almost completely communal activity.

This was the seemingly idyllic lifestyle that bewitched the early Europeans, but it embraced one particularly repellent aspect. The real business of Tupi men was fighting, and wars were waged as part of a cult of ritual cannibalism. All along the coast, battles would be fought with other tribes in an endless cycle of wars of revenge for previous acts of cannibalism. The battles were fought ferociously and, though many were killed, the aim was to take prisoners who would then be treated almost as guests until the time came for their execution. At the ceremony women ran round the victim, taunting him with his fate. An executioner was selected who would say: 'I am he that will kill you, since you and your people have slain and eaten many of my friends.' The victim would then reply: 'When I shall still

DANCING FOR VICTORY Brazilian tribesmen perform a ceremonial war dance before going into battle against their enemies.

have many to avenge my death.' A ceremonial club was wielded, the dead body torn open and its various parts distributed during a feast that lasted three days. The executioner did not join the celebrations; he was left to fast and recover, adding his victim's name to his own.

This custom gave an added missionary incentive to Christians. Genuine religious motives were always strong among the Portuguese, but they wanted the benefit of trade too and, though Brazil had produced none of the riches of Mexico and Peru, King John III decided, in the 1530s, to embark on a true colonial policy. Between 1534 and 1536 he divided the coastal region into some 15 hereditary captaincies, stretching from the Amazon in the north to Sao Vicente in the south. Each was given to a prominent Portuguese who, at his own expense, was charged with creating permanent settlements. In return, he was given wide-ranging powers and privileges, including the right to parcel out the coastal stretch with its unlimited hinterland as he wished; a 40 mile (65 km) length of coast for his own estate; the power of life and death in his judicial capacity; the right to take Indian slaves; and the right to keep the profits from trade, except for items which were reserved for the Crown, such as brazilwood.

Inevitably, this planned policy of settlement, with its official sanction for Indian slavery, undermined whatever good relationships had developed. Wars broke out between settlers and Indians, continuing with victories and defeats on both sides, for the rest of the age of exploration. Moreover, Portugal's European enemies, notably France, now had more opportunities to forge alliances with tribes hostile to the Portuguese. Through it all, the most obvious casualty was the lifestyle of the Indians, whose nomadic customs and slash-and-burn mobility were the very opposite of any concept of settlement.

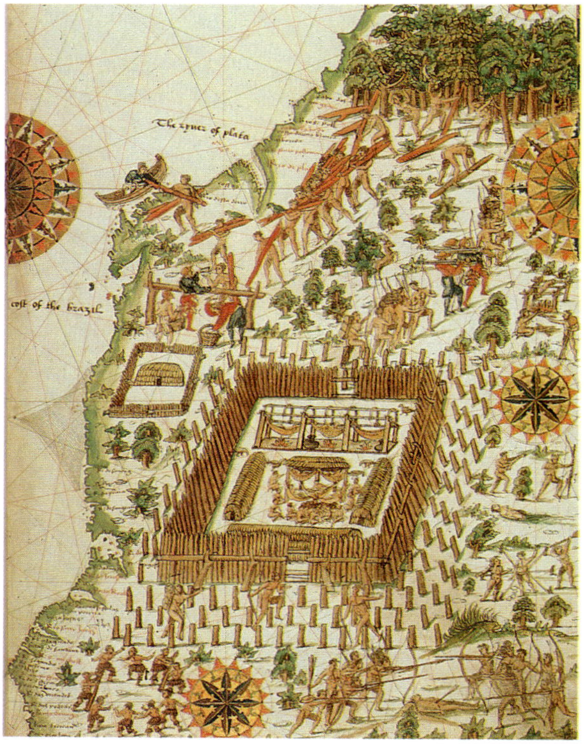

UNDER THREAT Indians fortified their villages against attack, but many thousands ended up as slaves.

SUGAR AND SLAVES

A few of the colonies, such as Bahia, Sao Vicente and Pernambuco, made progress due to the annual crops of sugar which flourished in their climate and soil. In the early 17th century, Pernambuco alone had over

TIMBER TRADE French traders, who sought land in South America, load their ships with brazilwood.

EYEWITNESS

A Plea for a Family

RICH SETTLERS in New Castile (Mexico) and Peru worried about who would inherit their wealth, writing endless letters to encourage younger members of their family to join them. Here is an extract from Andres Garcia's plea to his nephew Pedro, written in 1571:

❝ But now, nephew, I am advanced in years and can no longer take care of all this. I wish, if it please God, that you would come to this land, as I have written you in other letters . . .

I am married here to a woman very much to my taste. And though there in Spain it might shock you that I have married an Indian woman, here one loses nothing of his honour, because the Indians are a nation held in much esteem. And besides, I can tell you that in the ten years that we have been married we have had no children, praised be our Lord. And she is after me more every day, ever since I told her that I have a nephew whom I raised from infancy and love as if he were my son; she is of the opinion that if God our Lord brings you to this land, we should leave you our property . . . And if you could, bring along your cousin Pedro Lopez . . .

Nephew, I entreat you again to come . . . don't imagaine remote regions far from your native land, or the hardships that are usually met on the way, but rather the ease you will have here. ❞

MIXED MARRIAGE An Inca lady (left) in full traditional dress marries a Spanish man.

100 plantations. Sugar was not suitable for peasant agriculture. The planting, gathering, milling and transporting were all backbreaking activities. And the Indians considered farming and milling to be women's work, and the settlements to be the antithesis of their mobile, village lifestyle. As a result, many Indians refused to work on the plantations. They fled, revolted or committed suicide. From the middle of the 16th century, ever-increasing numbers of black slaves were brought from Africa to replace the Indian labour; by the end of the century, when they were coming at a rate of up to 8000 a year, a total of some 60 000 had arrived to work for a white population of around 30 000.

Gradually, a colonial society of Europeans, Indians and African slaves evolved, and it included the offspring of mixed parentage. The Mamelukes, children of white men and Indian women, became so numerous in Sao Paulo that the name for its inhabitants, 'Paulistas', was used as a synonym for the Mamelukes. No colonising Europeans bred inter-racially as thoroughly as the Portuguese in Brazil. In part this was due to the shortage of European women, and in part it may have been due to Portugal's own multiracial mix of European, Jew, Arab and North African descent.

The first governor of Brazil, Thomas de Sousa, arrived in 1549 with instructions to establish central authority from a new capital city – Salvador, in Bahia. Soon the city had stone buildings for the governor's residence, for public buildings, and for churches and religious orders; supplies of cereals, fruits, horses and

RIVALRY French and Portuguese ships battle it out while Indian archers fire from the shore.

EYEWITNESS

THE SLAVE ON THE PLANTATIONS

DURING THE AGE of exploration, vast plantations of sugar, tobacco or cotton, all depending on slave labour, emerged in the New World. The advice of a 17th-century Jesuit priest, John Andreoni, on how the slaves on a Brazilian sugar plantation should *not* be treated conjures up a vivid picture of their lives:

❛ The overseers must on no account be permitted to kick slaves – in particular to kick pregnant women in the belly – or to strike slaves with a stick because they may inflict a mortal head wound on some valuable slaves . . . To tie up a slave girl and lash her with a liana whip until the blood runs, or to place her in the stocks or in chains for months at a time (while the master is in the city) simply because she will not go to bed with him, may not be tolerated on any account.

The slaves are the hands and feet of the plantation owner, for without them you cannot make, increase, or preserve a fortune or operate a plantation in Brazil . . .

Some masters have the custom of giving their slaves one day a week to plant for themselves. This helps to keep them from suffering hunger. To deny them both flour and a day for planting, and to expect them to work in the fields by day, from sunrise to sundown, and in the sugar mill by night – and if on top of this the punishment is frequent and excessive, the slaves will either run away into the woods, or commit suicide, as is their custom, by holding their breath or hanging themselves. ❜

cattle were introduced from Europe; and a shipyard was built. In sum, Salvador's establishment symbolised the eclipse of the ways of the hunter-gatherer. More changes were to come with Governor Mem de Sa (1558-74) who ordered, without total success, an end to cannibalism and inter-tribal wars and demanded the adoption of Christian ethics.

As the settlements took on a colonial character, so the more fortunate settlers – most notably, the owners of great sugar plantations in Pernambuco – prospered. The Jesuit Fernando Cardim wrote wonderingly of 'the great facility with which they welcome guests. For, at whatever hour of day or night we arrived they gave us all food in the shortest time . . . every variety of meat, chickens, turkeys, ducks, sucking pigs, kids and other meats all raised by them . . . They, their wives and children dress in all sorts of velvets, damasks and other silks . . . They are unduly fond of banquets . . . every year they commonly drink 50,000 cruzados' worth of wines from Portugal . . . In short there is more luxury to be found in Pernambuco than in Lisbon.'

Cardim doubtless exaggerated, for nowhere in Brazil was there anything like the city splendours of a Mexico or a Lima, let alone Lisbon, while the interior remained largely virgin territory. Much of the country was insect-infested, alternately in flood or drought, and almost impassable. Europeans could find few ways to move about inland.

HOME FROM HOME A 17th-century settlement in Brazil. Europeans transported their lifestyles to the New World.

When they did, it was by river on uncomfortable canoes and rafts, or by making their way along jungle paths by horse, donkey or mule, accompanied by natives carrying supplies balanced on their heads.

Christian Villages

When the first governor arrived in Bahia in 1549, his fleet also brought the first Jesuits – half a dozen dedicated, intellectual members of a new order founded on military lines to lead a Roman Catholic counterattack against the Reformation. They were shocked to find so much immorality in the colonies, and horrified by the slavery of Indians. Under their formidable leader Manuel da Nobrega they set about acquiring such an influence that by 1600 – although there were only 128 of them in all Brazil – they would control the lives of most Indians under Portuguese rule.

From the first, the Jesuits were welcomed by the oppressed Indians. It was obvious that they were respected by the colonists despite being opposed to many of their excesses. It seemed to many Indians that safety lay in association with these men and in becoming Christians. Therefore, in the first years, there were baptisms, conversions and Roman Catholic marriages on a massive scale – hundreds and even thousands at a time. Everywhere they went, the Jesuits won respect: they learned the Tupi language, went to the villages and made no material demands. Yet the Jesuits' own early euphoria soon gave way to disillusion as their new converts rapidly lapsed into the old ways of polygamy, nudity and – possibly worst of all – a continued belief in the shaman.

Spreading the Faith Brazilians (right) were converted in large numbers. Below: Europeans exploring the Brazilian coastline traded with the local inhabitants.

The Jesuits' solution radically disrupted tribal life: they created enormous mission villages, or *Aldeas*, where thousands of Indians, protected from outside temptation, were encouraged – and later compelled – to live for the sole purpose of instruction and conversion. The *Aldeas* consisted of long rows of houses enclosing a courtyard, where a church and school were built. The daily routine of the village compounds, each run by two Jesuits, was based on European models. The day began with Mass, followed by religious instruction in the native tongue and prayers. There were classes – in reading, writing, singing and other musical skills – in the morning and afternoon. The day would end with a procession to church and prayers in the native language.

The Jesuit villages did not exactly fail; there were about 30 of them operating at the end of the 16th century, and they provided the foundations for the conversion of a continent. But they did not succeed as had at first seemed likely. This was in part because the villages were attacked by slave-hungry colonists; in part because they added to the demoralisation of the Indians by removing not only men but women, the labour force, from the countryside; but, most of all, because they created densely packed communities that were vulnerable to epidemic disease.

Terrible epidemics broke out in the 1550s, and recurred at intervals throughout the age of exploration. As thousands upon thousands died, the Jesuits worked, prayed, wept, gave the last sacrament and buried the dead without any thought of personal safety. They tried to explain that God was punishing former wicked ways, but they and the Indians knew that it was the settlers who had brought the devastation.

By the end of the age of exploration, little of Brazil had been settled apart from the coastal fringe. Yet also by the end of the age, Portugal had lost most of her worldwide trading supremacy to the Dutch and British, and it was Brazil that would provide the key to her colonial future.

THE POX European diseases such as smallpox spread rapidly among native populations, causing a rapid decline in numbers in areas of European settlement.

LAND OF HOPE Time would demonstrate that Portugal's colonial future was in Brazil, not the Indies.

SETTLERS IN NORTH AMERICA

The age of exploration brought the Europeans to North America. In time, their first tentative explorations led to the growth of new nations: to the powerhouse that became the United States, and, to the north, Canada. But these lands also became battlefields of colonial rivalry, bloody sites of warfare with native Indians, and a 'melting pot' where nationalities from all over the world found new lives and homes.

SEAMEN IN ATLANTIC WATERS

European seafarers continued to search for the North-west Passage on behalf of France and England. Instead of establishing new trade routes to India, however, they laid the foundations of French and English colonial futures in North America.

RICH PICKINGS **Waters teeming with fish and an uncharted land inhabited by Indian tribes awaited European explorers. Below: On his first voyage, John Cabot claimed Newfoundland for Henry VII of England.**

FOR A CENTURY or more after Columbus, explorers continued to look for a sea route to the Indies through North America. The first to do so was the Venetian John Cabot, who had no idea that there was a great continent between the Atlantic and the Indies when he set out to 'discover, and finde, whatsoever iles, countreyes, regions or provinces of the heathen and infidelles . . . whiche before this time have beene unknowen to all Christians'. These instructions were contained in the letters patent granted to Cabot by King Henry VII of England.

In May 1497 Cabot sailed from Bristol in the *Mathew*, taking 53 days to make landfall on what is now Newfoundland. He explored parts of the coastline and took possession of his 'new found land' in King Henry's name. If he had failed to reach China, he had made one notable discovery – the richest fishing grounds yet known to Europeans. The waters off

DETERMINED PILOT Jacques Cartier negotiated rip tides, sandbanks and rocky islands along the St Lawrence.

Newfoundland teemed with cod, herring and mackerel. Around July 20, Cabot turned for home, and made much better time thanks to the prevailing westerlies.

Other explorers of northern waters included the Portuguese brothers Gaspar and Miguel Corte Real, who captained separate expeditions to Newfoundland and Nova Scotia between 1500 and 1502. However, one of the greatest North Atlantic explorers sailed under the auspices of the King of France. Giovanni da Verrazzano was a Florentine who had moved to Dieppe, where his abilities attracted the attention of France's Francis I. The new king hired Verrazzano to explore a possible western route to the Indies, authorising him to take possession of any newly discovered lands for France. Francis lent Verrazzano a ship from the French navy – *La Dauphine* – in which he set sail on January 17, 1524. Verrazzano's course took him to the coast of North Carolina. From there he journeyed south, along the South Carolina coast, and then turned north to explore the entire coastline to Maine and Newfoundland.

Verrazzano returned to Dieppe in July, but he was not to survive his great voyage long. Four years later, in the Caribbean, he landed on an island, probably Guadeloupe, not knowing that it was inhabited by the fierce Caribs, who clubbed him to death almost as soon as he landed. If his success in charting large parts of North America's Atlantic coast had been followed up, it might have been France, not England, that colonised New England and Virginia.

EXPLORATION IN CANADA

Instead, voyagers continued the search for the North-west Passage, ignoring the opportunities Verrazzano had provided. Among them were two redoubtable explorers – Jacques Cartier and Samuel de Champlain – whose exploits resulted in the creation of New France.

In 1535, in an attempt to find a route to the Indies, Cartier set sail with a fleet of three ships. On August 10, St Lawrence's Day, he and his crews became the first Europeans to set eyes on the vast waterway that he called the St Lawrence, and which, in the next century, would take French explorers to the Great Lakes, and from there west to the Dakotas, and down the Mississippi to the Gulf of Mexico. Cartier followed the river as far as the site of present-day Montreal, but there, to his intense disappointment, a series of rapids made it impossible to continue. Cartier and his men suffered a terrible winter before they were able to make the return journey, reaching home on July 15, 1536.

Sixty years passed between Cartier's discoveries and Samuel de Champlain's first voyage to the St Lawrence in 1603. Over the next 30 years Champlain would make many voyages to New France and, by founding Quebec in 1608, lay one of the cornerstones of the future Canadian

VISIONARY Samuel de Champlain, founder of Quebec (below), started the French colonisation of Canada.

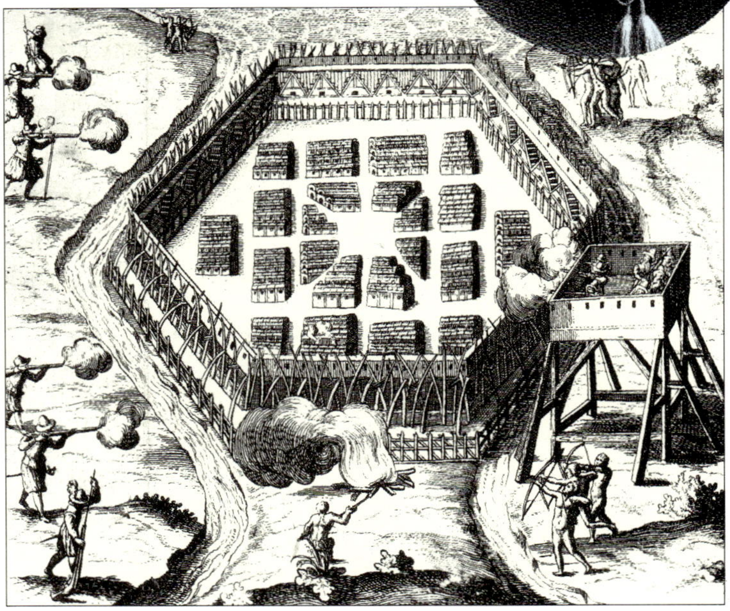

FROZEN WATERS Martin Frobisher's expedition met expert Eskimo canoeists, attacks from the land, and dangerous ice floes all around.

nation. He navigated hundreds of miles of the Ottawa River, penetrated Lake Huron's Georgian Bay and reached the eastern end of Lake Ontario. And he sent two colleagues, Étienne Brûlé and Jean Nicolet, on expeditions that largely completed the charting of the Great Lakes, which were to become the focus of new towns and cities, transport and trade.

Champlain never faltered in his belief in a French destiny in the New World. Yet at first there were few settlers, and many of them died quickly, while the itinerant fur traders, and dealers in alcohol and guns with the local Indians, were not interested in building a community. Indeed, in the early 1620s Quebec consisted of only three fortified houses and two settled families, one of them Champlain's own. Nevertheless, more settlers did, at last, begin to arrive; and by the time of Champlain's death, on Christmas Day 1635, France could look forward to a colonial future in Canada, laying a cultural legacy that has lasted to this day.

DID YOU KNOW?

While it was a Dutch colony, New York celebrated Christmas ten days earlier than the colonies in Virginia and Massachusetts. This was because most of Europe had adopted the new Gregorian calendar in 1582, while England – and her overseas settlements – stuck to the old Julian calendar, which differed by ten days, until 1752.

SEA DOGS AND PURITANS

While the French were making their tentative advances in Canada, England renewed her interest in finding the North-west Passage. Prominent among the advocates of a route to the Indies was Humphrey Gilbert, who searched for one in 1578, when he was forced by storms to return to England, and again in 1583, when he claimed Newfoundland for the Crown, as Cabot had done before him. Martin Frobisher made three voyages between 1576 and 1578, his journeys taking him to the far north, to Greenland, Labrador, Baffin Island and the Hudson Strait. Like John Davis, who followed him into the Canadian Arctic between 1585 and 1587, he was fascinated by the Eskimos. There are reports of organised wrestling matches with the crews, the English always anxious to produce their best men against their strong opponents; gymnastic displays in the ship's rigging; and accounts of a form of football.

However valiant they may have been, the Elizabethan sea dogs were unsuccessful. And no failure was more complete than that of the courtier Sir Walter Raleigh, whose ambition was to found an English colony in the New World. He

MOTHER CARE An Eskimo woman from Baffin Land carrying her baby, which can be seen peering out from her head-covering.

THE FAILED COLONIST Sir Walter Raleigh, whose attempts to found colonies in Virginia ended in disaster.

obtained the necessary letters patent from Queen Elizabeth, and in 1584 chose an island called Roanoke off the Virginia coast. However, an expedition led by Sir Richard Grenville in 1585 was almost exterminated by famine and disease, and the few survivors were only too pleased to return home with Sir Francis Drake, who called there the following year.

The English did succeed in planting a colony, albeit a shaky one, at Jamestown in 1607, and after the introduction of the tobacco crop in 1612, Virginia prospered. In 1609 the Dutch settled in New Amsterdam – New York. And, in 1620, came the most famous colonial voyage of all – that of the Pilgrims on board the *Mayflower*.

Edward Winslow, a leading Pilgrim, recorded the ship's departure: 'Wednesday, the sixth of September, the wind coming east-north-west, a fine small gale, we loosed from Plymouth, having been kindly entertained and courteously used by diverse friends there dwelling.' It was midwinter before they chose a site for their settlement, calling it New Plymouth.

MANHATTAN SKYLINE New Amsterdam, later re-named New York by the English. Above: The title page of John Smith's account of the first English colony in Virginia.

Arctic Ocean
GREENLAND
Baffin Bay
Baffin Island
Davis 1587
Cumberland Sound
Davis Strait
Frobisher Bay
Hudson Strait
Hudson 1610
Frobisher 1576
Hudson Bay
Frobisher 1578
Miguel Corte Real 1501–02
Davis 1585
LABRADOR
James Bay
Gaspar Corte Real 1500
Gilbert 1583
Cabot 1497
Lake Superior
Lake Huron
Cartier 1535–36
Quebec
Champlain 1608–16
Montreal
St Lawrence
NEWFOUND-LAND
Gulf of St Lawrence
NOVA SCOTIA
Lake Ontario
Lake Champlain
Boston
New Plymouth
New Amsterdam (New York)
Mayflower 1620
Washington D.C.
Jamestown
Roanoke
Verazzano 1524
NORTH AMERICA
North Atlantic Ocean
Azores
Canary Islands
Cape Verde Islands
ARCTIC CIRCLE
TROPIC OF CANCER
Routes are plotted according to the best estimates of modern scholarship. In some cases, however, accurate information is available only for parts of a voyage.

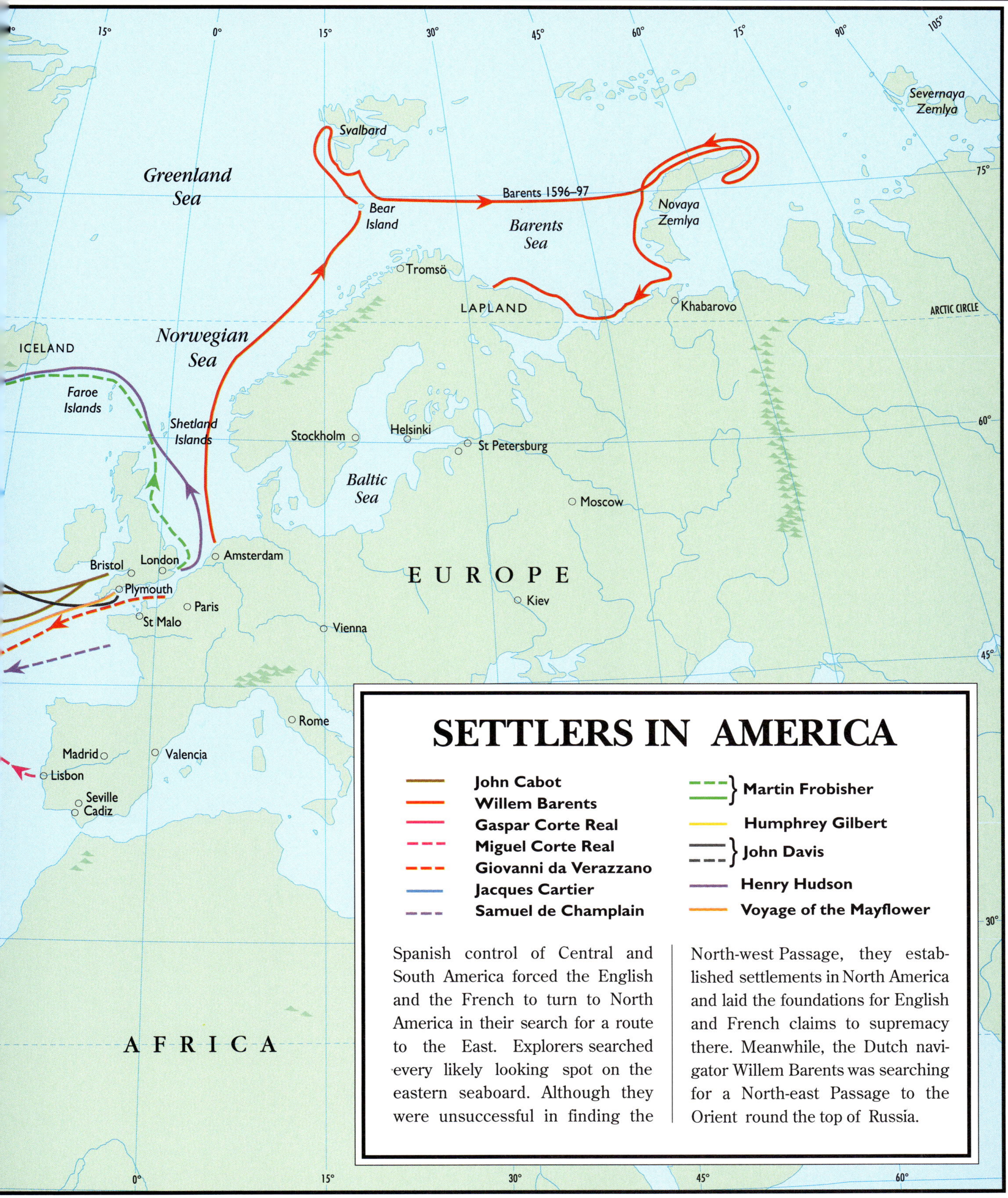

SETTLERS IN AMERICA

- John Cabot
- Willem Barents
- Gaspar Corte Real
- Miguel Corte Real
- Giovanni da Verazzano
- Jacques Cartier
- Samuel de Champlain
- Martin Frobisher
- Humphrey Gilbert
- John Davis
- Henry Hudson
- Voyage of the Mayflower

Spanish control of Central and South America forced the English and the French to turn to North America in their search for a route to the East. Explorers searched every likely looking spot on the eastern seaboard. Although they were unsuccessful in finding the North-west Passage, they established settlements in North America and laid the foundations for English and French claims to supremacy there. Meanwhile, the Dutch navigator Willem Barents was searching for a North-east Passage to the Orient round the top of Russia.

NEW FRANCE IN THE NORTH

Life was cruel to all but the wealthy and privileged in Europe at this time. Some Frenchmen sought an alternative in the inhospitable lands of the far north and, in doing so, created the Canadian nation.

BY THE END of the age of exploration, the French had explored Canada and established colonies there. These were small, precarious communities strung along the St Lawrence, plagued by insects in summer and paralysed by the arctic cold of winter. Moreover, there was the ever-present danger of attack by hostile Indians. Why should anyone have sought a new life in such an environment?

There were opportunities in the fish and fur trades in Canada, but more important than this was the absence of a better alternative at home. The assortment of labourers, peasant farmers, vagrants and convicts who comprised most of the first colonists had little enough to keep them in France.

THE RICH ARE DIFFERENT **A French peasant farmer brings produce to the landowner who rules his life.**

Peasant life in Europe before the Industrial Revolution was nothing like the carefree round of harvestings, dances, festivals and rural delights of popular imagination. For perhaps a century after the Black Death of 1348, when Europe's population fell by a third, there was a slight improvement in conditions as a shortage of labour compelled landowners to relax some of their feudal rights. But from 1450, and throughout the age of exploration, these worsened again – and in few countries as conspicuously as in France. There the aristocratic landowners, with no interest in farming, commuted many of their 'payments in kind' (a head of cattle, a gallon of milk, a bushel of wheat) into increased money rents. This meant that the peasant not only had to provide for himself and his family but somehow also had to earn the money to pay the rent, the tithes he paid to the Church and the *taille* – a tax he paid whenever the king decided to levy it for a special occasion.

BEGGING BOWL **Many dispossessed farming families turned to begging.**

The French peasant, therefore, worked from dawn to dusk for his superiors. Most of his daylight hours, and those of his family, were spent in the fields, tilling, sowing, harvesting; or perhaps tending a few

INDIAN INGENUITY The Indians disguised themselves with deer skins in order to advance on their prey.

head of livestock, which manured the fallow fields or were slaughtered for meat. This rarely found its way to his own family table, however; nor did the white bread made from wheat. These luxuries were sold at the village markets while the peasant household made do with bread, porridge or gruel made from oats, barley and rye.

The peasant's diet might sometimes include eggs, cheese or salt fish, but on the whole it was dominated by cereal, which resulted in malnutrition and also made peasant farmers very vulnerable when the crop failed. In this event, they would not earn enough to pay the rent and could be taken to court and dispossessed; the prospect of becoming landless lent a permanent sense of panic to the lives of many peasant families.

The families were heavily dependent on the goodwill or otherwise of their landlords. And among the greatest landowners was the Church, which

FRIENDLY WELCOME Local Indians show French explorers a column in Florida that had been constructed by earlier European visitors.

pervaded every aspect of daily life. At their best, the churches and monasteries remained close to the people, with priests and monks acting as teachers, doctors, agriculturalists, lawyers and providers of hospitality and welfare. The Church determined the structure of the year through its calendar of feast days and fast – or fish – days, of which there were 166 a year in a Roman Catholic country like France. Village church bells marked the time of day and gave the news: they rang to warn of invasions, to celebrate victories, to announce royal births; and they tolled for funerals. How else could a peasant know the time if the Angelus bell did not ring at six in the morning, at noon and at six in the evening? These were the hours to snatch a quick breakfast, to take a brief lunchtime break, and to come home for the evening meal. The activities of the Church reached everywhere, as it was also to its courts that you went to complain that your neighbour had fed his cattle on your land or to denounce a witch.

Yet at its worst the Church was remote, greedy and corrupt, its powerful bishops worse than many secular landlords, and it was against this that the Protestant reformers reacted. France remained Catholic because her monarchs did, but there were plenty of Protestants there whose rebellious spirits urged them to sea in the age of discovery. The port of La Rochelle, for example, became virtually an independent Protestant city-state.

The Lives of the Rich

French grandees led very different lives. The nobleman's bread was white; his wines were new and made from the finest regional grapes (corks and the idea of 'vintage' wines were unknown). He probably

TREASURE-SEEKERS The Descaliers Planisphere of 1550 shows the route explored by Cartier, the Indian town of Hochelaga (modern Montreal), and the area of 'Sagne', or Sanguenay, site of untold but non-existent wealth.

enjoyed fashionable new drinks such as brandy – for distilling wine, though wasteful, was becoming popular among those who could afford it. Unlike the peasant's, his fast days featured a variety of fresh fish. Feasts, which marked important saints' days, family celebrations, or perhaps the special day honouring the rich man's own patron saint, often lasted three days – or rather days and nights because the rich could afford candles and torches.

The rich, of course, ate meat – and lots of it: beef, mutton, partridge, pheasant, peacock, swan and, after 1550, turkey from the New World. Meat was served with vegetables and spices, with the emphasis on quantity rather than quality. In France it was the custom to place food on an enormous dish, on top of which came a pyramid-shaped construction of smaller plates, each filled with other delicacies. The whole pyramid, called a *mets*, comprised a single course. Thus an eight-course meal would consist of eight of these laden constructions, the aristocratic assembly served by armies of servants rushing about with fresh napkins that they supplied after every two platefuls.

Some of Europe's table manners were born in the 16th century. Before then it had been customary for guests at table to bring their own knives, but to eat with their fingers. Now a knife was always provided, and often a spoon as well. More radical still was the increasingly widespread use of forks, once derided as quite unnecessary for those who had the use of their fingers. Drinking from individual glasses was

CAPITAL CITY Samuel de Champlain's 'residence' and 'colony' at Quebec, founded in 1608. Below: Walrus, 'beasts like large oxen with tusks like elephants', amazed many voyagers.

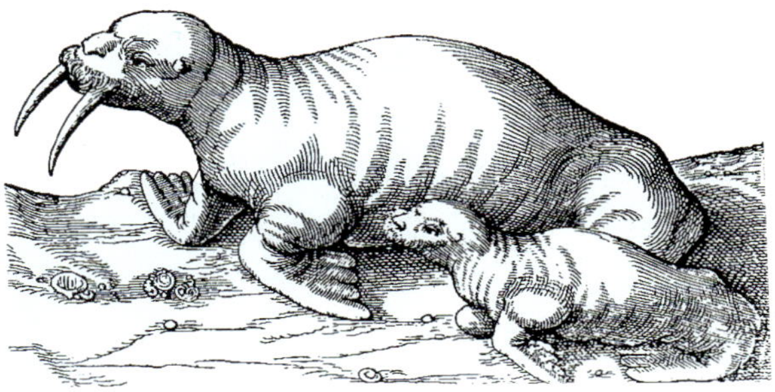

DID YOU KNOW?

When Cartier returned to France in 1542 with eleven barrels of 'gold', seven of 'silver' and a basket of 'precious stones', the whole lot was revealed to be worthless, giving rise to the expression 'a Canadian diamond', which is used by the French even today to describe something that promises much but delivers nothing.

Life in an Indian Village

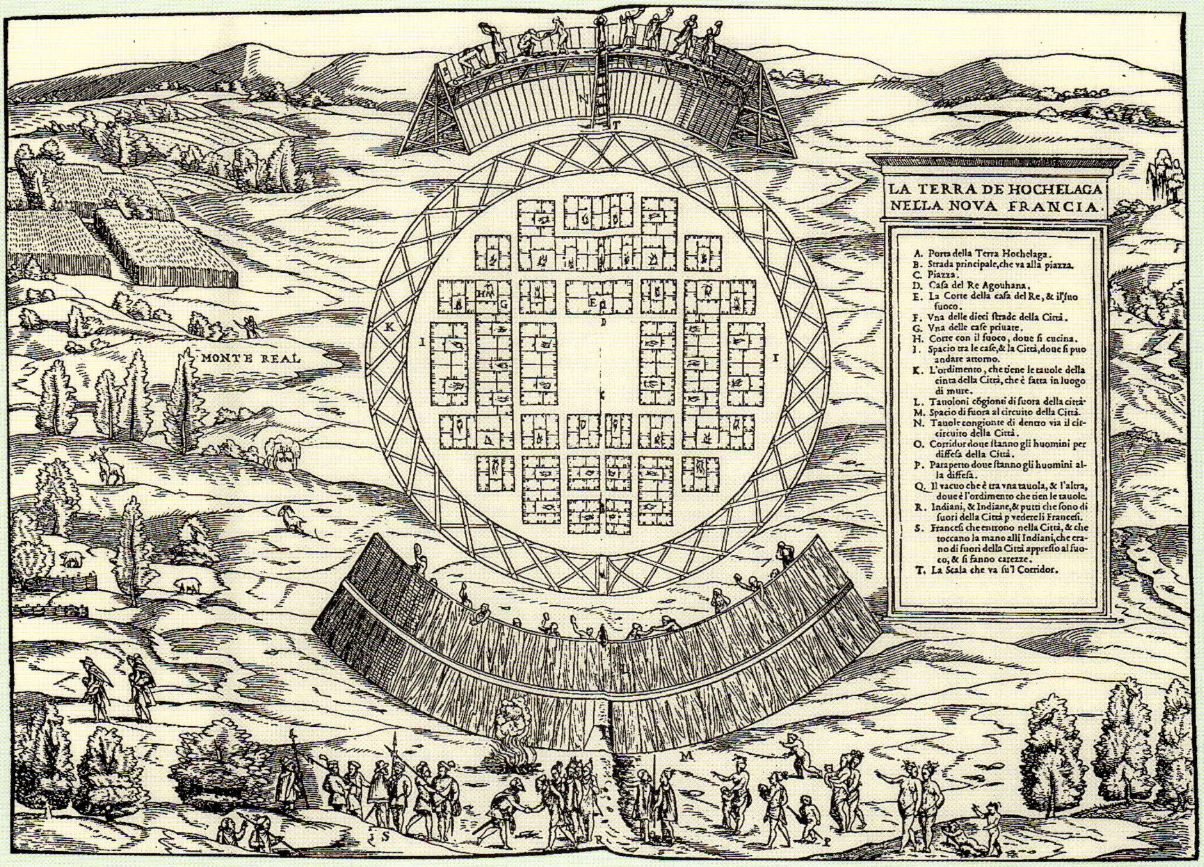

At least 1000 Indians – one in 20 of the Huron people – lived in the Indian village of Hochelaga. Built primarily for defence, it was surrounded by wooden palisades equipped with galleries where warriors stood on guard. The village had a principal street leading to a central plaza, at the end of which was the largest dwelling – the chief's. The longhouses, each accommodating up to 20 families, were built of bark and wood, with several rooms and an open fire.

The Indians grew corn, beans, pumpkins, sunflowers, hemp and tobacco in fields outside the palisades. Women did the work in the fields as in the home, while the men hunted, fought and bartered their corn surpluses for furs and meat. Village social life included feasts, ordered by the medicine man, that lasted up to a fortnight. On these occasions farewells were made to a hunting expedition; or a successful deer hunt or fish catch, or a good harvest, was celebrated.

Jacques Cartier disapproved of some of their social customs:

'They maintain the order of marriage except that the men take two or three wives. On the death of their husband, the wives never marry again, but wear mourning all their lives by dying their faces black with . . . charcoal and grease as thick as the back of a knife-blade; and by this one knows they are widows.

'They have another very bad custom connected with their daughters, who as soon as they reach the age of puberty are all placed in a brothel open to everyone, until the girls have made a match. . . . And furthermore betting, after their fashion, takes place in these wigwams, in which they stake all they own, even to the covering of their privy parts.'

The Future Montreal Ramusio's plan of the Huron village Hochelaga, published in 1565. Key: A, gate; B, principal street; C, plaza; D, house of the chief; E, courtyard of the chief's house; F, street; G, private house; H, courtyard/kitchen; K, palisade; L, palisade from the outside; N, palisade from the inside; O, P, gallery.

supplanting the traditional custom of swallowing from a communal cup passed from diner to diner.

The aristocrats of France, then, had little incentive to get involved in the world of fish and fur. Those who went overseas were propelled by either missionary zeal or fear of dispossession – very much the characteristics of the first French Canadians.

The Hurons of the St Lawrence

The main centre for the early colonists was Quebec, which was sited in Huron territory. The Hurons had not impressed Cartier, who wrote that they 'could well be called savages, for they are the poorest people that can be in the world; all their possessions, apart from the canoes and fishing nets, were not worth five sous'. The word 'Huron' came from *hure*, meaning ugly and bristly, reflecting the first French impressions; it does them no justice at all. The Hurons were an intelligent and resourceful group of hunters and farmers, and those 'poorest people' described by Cartier were simply travelling, as lightly as possible, on their summer visit to the coast to catch fish, seal and birds. After the hunting season they returned to the region around Quebec, to their families and a busy village life. The 19th-century American historian Francis Parkman wrote an evocative description of life in a Huron home on a winter's evening:

'He who entered on a winter's night beheld a strange spectacle: the vista of fires lighting the smoky concave; the bronzed groups encircling each, cooking, eating, gambling, or amusing themselves with idle badinage; shrivelled squaws, hideous with threescore years of hardship; grisly old warriors, scarred with Iroquois war clubs; young aspirants, whose honours were yet to be won; damsels gay with ochre and wampum; restless children pell-mell with restless dogs. Now a tongue of resinous flame painted each wild feature in vivid light; now the fitful gleam expired, and the group vanished from sight, as their nation has vanished from history.'

The first French settlers owed a lot to the friendship of the Hurons, who taught them Indian ways of hunting seal and trapping beaver. The French learned to use snowshoes in winter, calling them *raquettes*; they rode on toboggans; and they even encountered a strange game that the Indians played with a ball, carried cradled in a specially cupped stick called by the French *La Crosse*. It was a brutal affair: the main concern at the start seemed to be to incapacitate as many opponents as possible. Only when the field had been reduced to a manageable number of active players did those left turn their attention to scoring goals.

It was a long time before the Canadian colony came to resemble a real settlement. As late as 1627, when Louis XIII's chief

EYEWITNESS

'Their Soul is a Soil which is Naturally Good'

Writing in the 1630s, the Jesuit Father Le Jeune compared the intelligence of the Hurons favourably with that of the French peasant:

❛ As to the mind of the Savage, it is of good quality. I believe that souls are all made from the same stock, and that they do not materially differ; hence, these barbarians having well-formed bodies, and organs well regulated and well arranged, their minds ought to work with ease. Education and instruction alone are lacking. Their soul is a soil which is naturally good, but loaded down with all the evils that a land abandoned since the birth of the world can produce. I naturally compare our Savages with certain villagers, because both are usually without education, though our Peasants are superior in this regard; and yet I have not seen anyone thus far, of those who have come to this country, who does not confess and frankly admit that the Savages are more intelligent than our ordinary Peasants. ❜

Huron Warrior
The Hurons, who befriended the early French settlers, were exterminated by their Iroquois enemies.

minister, Richelieu, set up the Company of New France to encourage emigration, there were only 107 Frenchmen living in the St Lawrence region. The farmers in these minuscule settlements resented the far richer fur trappers, who fostered contacts with the Indians and succeeded in building their exports of beaver pelts to 15 000 a year during the 1620s.

Missionaries in Canada

There was one group of Frenchmen, even fewer in number than the settlers and the traders, who worked tirelessly to change the lives of the native inhabitants. These were the Jesuit missionaries. The first two Jesuits came to the St Lawrence in 1611, and by 1640 had built five churches and performed 1000 baptisms in Huron territory.

The missionaries had to be extremely dedicated to the Jesuit crusade to work in the dangerous, inhospitable regions of Canada. Indeed, part of their rigorous training stressed the anticipation of a martyr's death, whether it happened among savages or at the hands of Protestant governments in Europe. In 1535 Father Le Jeune wrote:

'Three mighty thoughts console a good heart which is in the infinite forests of New France, or among the Hurons. The first is: "I am in a place where God has sent me, where he has led me as if by the hand, where he is with me, and where I seek him alone." The second is, in the words of David: "According to the measure of the pain I endure for God, his Divine consolations rejoice my soul." The third, "that we never find crosses, nails, nor thorns, in the midst of which, if we look closely, we do not find J.C. [Jesus Christ]".'

The Jesuits found much to admire in the Hurons' way of life: their simplicity, their lack of interest in material possessions, the unfailing way in which they honoured treaties, and their love of their families. Of course, the Jesuits also found much that they strongly condemned, such as polygamy, premarital sex and nudity. However, if the Indians' gods of nature could be supplanted by the true God, then, the Jesuits believed, an intelligent and resourceful people could be brought into the Roman Catholic fold.

And so the handful of Jesuits went to work with their usual thoroughness: they worked with the Hurons in their villages; they sought to protect them from the settlers' alcohol and firearms; they learned their language; and they hunted, fished and worked in the fields alongside them.

Nevertheless the Jesuits failed, in part because the Huron language was incapable of expressing those concepts, such as 'guilt' and 'faith', that were central to Christianity; and partly because the Indians were just not interested in what the missionaries tried to teach them. The Jesuits admitted the difficulties they had with a sharp-witted and practical people. For

Barents's Search for the North-East Passage

The Dutch navigator Willem Barents, born in about 1550, made three voyages between 1594 and 1597 in search of a North-east Passage to India for the Dutch.

Barents left Amsterdam on his third voyage, undertaken with two ships, in 1596. The ships separated, but on the edge of the Arctic Ocean Barents discovered West Spitzbergen, before he was forced by ice to seek shelter on Novaya Zemlya. His ship, cracked in the hard ice, had to be abandoned. The crew salvaged what they could and wintered on Novaya Zemlya. No Europeans had ever wintered so far north and soon the men were immobilised through cold in their primitive quarters.

The Dutchmen survived the winter, and Barents decided that their only hope was to make for the nearest mainland, the Kola Peninsula, some 1600 miles away. They undertook the journey in two open boats rescued from their ship and finally reached the peninsula. But Barents was not among the survivors. On June 20, 1597, just seven days after they had set off, he died. The sea that lies east of the North Cape on the northern tip of Norway is named in his memory.

Endurance Test Barents and his crew abandon their ship and take to open rowing boats.

example, the Hurons could not understand why anyone should be so anxious to go to a heaven that was likely to be swarming with Frenchmen; or to a heaven where there was no hunting, feasting, polygamy or warfare. And they argued that it seemed most unfair of God to allow all mankind to bear the guilt of Adam's fall, yet grant salvation only to the half who then became Christians.

The Indians preferred to continue to worship their own Great Spirit, whose favours were granted in this world, not the next; who existed in the trees and streams, in the sun and rain, in the growth of corn or the availability of deer, in the arrival of friends, and in the elimination of enemies. Finally, they preferred to reach their Spirit through song and dance rather than prayer.

Some of the Jesuits in Canada deliberately sought martyrdom. They could not hope to match the glories of those of their order who had performed conversions by the tens of thousands in Japan and South America; but they could die at the stake in a manner symbolic of Christ's own crucifixion. As a result, there were priests who escaped from the Indians only to return to the same territory and face certain death.

Whale Hunting The whale was hunted by the Indians and Eskimos for its hide, blubber and meat. Whaling proved a valuable new industry for Europeans, shown here slaughtering the animals off Newfoundland.

TOBACCO: 'HERBS TO DRINK THE SMOKE THEREOF'

NOXIOUS WEED A Dutch illustration of a 'smoking club'.

DURING THE age of exploration, habits long established in other parts of the world began to spread to Europe. There was the drinking of tea, from China; of coffee, from the Muslim world; and of chocolate, from Mexico. And tobacco rapidly conquered the Old World after its introduction in the 1560s.

Columbus discovered tobacco on Cuba, where he found 'many people who were going to their villages, both women and men, with a firebrand in the hand and herbs to drink the smoke thereof, as they are accustomed'. Forty years later, and thousands of miles away along the St Lawrence, Jacques Cartier wrote of a plant that the Indians 'hold in high esteem, though the men alone make use of it in the following manner. After drying it in the sun, they carry it about . . . together with a hollow bit of stone or wood. Then at frequent intervals they crumble this plant into powder, which they place in one of the openings of the hollow instrument, and laying a live coal on top, suck at the other end to such an extent that they fill their bodies so full of smoke that it streams out of the mouths and nostrils as from a chimney. They say it keeps them warm and in good health, and never go about without these things. We made a trial of this smoke. When it is in one's mouth, one would think one had taken powdered pepper, it is so hot.'

All explorers of America encountered this, seeing tobacco taken as snuff, smoked in pipes or cigars, or simply chewed. It was said that it had a whole range of wonderful properties. In England it was believed to open pores, cure ague and gout, reduce fatigue and hunger, and prevent hangovers.

Every new large-scale trade interferes with some vested interest. Established merchants did not like this rival to their traditional cargoes, but governments disliked it even more because, initially, it carried no tax. Its conquest of the world can be plotted by the years in which it was 'banned' in a spread of countries: England (1604); Japan (1607-9); the Ottoman Empire (1611); Mogul India (1617); Sweden and Denmark (1632); Russia (1634); Naples (1637); Sicily (1640); China (1642); the Papal States (1642); and Cologne, Germany (1649).

The English Colonists

England was late entering the colonial race, but in the early 1600s founded successful colonies at Jamestown, Virginia, and at New Plymouth in New England. A new age of colonial supremacy had dawned.

THE MOST celebrated of all the colonial settlers arrived at the place they called New Plymouth on the morning of Monday, December 11, 1620. Although an English colony had already been established in Virginia, it was the Pilgrims of the *Mayflower* who went down in history as the true founders of English-speaking North America. One reason for this is that their voyage was inspired by ambition not for fame and fortune but for liberty: freedom to practise their religious beliefs in a new world without interference from the oppressive government they had known at home.

In fact, the oppression suffered by Puritan communities at home was, by contemporary standards, light. Neither the Elizabethan nor the Stuart government practised persecution in the manner of, for example, the Spanish Inquisition. Nevertheless, those who failed to conform to the practices of the Anglican Church suffered occasional fines or imprisonment, or lost their jobs. In particular, ministers were required to adopt the vestments and rituals of the Anglicans or lose their livings. For Puritans, the minister was the focal point of religious life, and many decided that if their ministers were to be driven from the churches, they would just have to set up their own congregations outside the Anglican Church. These Separatists included a group, mainly from the eastern counties of England, who moved their congregation to Leyden, where the authorities in the newly independent Netherlands were more

PURITAN PERSECUTION Puritan worshippers, oppressed by 'High Anglican' laws in Stuart England, are arrested.

TINKER TAILOR Puritan settlers in North America came from a variety of professions.

The Puritan Home

The first New Plymouth dwellings were little more than mud-and-thatch shelters, and were soon replaced by clapboard houses with shingled roofs, each with its kitchen garden and orchard nearby. These were very basic: a low doorway led into the only real room in the house, called the hall. There were no separate bedrooms, nor was there a living room; and there was no lavatory – everybody relieved themselves in the outside privy.

The hall was dominated by a central fireplace, a construction at least double the size of that in a yeoman's house in England. This was in permanent use – for warmth, for cooking, and for light by which to mend, sew or read at the end of the day. At one end of the fireplace a kettle would be warming; at the other an oven heating; and in the centre stood, or hung, a pot for the stews that comprised most meals. Early settlers in New England did not take readily to local foods, such as venison, goose, turkey, oysters, bass, cod and wild strawberries, preferring stews made with familiar ingredients. These were served for dinner, the main meal of the day, which was taken any time between noon and three o'clock; they also appeared at breakfast and suppertime.

Since it took well over half an acre of timber each year to provide fuel for one fireplace, much of the settlers' time was spent in the woods, and landscapes were quickly transformed by trees that had been felled or 'girdled' – that is, stripped of a section of bark and left to die. Sawn timber was also used to build houses, mile after mile of fencing, and furniture. This was usually quite simple. A long, crude table called a board (a hired servant would expect 'room and board') sufficed for all meals. People paired off to share from a wooden bowl, and everyone sat on benches – adults and guests above a salt cellar in the middle, children and servants 'below the salt'. It was very rare for one of these early houses to have a chair, but when it did, this was reserved for the head of the household – hence the word 'chairman'.

High Minded **Puritan family life emphasised piety and hard work.**

As well as serving as a dining room, the hall was also a bedroom. Bedding was rudimentary: most mattresses were made from a bag stuffed with bits of rag, wool and feathers, which could be rolled up and stacked during the day. Walls were plain, too; needless to say, there were no crucifixes or holy pictures, and the main decorations were generally firearms and tools hung up in the hall simply because there was nowhere else to put them.

Time, of course, brought some changes. Quite soon a loft might be added, providing room for the children to sleep, and a lean-to addition to the house, to which the cooking was transferred. But the hall remained the focus of family life. It was here that the Bible was read aloud and children were given lessons in reading and writing. The historian David Hooke has summarised the functions of the Puritan home in early America as 'a business, a vocational institute, a house of correction, a church, a welfare institution'. It was that basic unit of family life which would in time create a whole new society and set of values around it.

Chairman **Chairs were reserved for the head of the household.**

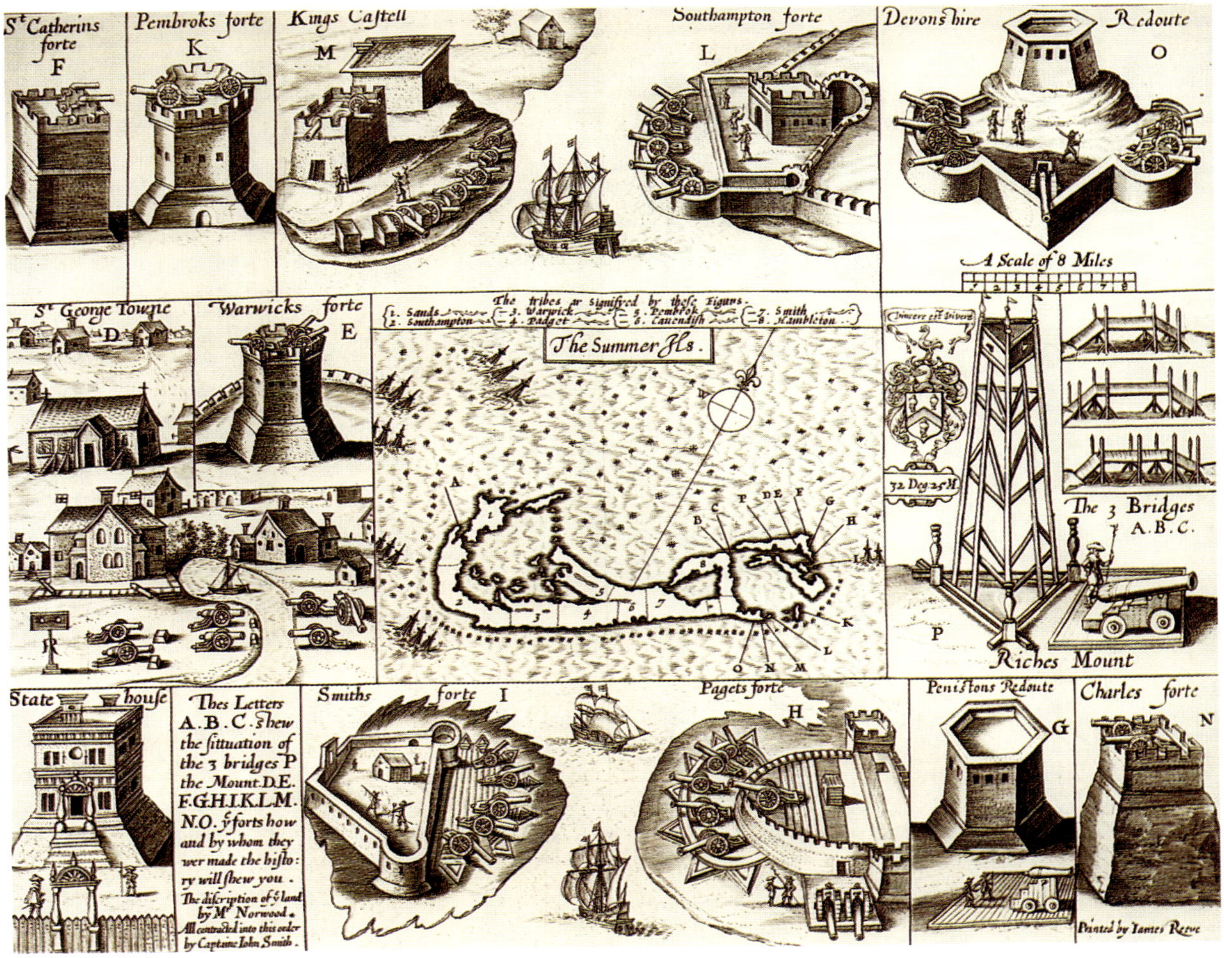

FOUNDATION OF EMPIRE An engraving of the fortifications of Bermuda.

tolerant. And it was the Leyden congregation that decided to move further afield, away from all the temptations of city life in old Europe, and start afresh in the New World.

THE PURITAN WAY

All the attitudes and activities of the Pilgrims stemmed from their religious beliefs. Their strict morality defined both their life in Leyden and that of the New Plymouth colony they founded. Every day began and ended with readings from the Bible; every meal was preceded and followed by prayer. Sunday effectively began at 6 pm on Saturday, after which all travelling to and from towns was forbidden. The Sabbath itself was spent largely in church – four hours in the morning, three or four hours in the afternoon, with prayers and meditation at home afterwards. In New Plymouth the spiritual leader, William Brewster, preached three times a week. Church attendance was compulsory and the sermons were very long; the minister would set up an hour-glass, but he – and his congregation – would expect it to go well over the hour. Hour after hour in church was not to everybody's taste, especially that of young children on swelteringly hot days. But any sign of restlessness, fidgeting or sleepiness would bring along an official called a tithingman, who walked up and down the

DID YOU KNOW?

Many Indian words have found their way into the English language, including persimmon, skunk, moccasin and canoe. Difficult words were altered, so that *pawschoicora* became 'hickory'; *isquotersuash* became 'squash'; and *arathkone* turned into 'raccoon'.

INDIAN VILLAGE The longhouses are arranged in a circle to provide protection in case of attack.

benches brushing the chins of the backsliders with a stick. Giggling or whispering would also attract his attention, and culprits were fined.

Most forms of frivolity constituted even more serious offences. Sports, games and drama, and above all that most pagan of pleasures, the Maypole, were forbidden; even Christmas Day was treated as a normal work day. One early group of newcomers to New Plymouth declined to work on the town's defences, claiming that it was against their principles to work on Christmas Day. However, when he returned from work at noon, Governor William Bradford was horrified to find them playing games, 'some pitching the bar, and some at stool-ball and such like sports'. He 'went to them and took away their implements and told them it was against *his* conscience, that they should play and others work. If they made the keeping of it a matter of devotions let them keep their houses, but there should be no gaming or revelling in the streets.'

Newcomers soon introduced even more problems for the New England Puritans. One was a Mr Fells, whose maid became pregnant; the Elders promptly 'packed them away as soon as possible'. Then there was Sir Christopher Gardiner, whose 'cousin' turned out to be his mistress. Worse than that, a notebook was discovered recording Sir Christopher's conversion to Rome, whereupon he, too, left the colony. The most colourful of the troublemakers was Thomas Morton, dissolute, witty and certainly at least half mad, who set up his own establishment at a place he called Merrymount, where he and his followers spent their time drinking, gambling and making love to Indian women. They even set up a Maypole, while Morton presided as Lord of Misrule. He was, of course, expelled – but not before he had begun engaging in the more sinister crime of gun-running for the Indians.

The sober pattern of life in New England was not typical of North American settlements as a whole. Sunday in Virginia, for example, was a more relaxed

EYEWITNESS

ALL QUIET ON THE LORD'S DAY

THE PURITAN SUNDAY could be a miserable experience for the unsuspecting traveller. Here is one view of the Sabbath in Boston:

❛ All their religion consists in observing Sunday by not working or going into the taverns on that day; but the houses are worse than the taverns. No stranger or traveller can therefore be entertained on a Sunday, which begins at sunset on Saturday and continues until the same time on Sunday. At these two hours you see all their countenances change. Saturday evening the constable goes round into all the taverns of the city for the purpose of stopping all noise and debauchery, which frequently causes him to stop his search before his search causes the debauchery to stop. ❜

DID YOU KNOW?

Harvard College was founded in Newetowne in 1636, but was given its current name only in 1639, after the Puritan minister John Harvard, who left the college £780 plus his 400-volume library when he died. At the same time, Newetowne was re-named Cambridge after Dr Harvard's old university in England.

affair, with trading, gossip and home entertainment. The late finish to the tobacco season in early December combined the harvest festival with Christmas, which became the settlers' great holiday and the main time for weddings. New Amsterdam practised a 'continental' Sunday with the taverns open and recreations that included dancing and horse-racing. Racing was even more popular in Virginia, as were hunting hares, raccoons and opossums, bull-baiting and cockfighting.

Even New England had its recreation days: the harvest festival merged with Thanksgiving; the annual town meetings, which were as much social as political occasions; Election Days, and the twice-yearly Muster Days for the militia, which were criticised by the more devout as opportunities for drunkenness. Nonetheless, by ignoring saints' days, folk customs and the festivities associated with particular crafts and trades in Europe, the colonists had by far the dullest calendar in the 'western' world.

FOOD AND DRINK

If the Puritans of New England seem severe, it was partly because the inhospitable nature of their land demanded it. After all, the Pilgrims had very nearly failed to survive their first winter – a time when they had taken to burying their dead in

SPORTING LIFE An idealised picture of the sporting pleasures of Virginia. In reality, hunting was less a sport than an essential means of getting food. Below: Settlers and Indians celebrate the first Thanksgiving.

Pilgrim Village

The pilgrim settlers in New England constructed well-defended, close-knit villages which, in the course of a few years, became virtually self-sufficient.

This village, based on New Plymouth in the 1620s, occupied a site overlooking an estuary. A steep slope led down to salt marshes on one side, and the cleared land made a surprise attack difficult. A wooden stockade, together with a redoubt in the centre of the village and a look-out point guarding the landing-stage, were constructed to defend the village against Indian attack.

Wooden houses surrounded by neat kitchen gardens lined the main street, together with a communal baking oven, storehouses and a barn. The common house was used for meetings and services. Everyone helped with looking after livestock and growing crops, and these supplies were supplemented by goods brought in by Indian traders.

COW SHED
REDOUBT

Pocahontas

Of the millions of Indians who have ever lived in North America, most people could probably name only three: Hiawatha, the chief who organised the Iroquois into a federation of Nations; Sitting Bull, who destroyed General Custer and his troops; and a young girl called Pocahontas.

Pocahontas's story begins with the foundation of the British colony at Jamestown, Virginia, in 1607. This was a vulnerable settlement 60 miles (96 km) up river in mosquito-infested territory, surrounded by hostile Indians under their chief Powhatan. Within three months, 46 colonists, nearly half the total, had died of disease. The rest faced starvation as they were too weak to farm the land and unfamiliar with the native fruits and berries that could save them. In desperation, the ruling council turned to the strongest man among them, John Smith, and begged him to undertake the dangerous task of seeking help and supplies from the Indians.

Smith, an experienced mercenary soldier, travelled 50 miles (80 km) up the James River before being captured by Powhatan's warriors. He might have been killed there and then, but he resourcefully played for time by showing the Indians his 'magic' compass with its needle moving apparently unaided. Eventually he was taken to Powhatan's camp, where the chief and his elders debated his fate. The sentence was death.

Indian Bride 'Lady Rebecca', as Pocahontas was known in England, in European dress.

Smith was stretched out on the ground, where he was to be clubbed to death. But just as the first blow was about to be struck, the chief's 12-year-old daughter, Pocahontas, rushed forward and flung herself protectively across Smith's body, begging for his life. Smith was freed, adopted by the tribe, given Indian names and returned to Jamestown with provisions.

Jamestown soon needed saving again. Although some 900 settlers had made the voyage in the first two years, there were only 100 left by 1610. However, in 1612 John Rolfe introduced tobacco and founded the basis of further prosperity. Two years later, with the agreement of her father, Rolfe married Pocahontas and in 1616 he took her to England. There she was given celebrity status as 'Lady Rebecca, alias Pocahontas, who was taught by John Rolfe, her husband, and his friends, to speak English and learn English customs and manners'. The marriage brought about a peace treaty with the Indians and heralded a period of growth and stability for the Jamestown settlement. Once again, Pocahontas had played her part in saving the colony. But, at the age of 21, just as her husband was about to return to Jamestown with her, she contracted smallpox and died. Six years later, the first of a series of devastating wars between Indians and settlers broke out. These were to destroy the Powhatan Indians and establish the military supremacy of the English in Virginia.

Saviour Pocahontas kneels beside the condemned John Smith and implores her father to spare his life.

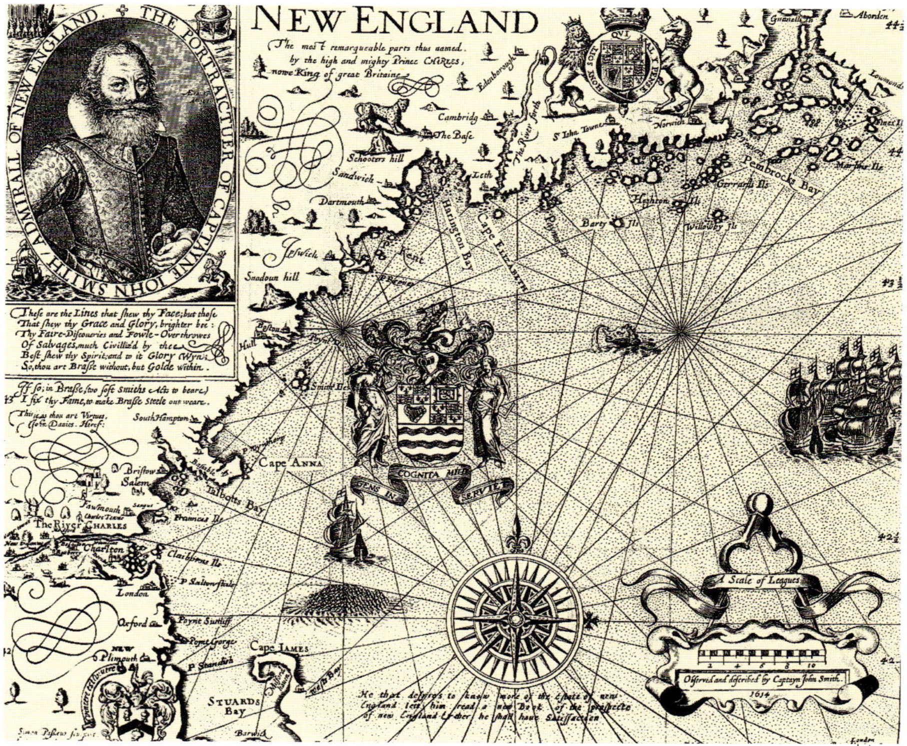

NEW ENGLAND John Smith's map of 1614 showing the colonial lands around Virginia.

flat graves at night, so as not to alert the Indians to their plight. In fact, it turned out to be Indians who saved them.

The local Indians were Wampanoags, farmers and hunters who traded and occasionally fought with neighbouring tribes. One of the Pilgrims described their rounded huts 'made with long young sapling trees, bended and both ends stuck in the ground. They were made round like an arbour, and covered down to the ground with thick and well-wrought mats, and the door was not over a yard high, made of a mat to open . . . Round about the fire they lay on mats which are their beds.' Inside the huts, the Pilgrim noted wooden bowls, trays, dishes, baskets made of crab shells, the remains of fish and deer, and tobacco seeds. It was certainly fortunate for the first settlers that they established good relations with the local tribe. The governor, William Bradford, wrote home: 'We often go to them and they to us. We entertain them familiarly in our houses and they as friendly bestowing their venison on us.'

When the colonists' seed crops failed to grow, a local Indian, Squanto, introduced them to maize; he taught them how to plant it in small mounds, and how, when the stalks were 3 ft (1 m) high, to use them as supports for beanshoots. He also showed them how to trap the swarms of herring that came in spring – sometimes 10 000 on one tide. Maize became an immediate staple, though the settlers preferred more familiar foods. Once established, their orchards grew apples and peaches – and their gardens parsnips, turnips, onions, peas, cabbage and carrots. From Virginia to New England, the colonists were wary of both the sweet potato and the white potato, clams and other shellfish, not to mention the unfamiliar blueberries and huckleberries. In time, of course, a taste for local food did develop – chowder, Boston beans, turkey, pumpkin, and corn-based meals such as samp and succotash – though nothing rivalled the popularity of pork once hogs and pigs began arriving from England.

BARBECUE The settlers learned new ways of gathering and cooking food from the Indians.

Another local staple of which the settlers were wary was water. In New England they favoured milk, from goats or cows, or alcohol. Breweries appeared early in New Plymouth, Boston, Charlestown and New Amsterdam, although a great deal of whiskey, rum, brandy and cider was home-made. It is hardly surprising that drunkenness was normally top of the list of offences dealt with by the colonies' courts.

GOVERNMENT AND LAND

Representative institutions of a kind unknown in Europe came early to North America, with the male settlers electing magistrates and officials, and Virginia

VARIETY IN SECOTA A detailed drawing by John White of the Indian village of Secota, Virginia.

establishing a House of Burgesses in 1619. For the first time, political, civil and criminal regulations were being made by ordinary, inexperienced men, who also dealt with matters handled in Europe by the Church authorities; marriage licences, for example, were handled by town clerks in New England and county clerks in Virginia. As a result, the colonists learned how to govern themselves, and how to select leaders from among their own numbers. Of course there were class distinctions, but these tended to come from wealth earned by hard work, rather than from inheritance and 'good breeding' as in Europe.

All work was done in common and all men were treated as equals. For example, the amount of land allotted to each individual in New Plymouth was based on an oddly narrow unit of 8 ft (2.4 m) by 49½ ft (15 m). These plots accommodated the first mud-and-wattle shelters, and later the clapboard-and-shingle houses that characterised the close-knit 'village' communities of New England's towns. Virginia, with its 2000 miles (3220 km) of shoreline and a hinterland of tobacco plantations, adopted a different approach. There, land was so plentiful that the planters abandoned their flimsy farmhouses when they had exhausted the land, and moved on. The spaciousness of the south changed the meaning of the word 'neighbourhood', from the area you could see from your house to any distance within a day's ride.

In New Plymouth, in 1623, many settlers objected to working on behalf of other people; the young and strong, for example, did not see why they should work just as hard for the elderly, whose needs were less; and the women objected to washing, planting, cleaning and mending for those outside their own households. New taxes were introduced to provide for defence, and for fishing and hunting expeditions, which were all necessarily communal activities. Otherwise, life changed to one of private enterprise, and it worked: 'It made all hands very industrious, so as much more corn was planted than otherwise would have been. The women now went willingly into the field, and took their little ones with them to set corn, which before would allege weakness and inability . . .'

The biggest change of all, however, came with the very success of the colonies and the massive influx of new arrivals. On Easter Monday 1629, eight ships carried 900 settlers to the new colony to be settled at Massachusetts Bay. The supremacy of Massachusetts and its chief town, Boston, was now inevitable. By 1700 Boston was a busy, powerful city of 7000 inhabitants, and New Plymouth had been absorbed into the colony of Massachusetts.

At the same time, the massive influx of colonists eroded the New England Indians' territory and led, as everywhere else, to their decline. It is ironic, therefore, that the first Thanksgiving Day, held in New Plymouth in the autumn of 1621, had been a joint celebration with an Indian people who would so soon have nothing to be thankful for.

LANDS OF SILKS AND SPICES

With the opening of the Cape route to India and the Far East, European civilisation was brought into direct contact with the rich traditions of East Africa, Persia, the Indian sub-continent, the Far East and Indonesia. The clashes with Arab, Hindu, Buddhist and Confucian worlds created a culture shock for the Europeans, and left indelible marks on all the communities that they encountered.

TRAVELLERS IN THE EAST

The Portuguese led the way, with other Europeans following in their trail. Traders and colonists from the Netherlands, England and France seized land and influence that the Portuguese had wrested so bloodily from the native inhabitants of the East.

WHEN VASCO da Gama, the Portuguese navigator, rounded the Cape of Good Hope in 1497-8 and sailed into the Indian Ocean, he entered a busy world of seaborne trade that, although new to him, was long established among the Muslim traders of the region. Arab fleets dominated the seas; they took gold and ivory from East Africa to the Malabar coast of south-west India, and brought cinnamon from Ceylon, pepper from India and spices from Indonesia to Europe via the Levant. Da Gama had indeed found the route to the Indies.

On May 21 1498, da Gama reached Calicut, a thriving port on the Malabar coast. For his meeting with its ruler, a Hindu Samorin, or Sea-Rajah, da Gama came enthroned on a palanquin – the oriental sedan chair – with guns booming in salute, drums beating and flags waving. The Portuguese were taken to a Hindu temple, which they took to be some kind of Christian church. They worshipped before statues of goddesses, mistaking them for the Virgin Mary,

CAPTAIN AND CAPE **Vasco da Gama established the route to the Indian Ocean via the Cape of Good Hope. Below: English ships of the East India Company followed the path pioneered by da Gama.**

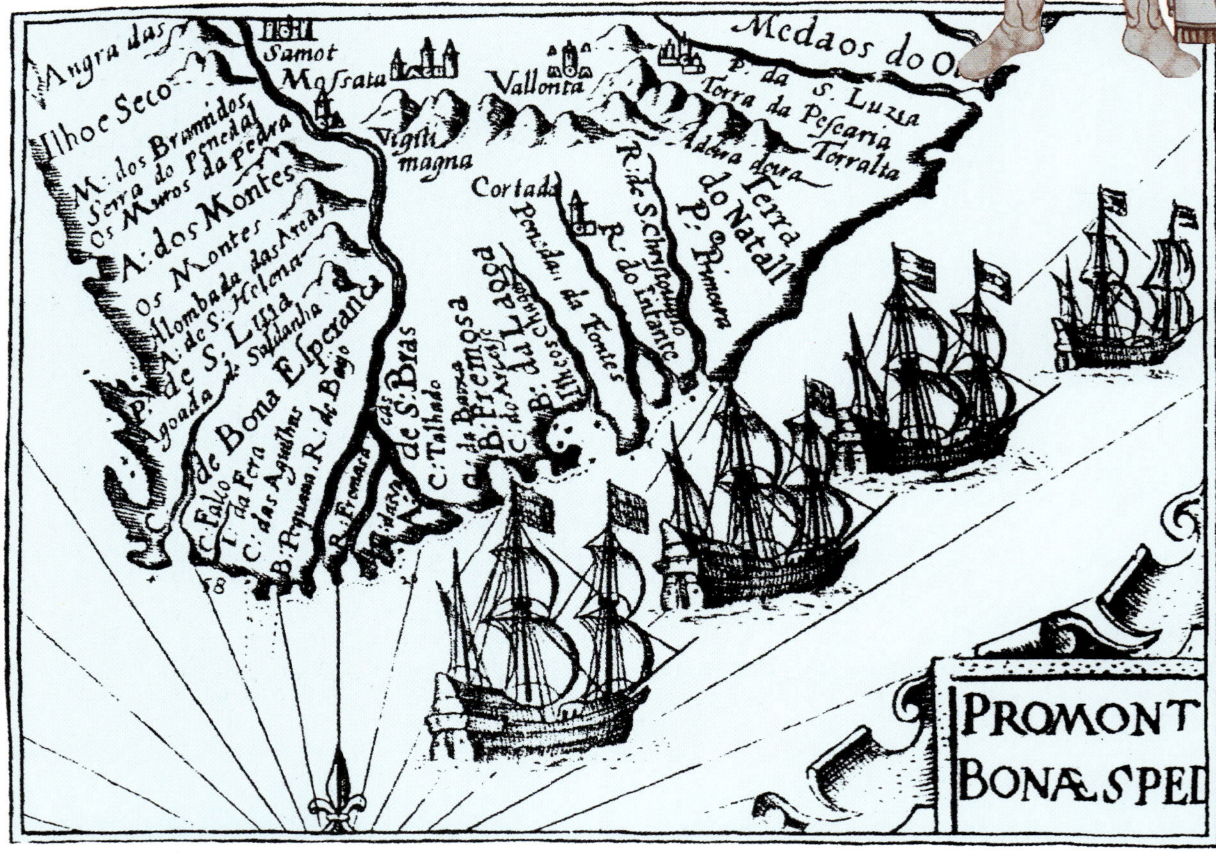

which scandalised the Hindus. Following this, da Gama had an audience with the Samorin, recorded by the chronicler of da Gama's voyage: 'In his left hand the King held a very large golden cup, having a capacity of half an almude [8 pints/4.5 litres] . . . On the right side of the King stood a basin of gold, so large that a man might just encircle it with his arms . . .' The Samorin made it clear that he was insulted by da Gama's gifts, very likely a piece of coral, a hat, a few copper bowls and bells. After the behaviour in the temple, this made da Gama's negotiations for a trading treaty hopeless. Months of bickering followed, and on August 29, 1498, he sailed for home.

Of da Gama's original crew of 170, only a third lived to see Portugal again. But da Gama himself arrived to a hero's welcome early in September 1499. He had brought precious stones, gold, ivory and spices; he had rounded the Cape and found the ocean route to the Indies; and he had also produced a new

DID YOU KNOW?

The triangular lateen sail takes its name from the word 'Latin'. Triangular sails were features of Arab ships of the 'Latin' Mediterranean, and they were adopted for use, in combination with the square-rigged sails of north European tradition, for many of the ships in the exploration fleets.

FAILURE AT ADEN **In 1513 the Portuguese failed to capture Aden, leaving Red Sea trade in Arab hands. Below: A variety of warships, cargo vessels and armed merchantmen plied the oceans in the 16th century.**

EYEWITNESS

'A Difference of One Day'

Before the International Dateline, calendars became confused, as this extract from Francesco Carletti's *My Voyage Around the World* demonstrates:

❛ And we found a difference in reckoning the days between us, who had come from the city of Manila, and the Portuguese who had come from that of Macao, an island off China. Those Portuguese, having left Lisbon and navigated constantly eastward, had reached Japan as the farthest point of their journeying. During their voyage, the sun having risen for them constantly earlier, they had gained twelve hours of a natural day. We, on the contrary, having left the port of Sanlucar de Barrameda in Spain and navigated steadily westward and having lost daylight constantly because the sun kept rising later, had lost twelve hours. So when we discussed it with them, we found that we had reached a difference of one day. And when they said that it was Sunday, we counted up to Saturday. Had I pursued my voyage around the world without having met those Portuguese, by the time of my arrival in Europe, whence I first had departed, I should have lost exactly a whole day of twenty-four hours. ❜

mission for Portugal – a crusade in Asian seas against the Muslims, whom the Portuguese considered heathens as well as commercial rivals.

Da Gama was given the title Admiral of the Seas of the Indies, though he declined to lead the next voyage. Command of this went to Pedro Cabral, whose fleet of 13 well-armed ships and 1500 men left on March 9, 1500. Cabral's first mistake was a happy one – the discovery of Brazil, when he was blown off course. Others were less fortunate. At Calicut he was well received by the Hindu ruler, given a warehouse and his crew provided with lodgings. Some Muslims, however, launched an assault on the warehouse, killing half the 70 Portuguese occupants, to which Cabral responded by sinking ten Muslim ships and murdering their crews. He also bombarded Calicut, terrorising the Hindus and their ruler, who had taken no part in the assault. He filled his ships with treasure and left for home on January 15, 1501. Only seven of the original 13 ships reached Lisbon, but Cabral's valuable cargoes ensured not only his welcome from the king but also rapid plans for a new expedition.

Downfall of Diu The Portuguese annexed the vital port of Diu, killing its sultan, in 1537.

Vasco da Gama set sail on his second voyage on February 10, 1502, with a large fleet divided into three squadrons. The aims were to impose Portugal's trading supremacy and to plunder Arab shipping in the Indian Ocean, as well as to punish the Samorin of Calicut, which he did by devastating the town with Portuguese artillery.

An Empire is Founded

King Manuel of Portugal realised that no long-term aim was to be served by such hit-and-run missions and so he appointed first Francisco de Almeida, in 1505, and then Alfonso de Albuquerque, in 1509, as Viceroy of the Indies.

OUTGUNNED **Arab and local pirate ships (above) were no match for the heavily armed ships of the Portuguese, shown below in possession of Calicut, an important trading post and one of their earlier conquests on the Indian coast.**

DID YOU KNOW?

Silver was used as currency in China and Japan, but not in the form of coins. Instead, people had silver 'loaves', shaped like small boats, which they cut expertly with large scissors and then weighed on portable scales. In 1626 Father de las Cortés reckoned that every child in China could guess the amount of metal and its purity in any 'loaf'; he also observed that children picked up every scrap, however small, to put in small bell-shaped containers made of wax. When a child thought there was enough silver, he would simply melt the wax.

Albuquerque brought both statesmanship and military prowess to the job. It was largely his strategic insight that identified the crucial points that controlled trade. One was Hormuz, the key to the Persian Gulf; the second was Malacca (near present-day Singapore), reputed to be the richest city in the East, which dominated trade to and from the Spice Islands; and the third was Goa, which he attacked with 20 ships and 1000 men. Battles continued around Goa even after its surrender in February 1510, but it soon became the jewel in the crown of Portuguese Asia and capital of the Empire of the Indies. Malacca

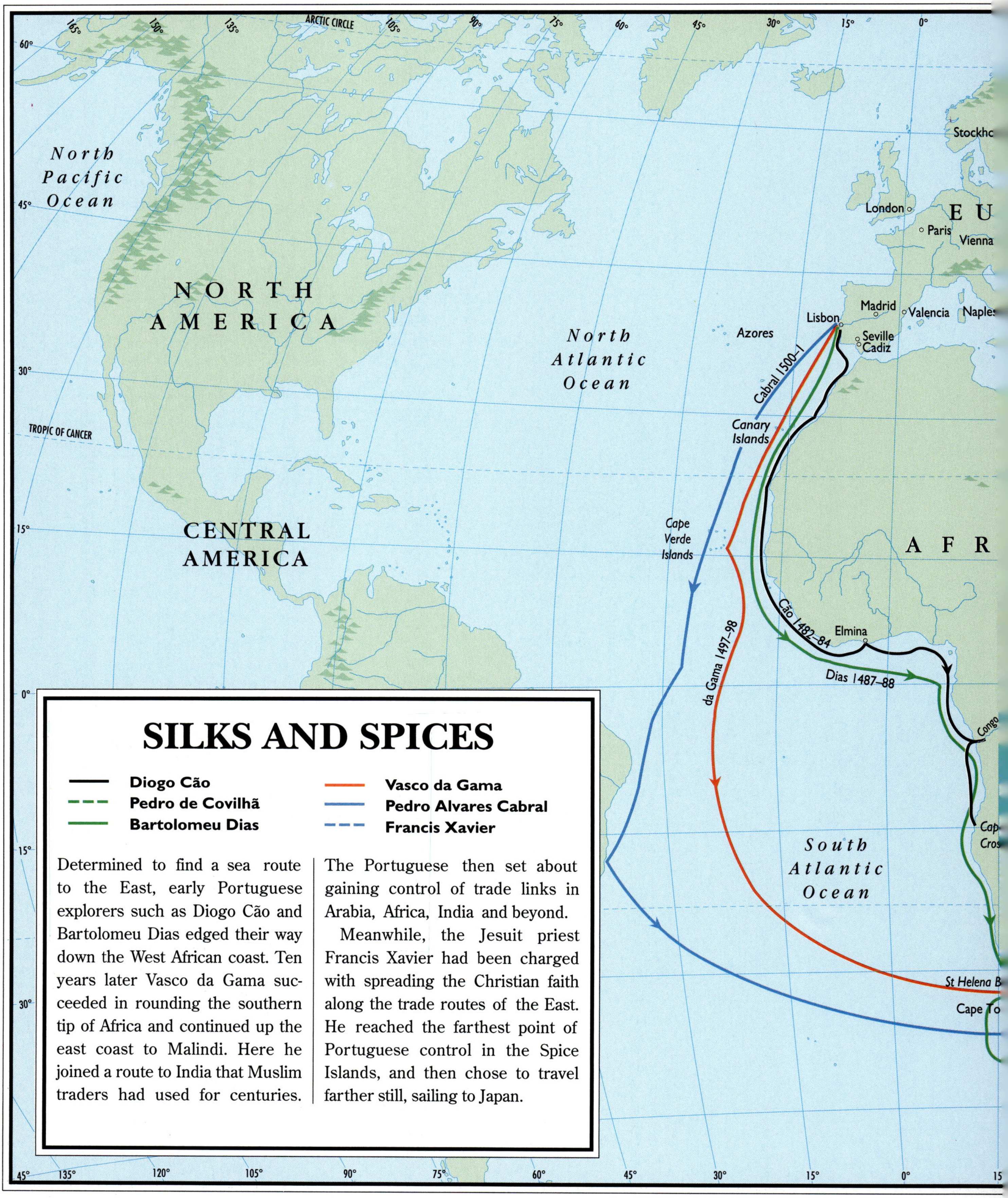

SILKS AND SPICES

- Diogo Cão
- Pedro de Covilhã
- Bartolomeu Dias
- Vasco da Gama
- Pedro Alvares Cabral
- Francis Xavier

Determined to find a sea route to the East, early Portuguese explorers such as Diogo Cão and Bartolomeu Dias edged their way down the West African coast. Ten years later Vasco da Gama succeeded in rounding the southern tip of Africa and continued up the east coast to Malindi. Here he joined a route to India that Muslim traders had used for centuries.

The Portuguese then set about gaining control of trade links in Arabia, Africa, India and beyond.

Meanwhile, the Jesuit priest Francis Xavier had been charged with spreading the Christian faith along the trade routes of the East. He reached the farthest point of Portuguese control in the Spice Islands, and then chose to travel farther still, sailing to Japan.

Routes are plotted according to the best estimates of modern scholarship. In some cases, however, accurate information is available only for parts of a voyage.

was stormed in 1511, and Hormuz taken in 1515. Of the strategic points identified by Albuquerque, only Aden, which commanded movement to and from the Red Sea, remained unconquered.

Albuquerque's rule laid the foundations for other conquests and discoveries. The Spice Islands of the Moluccas were taken in 1512; a Portuguese trading mission reached Canton in 1514; Ceylon, home of gold, elephants and cinnamon, was taken in 1518; and Diu on the north-west coast of India was captured in 1537. In 1542 a party of Portuguese landed accidentally in Japan, opening a trading and missionary territory rich in promise, while in 1557 a trading settlement was established at Macao off the Chinese coast.

By the mid-16th century Portugal's Asian empire was essentially complete. It consisted of some 40

LANDFALL The Portuguese established trading posts all along the east coast of Africa.

EYEWITNESS

TRICKS OF THE TRADE

EUROPEAN CANNON were generally superior to that of the East, but there were severe penalties for passing on the art of making and firing cannon. Here is an early 16th-century account, by the Italian traveller Ludovico di Varthema, of rule-breaking in India:

❛ Being then arrived in Calicut (1506) I found two Christians who were Milanese. One was called Ioan-Maria and the other Piero-Antonio, who had arrived from Portugal with the ships of the Portuguese and had come to purchase jewels on the part of the King. And when they had arrived in Cochin, they fled to Calicut . . . They told me that they would willingly have returned to their country, but that they did not know by what way. I answered them: "Return by the way you came." They said that was not possible, because they had escaped from the Portuguese and that the King of Calicut had obliged them to make a great quantity of artillery against their will, and on this account they did not wish to return by that route. And they said that they expected the fleet of the King of Portugal very soon. I answered them, that if God granted me so much grace that I might be able to escape to Cananor when the fleet had arrived, I would so act that the captain of the Christians should pardon them, and I told them that it was not possible for them to escape by any other way, because it was known through many nations that they made artillery and many kings had wished to have them in their hands on account of their skill, and therefore it was not possible to escape in any other manner. And you must know that they had made between four and five hundred pieces of ordnance large and small, so that in short they had great fear of the Portuguese. And in truth there were reasons to be afraid, for not only did they make the artillery themselves, but they had also taught the Pagans to make it, and they told me, moreover, that they had taught fifteen servants of the King to fire spingarde. And during the time I was here, they gave a Pagan the design and form of a mortar, which weighed one hundred and five cantara and was made of metal. ❜

NEW MASTERS A Dutch captain shakes hands with King Kandy of Ceylon, an island that fell in 1658 after more than 100 years of Portuguese control.

towns and trading posts stretching along the Indian Ocean; it held extraterritorial rights in Japan and China; and it had a presence in Ceylon and South-east Asia. But Portugal's impact was not confined to her merchants and conquerors, for her influence also involved the work of the Catholic missionaries. Of these, the greatest was the Spaniard Francis Xavier – later canonised by the Church.

Arriving in Goa in 1542, Xavier spent more than two years among the Hindus of both the east and the west Indian coasts before sailing for Malacca in 1545 and working in Malaysia and Indonesia. In 1549 he went to Japan, preaching in many regions of the south; despite, or perhaps because of, his uncompromising message – that there was no possibility of salvation outside the Roman Catholic Church – he had made over 1000 converts in Japan by the time he left in 1551. His next ambition was to begin the conversion of the Chinese, but he died of fever, at the age of 46, on an island off the Chinese coast, waiting for permission to enter the country.

After Xavier's death, the missions achieved some startling successes; in the late 16th century, Japan alone had some 300 000 converts. But neither the work of the missionaries nor the Portuguese Empire itself was to survive. The Jesuits were expelled from Japan and Christianity outlawed there in 1614. Meanwhile the Portuguese Empire was rapidly disintegrating at the hands of the English and Dutch. The Dutch East India Company, formed in 1602, spearheaded a series of attacks on the Portuguese, effectively supplanting them with a Dutch empire centred on a new capital, Batavia (now Jakarta), on Java. By the second half of the 17th century, Portugal's vast eastern empire had been reduced to Goa, Macao and a few of the less important islands.

DID YOU KNOW?

The Chinese word for Europeans was *Folangchi*, and occasionally *Fancui*. The words probably came from the European word 'Franks', one of the barbaric tribes that harassed the Roman Empire, and was taught to the Chinese by Muslims, who had no liking for Europeans.

SPICE WARS A Dutch squadron storms the Portuguese-held stronghold of Bantam.

THE PORTUGUESE COLONISTS

From vulnerable fortified warehouses to sumptuous cities, the Portuguese established settlements across Asia, some of them the envy of European visitors who marvelled at what had been created.

THE PORTUGUESE broke into the busy world of Indian Ocean commerce by brute force, destroying Arab and Muslim fleets and conquering historic towns and city-states. There were places, such as Malindi on the East African coast and Hormuz at the entrance to the Persian Gulf, where they reached an accommodation with the local rulers, but on the whole the Portuguese employed force of arms. They completely disrupted the ancient trading network that they invaded, and, though they never established a complete monopoly, they dominated enough of the trade in the area to ensure that the reduced and diminished commerce of the region benefited few others.

The Portuguese colonies stretched along the coasts of the Indian Ocean and beyond. They included settlements in East Africa and Arabia; the east and west coasts of India and Ceylon; Malaysia and South-east Asia; Indonesia and the Spice Islands. But, with the exception of Malacca and Goa, few could be called colonies in the modern sense. Most of the 40 or so

RICHES OF THE EAST **A 16th-century map of India shows the array of treasures sought by the explorers.**

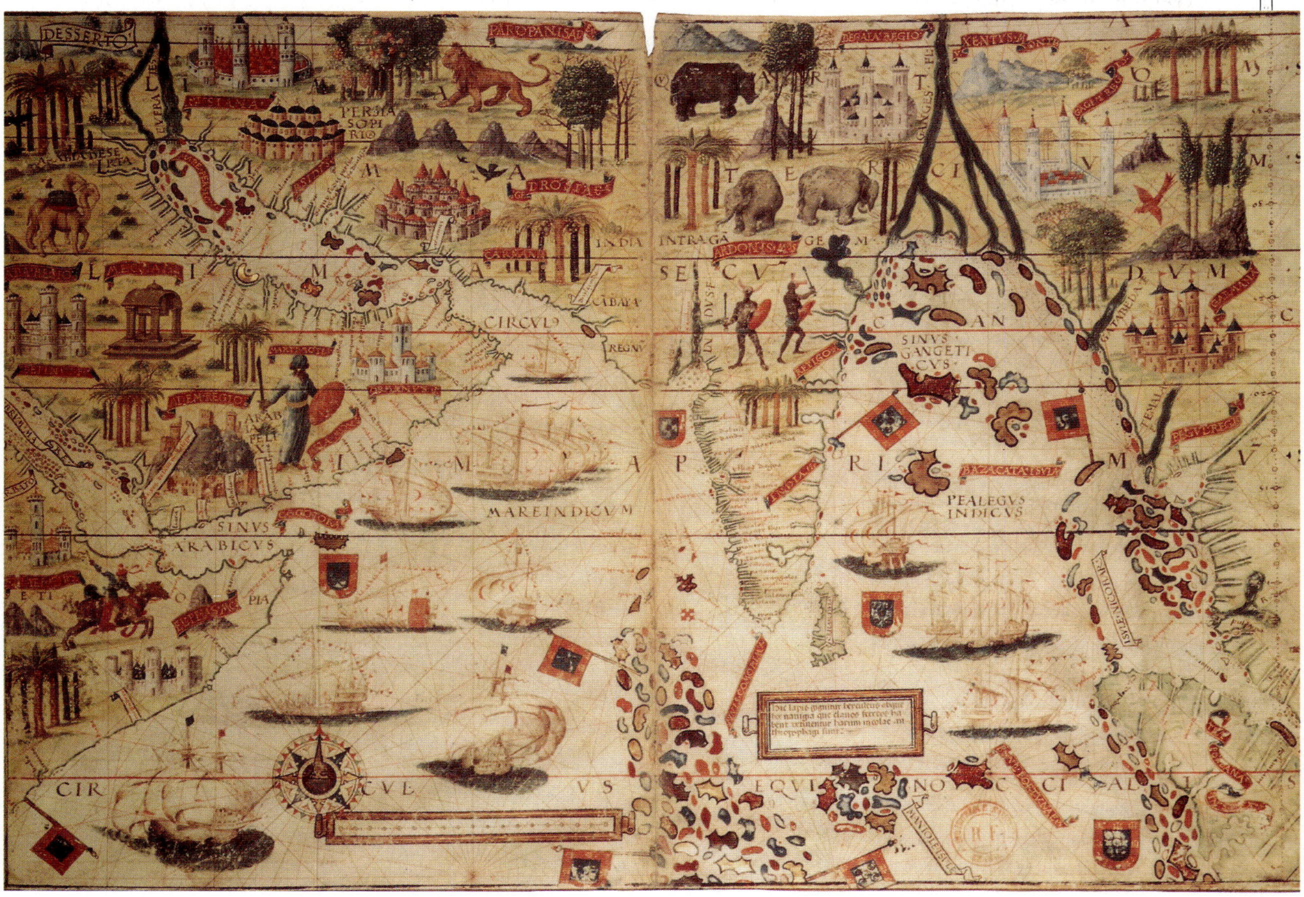

communities consisted of mere 'factories' or trading posts, a few hundred inhabitants clustered around a warehouse and its accompanying fortifications.

The Portuguese lived well enough in Hormuz, where the English merchant-adventurer Ralph Fitch paid a visit in 1583. He described 'the driest island in the world: for there is nothing growing in it but only salt'. Everything for daily life, including water and wood, had to be brought from Persia, about 12 miles (19 km) away. Yet: 'There is a very great trade of all sorts of spices, drugs, silks, cloth of silk, fine tapestry of Persia, great store of pearls . . . and many horses of Persia, which serve all India. They have a Moor to their King which is chosen and governed by the Portugals.'

At the other end of the scale, though, were the settlements like Mozambique. There were slaves, trade, some gold and ivory, but, like most of the African areas under Portuguese control, the settlement consisted of a few score soldiers. It also served as a penal colony, and the wives of captains or magistrates simply did not accompany their husbands. The Portuguese authorities made efforts to send prostitutes to such places, and even a few female 'state orphans'. But the death rate was appalling, and the Portuguese in the outposts of East Africa generally found partners among Swahili women. Exiles or convicts tried to escape, soldiers to desert, and officials to vie for the prestigious postings in Goa or Brazil.

For the most part, the presence of the Portuguese was precarious, and, with one or two exceptions, they made little impact on the varied local cultures that they encountered. Islam was not displaced, and the populations retained their traditional lifestyles.

DESERT DEFENCES This detail of a 16th-century map shows the coastal settlements on the Arabian peninsula. Below: The Mogul ruler Akbar gives an audience at his palace.

DID YOU KNOW?

Babur, the founder of the Mogul dynasty, despised worldly wealth. When his son, Humayan, was ill, and the doctors prescribed that Babur give up his most valuable possession, the Koh-i-Nor, largest and most famous diamond in the world, Babur replied: 'What good is worldly wealth?'

Thus Friday continued to be observed as a holy day; food forbidden by the Koran remained forbidden; and the traditional Muslim reliance on milk and dairy produce was unaffected. For many settlers, the customs of the country came to them rather than the other way round. And they sometimes lived, to their displeasure, in towns very different from the European cities they were used to.

Middle Eastern towns were almost invariably crowded and low-built, with a maze of narrow streets along which no wheeled vehicle could travel. The one-storey houses, made of mud, wood and occasionally stone followed the dictates of the Koran, which disapproved of all tall buildings except those built to the glory of God. The streets were never cleaned; refuse was thrown from the windows, and, when it rained, rivers of stinking mud and rubbish collected in gulleys.

The towns, radiating out from a mosque at the centre, consisted mainly of marketplaces; holy objects and perfumes were sited closest to the centre, followed by precious items such as silverware, gold, ceramics and silks, right out to the food stalls on the fringe. Here there was always water on the boil for tea and

GOLDEN GOA The marketplace at Goa, a city that was renowned for 'the good life' under Portuguese rule.

coffee, and all manner of cooked and uncooked foods, including meat. Wary travellers thought twice about the meat, suspecting that it was horse, camel or dog. Around these stalls were areas where the poorer patrons sat and ate their midday or evening meals. These markets were very much the centres of social life. There were entertainers, such as jugglers and acrobats, and storytellers, whose beautifully crafted tales have been immortalised for later generations in *A Thousand and One Nights*.

Eastern Ways and the Western Response

The Muslim communities made up only a small fraction of the populations encountered by European settlers in the East. And even where a country's rulers were Muslim, for example, in the territories of the great Mogul dynasty that controlled northern India, the great majority of indigenous people held to their age-old, and varied, Hindu and Buddhist religions and lifestyles.

In whatever form they encountered them, the Portuguese and all the other Europeans who followed in their wake were baffled by the lands of Hindu temples and Buddhist monasteries. For the Portuguese, there was the first disastrous error when Vasco da Gama's crew, taken to visit a Hindu temple by their hosts in Calicut, mistook representations of Hindu goddesses for likenesses of the Virgin Mary and proceeded to worship before them. Other errors followed: arrogant attempts at forcible conversion to Christianity and brutal efforts to requisition cheap labour that caused many native Indians to flee.

To the Western mind, Eastern beliefs were incomprehensible. The early voyagers could at least understand Islam with its one God and Day of Judgment, even if they detested it. But the bewildering mixture of gods, rituals and rites of ancestor worship confused them. The Catholic missionaries who

SELF-SACRIFICE At the Juggernaut ceremony, an image of the Hindu god Krishna was pulled along on a cart and the faithful flung themselves under its wheels.

DRESS SENSE The richly decorated fabrics worn in India entranced the Europeans. Designed to display the body's contours, they scandalised pious churchmen.

followed hard in the footsteps of the European soldiers and traders in China, India, South-east Asia and Japan could not even decide whether these Oriental practices constituted a religion at all. Until about 1540 they were generally tolerant, for they lived and worked alongside people of other faiths, Muslims included. However, from the 1540s the Portuguese became sterner in their attitudes to non-Christians. Hindu temples, Muslim mosques and Buddhist monasteries were destroyed; and in 1560 the Inquisition came to Goa, with many people burnt at the stake. However, not all the missionaries accepted the new approach. Many Jesuits came to argue that 'Malabar [Hindu] rites' could be accommodated without heresy into the Catholic doctrine. They studied the texts, discussed them with native priests and dressed as locals. In 1618 Father Roberto de Nobili appeared before the Archbishop of Goa dressed in Brahmin robes.

The methods of the more fanatical missionaries were hardly tailored to winning hearts and minds. Almost no Muslim converts were made, apart from the wives or concubines of the Portuguese. The Catholics refused to ordain Hindu converts as priests,

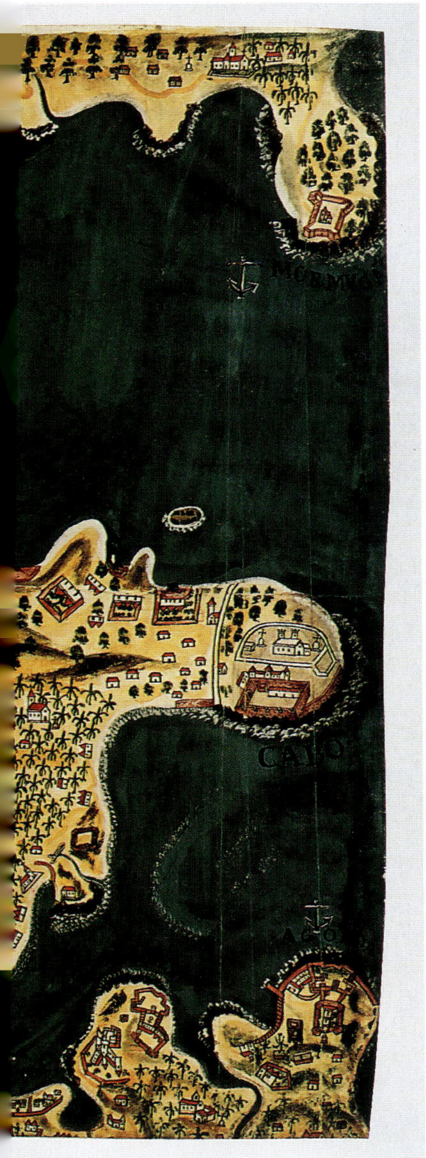

JEWEL IN THE CROWN **The settlement at Goa was the capital of Portugal's Asian empire, and her jurisdiction stretched, in theory, from East Africa to Macao, and from India to South-east Asia.**

DID YOU KNOW?

The Japanese emperor, whose capital was Kyoto, was a nonentity. Real power lay with the Shogun in his capital at Edo (Tokyo), where the great landowners had to spend several months and, when they left, were compelled to leave their families behind as hostages for good behaviour.

and moreover passed laws claiming possession of all Indian orphans in their territories – needless to say, the relatives of the children were often devastated.

Nevertheless, the numbers of converts were impressive. By the end of the 16th century there were 50 000 Christians in the area around Goa; 30 000 in Ceylon; a few thousand in Cochin and other Indian coastal towns; some 15 000 in the islands of Indonesia; and a total of roughly 10 000 in Malacca, Indochina and China. These figures exclude Japan, with its 300 000 converts in and around Nagasaki and the capital, Kyoto – a staggering figure considering that there were only 137 Jesuits in Japan in 1597. The lives of the converts were transformed; they were generally ostracised by their old communities, and regarded as inferior by those who had converted them. In time the local ruler, or shogun, concerned that the foreign ways would undermine Japanese values and culture, instigated the persecution of Christians, and many were tortured or executed by burning, beheading or crucifixion.

The conversion of a number of Buddhists and Hindus succeeded partly because their creeds had certain things in common with Roman Catholicism. There were prayers with beads like rosaries; incense and chanting; monasteries with monks and nuns; colourful ceremonies and processions; and temples with holy relics and images of deities. More fundamentally, though, the Christian doctrine of salvation being available to all appealed in particular to the victims of the caste system. Many Indians, and the inhabitants of Ceylon and South-east Asia, accepted that the condition of people in this life reflected a well-spent or ill-spent life in a previous incarnation – in contrast to Christianity, which revered a humble carpenter as God. The caste system of India dictated large areas of daily life – whom you could touch, whose home you could visit, whose meal you could share, with whom you could trade, and what kind of job was open to you. At their most aggressive, the missionaries tried to break the system down, for example by compelling Hindus to eat 'unclean' food or to associate with those of different stations in life.

But they failed to appreciate how deeply religion was ingrained in the social life and conventions of these countries. For example, they could not understand the taboos that prevented the Brahmins, the top layer of Indian society, from accepting invitations to visit European ships, where they might be forced into contact with lower-caste Hindu sailors. Nor did the Portuguese understand the Hindu practice of widow-burning, or *suttee*, which they abolished in their territories – despite the fact that it was central to the Hindu way of life, ensuring as it did that the dead man was accompanied into the afterlife by his faithful widow.

LIFE IN GOLDEN GOA

Goa was far more than the home of the Inquisition in India. The city was the residence of the viceroy and the archbishop, the second most important centre of Jesuit organisation outside Rome, and the administrative capital of all Portuguese possessions in

PEPPERS, PERFUME AND PORCELAIN: THE LUXURIES OF LIFE

THE OPENING of the new routes during the age of exploration made certain luxuries more accessible in western Europe: exotic spices from the East; ivory from Africa; porcelain, lacquered furniture and silks from China. Even in countries outside Europe, there were plenty of imported luxuries too, such as fine horses from Arabia and Persia, and elephants from Ceylon which were in great demand in India both for warfare and for work.

But it was Europe's craze for spices that made 'the Indies' so alluring. It had been largely in search of these that voyagers had first braved the Atlantic, looking for a northern sea route, and had then rounded the Cape, travelling to the Indian subcontinent and beyond to the remotest islands of Indonesia. For example, the Portuguese obtained their pepper from the Malabar coast, cinnamon from Ceylon, cloves from the Moluccas, and nutmeg and mace from the Bandas. They also found sandalwood in Timor, silk in China and lacquer in Pegu.

This enthusiasm was nothing new and was partly due to the fact that meat was rarely fresh, and that spices added greatly to the flavour. When Alaric the Goth had sacked ancient Rome in AD 410 he had found a storehouse containing 5000 lb (2265 kg) of pepper. And in the Middle Ages, even the poorer households of Europe had easy access to herbs and spices such as thyme, marjoram, bay leaves, aniseed, coriander and garlic. However, the passion grew throughout the age of exploration, with trade dominated at first by Venice, then by Lisbon, and eventually by Amsterdam, which supplied Russia and other latecomers.

Silk was the most fashionable fabric – and before the spread of the silk industry in Italy, the best came from China. It became a mark of rank, helping the rich to distinguish themselves from the mass of the people. In France, Henry IV forbade the wives and daughters of the bourgeois in Paris to wear silk; and in China itself only the poorest silks were allowed to those below the ranks of the nobility.

Other luxuries of the age included furs, precious stones, rare dyes, perfumes and fine porcelain. But as each became more widely available, another more fashionable item would take its place.

INTRICACY Indian fabrics were decorated by specialist craftsmen.

INDIAN KING The King of Cochin (in Southern India) is borne aloft by his attendants.

the East. Naturally there were other prosperous settlements, but it was 'Golden Goa' that captured the imagination. Here, built on an island, grew a walled city of spectacular wealth where Portuguese men lived in luxury with their Eurasian wives, their families, slaves, mistresses and servants. For the Portuguese overseas it became *the* centre of high life, corruption, intrigue and riches. As a great trading centre it took spices from other parts of India and Malacca; Venetian glass, playing cards, books and fashionable clothes from Europe; gold and precious stones from Burma; elephants and cinnamon from Ceylon; magnificent horses from Persia and Arabia; and silks, ceramics and luxurious furnishings from China.

The city grew on the site of a small native village to become a fair approximation of a wealthy European Renaissance-style city, with wide streets, public buildings and palatial homes for the Portuguese. Visitors envied them their lifestyle and the ready availability of beautiful Indian and Eurasian women with their heavy jewels and soft silk saris. Most Portuguese did no work – they were merchants living like princes. And even a humble artisan might own a dozen African slaves or more.

Yet for all its delights, life in Goa was doubtless more attractive to visitors than to settlers, who had to contend with disease and the threat of attack, their low numbers making them vulnerable. Portugal's population remained at little more than 1 million throughout the age of exploration, and while the 2500 or so who left her shores each year were a drain on her resources, they were a drop in the ocean when deposited among populations of tens of millions. A ship leaving Lisbon for India with 800 passengers was likely to carry no more than half a dozen females; it would probably pick up some 500 black slaves, male

PRESERVING WINE Wine in India was carefully preserved in square, covered ewers. Below: Different Indian boats were used for local coastal trade.

SHORT BUT SWEET Life in Portugal's Asian colonies was hazardous, but the lifestyle was enviable, with plenty of servants to cater for the *fidalgo*'s needs.

and female, in Mozambique, but half the passengers would be dead before they reached Goa and had to confront the problems presented by life in colonial Asia.

Because of the shortage of European women, the overseas settlers decided to mix with the local people, creating populations of *mestizos* (or Eurasians), and to depend where possible on the co-operation of local Hindus and Muslims. By the 1580s, Goa had a population of about 60 000, of whom only some 4000 were Portuguese.

IN SUPPORT OF COLONIAL LIFE

The determination of the settlers to make the most of their opportunities is not surprising. After all, it was the soldiers amongst them, the *soldados*, who protected the settlements, and the 'married males', the *casados*, whose trade provided the wealth. Trade was the life-blood of the communities. Malacca controlled the spice trade; Goa controlled trade along the Indian coast; and Macao dominated trade between China and Japan. The settlers in these trading posts felt few ties with the homeland: they adopted native food and light native costumes as well as native women, which naturally did not please the viceregal authorities at Goa, or the churchmen.

These officials played little part in colonial daily

TIME FOR TEA An English grandee of the East India Company watches a tea plantation, source of a world-wide export trade, being established.

life, however. More important were the voluntary groups of prominent citizens, which formed the 'twin pillars of colonial society': the town councils, or *camara*, and the lay brotherhoods, or *misericordia*. The *camara*, with its aldermen, an attorney, treasurer, market inspector, jailer and a superintendent of public works, was responsible for the distribution of common land, municipal taxation, licensing traders, price-fixing, the quality of goods sold, roads, buildings, bridges, fountains, jails, public health, the garrisons, public holidays and religious processions. The welfare role of the *misericordia* – Goa had as many as 600 lay brothers in 1609 – included the seven corporeal works of mercy: feeding the hungry; giving drink to the thirsty; clothing the naked; visiting the sick and imprisoned; ransoming captives; sheltering the weary; and burying the dead.

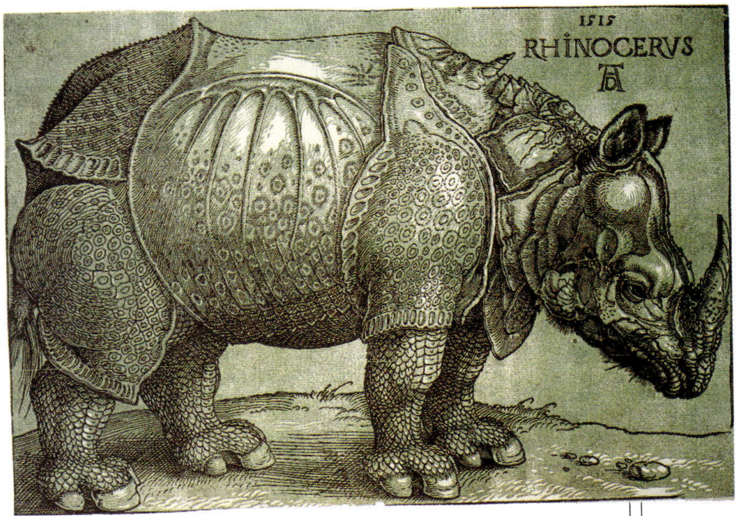

HORN OF PLENTY Albrecht Dürer executed this drawing of a Cambay rhinoceros in 1515 from descriptions sent to him from Lisbon by a friend. Below: An Englishman in India, a sub-continent that his nation was in time to dominate.

THE PORTUGUESE MIRACLE FADES

Portuguese institutions were in decline by the end of the age of exploration, as indeed was the 'Portuguese miracle' itself. Once Golden Goa had impressed Francesco Carletti, the Florentine traveller, for the way the Portuguese in their splendour were always 'going about on horseback . . . And when they ride out they have before and behind them goodly troupes of slaves, including one slave carrying a club in his hand in the manner of a mace, opening up the way; one with an umbrella, without which they never leave the house; one who drives off the flies with a red-and-white horse's tail; and one who acts as a footman and one as a page. And in that style they go all over the city as if in triumph.'

By the end of the 16th century, however, this was a lifestyle in retreat. There were many reasons for the decline of the great Portuguese settlements in the East: corruption and too much of 'the good life' in the more prosperous colonies; the realisation by local rulers that they had everything to gain by dealing with a wider group of traders; and the inability of Portugal herself to maintain and defend her territories.

Above all, however, was the challenge of the Dutch, who made a deliberate assault on the Portuguese monopoly of the spice trade, backed by vastly superior resources and the wealth of Amsterdam, which in the 16th century developed into the most important trading centre in northern Europe and one of the world's leading money markets.

Among the resources of the Dutch were their fleets. They had evolved small, virtually unarmed 'fly boats' that were geared to cargo-carrying, in

Dutch Power The Dutch East Indies Company's trading station on the Hooghly River, Bengal.

contrast to the oversized 'floating fortresses' that comprised the cumbersome fleets of Portuguese carracks. And Dutch warships were better armed and tactically superior to their rivals.

The Dutch predators were tough, and subject to ruthless discipline from the Dutch East Indies Company, which was founded in 1602 by a group of wealthy merchants to coordinate their efforts. The Dutch were thrifty with rations, which accounted for mortality rates even higher than those on Portuguese, Spanish and English ships. Punishments were severe: death for murder, mutiny and homosexuality; keelhauling and ducking; nailing a culprit's hand to the mast; and flogging in degrees up to 500 lashes. Fines for fighting, insolence, blasphemy and drunkenness were common. The Dutch also inflicted their own brands of punishment on the natives. In the 1620s the indigenous peoples of the Banda Islands (part of Indonesia) were exterminated en masse, or deported to serve as soldiers or slaves.

The intrusion of the Dutch, from the 1590s

onwards, marked a new phase in the European balance of power in the East. In the age of exploration there was little attempt at direct colonisation, though Amboina was captured in 1605 and in 1619 the Dutch established a new capital in Java at Batavia (modern Jakarta). However, they destroyed the power of local rulers in many parts of South-east Asia in order to maintain their own monopoly on the spice trade.

The ascendancy of the Dutch is, at first sight, quite as astonishing as the success of their Portuguese predecessors. It rested on the spectacular rise of the two maritime provinces of Holland and Zeeland, and it is not an exaggeration to say that for these provinces the sea became a way of life through sheer necessity. A 16th-century document makes the point clearly enough:

'It is noticeably true that the province of Holland is a very small country, small in length and even smaller in breadth, and almost enclosed by the sea on three sides. It must be protected from the sea by . . . dykes, sluices, mill-races, windmills and polders. Moreover the said province of Holland contains many dunes, bogs, and lakes which grow daily more extensive, as well as other barren districts, unfit for crops or pasture. Wherefore the inhabitants of this said country in order to make a living for their wives, children and families, must maintain themselves by

MERCHANTS OF ANTWERP **Antwerp marketplace in the early 16th century. Antwerp became one of the crucial trading centres of Europe, profiting from overseas ventures as well as from inter-European trade.**

NEW CAPITAL Batavia (now Jakarta) was the chief centre for Dutch activities in South-east Asia, which led to the downfall of Portuguese influence in the area.

handicrafts and trades, in such wise that they fetch raw materials from foreign lands and re-export the finished products . . . Consequently, the main business of the country must needs be in shipping and related trades, from which a great many people earn their living, like merchants, skippers, masters, pilots, sailors, shipwrights, and all those connected therewith.'

It was this seafaring tradition that was suddenly released onto the wider world when the Netherlands – Holland, Zeeland and five lesser provinces – broke free of Spanish domination and gained her independence. The trading way of life became not just a means of national survival but a route to increasing prosperity that would turn the new nation into the greatest maritime power in the world.

EYEWITNESS

RUBIES, DIAMONDS AND PEARLS

AFTER THE MOGUL dynasty had been established in 1526, the magnificence of Agra, the Mogul capital south of Delhi, dazzled European visitors, among them the Elizabethan merchant Ralph Fitch:

❛ From thence we went to Agra . . . Agra is a very great Citie and populous, built with stone, having faire and large streets, with a faire River running by it, which falleth into the Gulfe of Bengala . . . the King is called Zelabdim Echebar [Akbar]: the people for the most part call him The Great Mogor. From thence we went for Fatepore, which is the place where the King kept his Court . . . The King hath in Agra and Fatepore, as they doe credibly report, one thousand Elephants, thirtie thousand Horses, one thousand and foure hundred tame Deere, eight hundred Concubines: such store of Ounces [snow leopards], Tygres, Buffles, Cockes and Hawkes, that is very strange to see. He keepeth a great Court, which they call Dericcan. Agra and Fatepore are two very great cities, either of them much greater than London, and very populous. Between Agra and Fatepore are twelve miles, and all the way is a Market of victuals and other things, as full as though a man were still in a Towne, and so many people as if a man were in a Market. They have many fine Carts, and many of them carved and gilded with Gold, with two wheeles which bee drawne with two little Bulls about the bignesse of our great Dogs in England, and they will runne with any Horse, and carrie two or three men in one of these Carts: they are covered with Silke or very fine cloth, and bee used here as our Coaches be in England. Hither is great resort of Merchants from Persia, and out of India, and very much Merchandize of Silke and Cloth, and of precious Stones, both Rubies, Diamants, and Pearles. The King is apparelled in a white Cabie made like a Shirt tyed with strings on the one side, and a little cloth on his head, coloured oftentimes with red and yellow. ❜

The Spice of Life

Prized Plants Cinamon bark is collected in India for export to Europe. Above: The clove was grown in the Molucca and Banda islands.

Pepper and spices were dreams of the early explorers. 'As dear as pepper' was a saying in common use, while the quest for spices such as cinnamon, cloves, nutmeg and mace inspired exploration and conquest. The European craze for spices and pepper was part of the legacy of the Roman Empire. Pepper was so prized in ancient Rome that it was kept in its own specialised storehouses. Yet the use of flavourings of this kind were not an exclusively European fashion. A Hindu writer reflected: 'When the palate revolts against the insipidness of rice boiled with no other ingredients, we dream of fat, salt and spices.'

The spice craze was particularly powerful in Europe because, unlike most of the rest of the world, Europe was a continent of meat-eaters, at least among those of its population who could afford it. It was the inability to preserve meat, and therefore the need to disguise its taste, that made spices so sought after. Of course, they were used for other foods – fish, jam, soup, game, fruit and even certain drinks – and they were also thought to have medicinal properties. But it was as adjuncts to stale, tough and tasteless meat that spices were mainly associated.

And so, in the search for the 'lands of spices', the Europeans reached India, home of the best pepper; Ceylon with its cinnamon; the Moluccas with their nutmeg and cloves. Empires were built in the Indian sub-continent, South-east Asia and Indonesia. As supplies became more plentiful, demand slackened. Nevertheless, the empires, though they changed hands, remained – a legacy in part of the spice mania that had inspired so many to seek out the regions where wealth grew in the ground.

Spice Market The marketplace at Bantam, a trading city on Java dominated by the Dutch. It became a centre for the spice trade.

LIFE IN CHINA AND JAPAN

In the Europeans' dealings with China and Japan, unlike their experiences in other parts of the world, they found themselves very much the poor relations, holding on to their precarious positions only at the whim of powerful rulers.

IN A SENSE, the discovery of China and Japan by the Portuguese was the climax of the age. After all, reaching those countries had been the goal of Columbus's voyages, as well as those of John Cabot, Verrazzano, Cartier and Champlain. Yet they proved to be the very countries where the Europeans made the least impact in the 16th century. For one thing, their numbers were negligible. China alone had a population equal to the whole European continent, perhaps 100 million. And the rituals of administration built up over the centuries often proved exasperating and impenetrable. The few concessions that were made were on sufferance only: Portuguese rights to establish themselves in Macao on the Chinese coast

CELESTIAL EMPIRE **William Blaeu's map of China, 1623. As one would expect, it contains a number of inaccuracies such as the position and relative size of the Philippines.**

CITY ON SUFFERANCE The Portuguese settlement of Macao around 1600. Prosperous and distinctive, it was dependent on the good will of its giant neighbour for survival. Right: European 17th-century illustrations of Asia's 'exotic' inhabitants.

and Nagasaki in Japan involved no territorial conquest or surrender.

The first Portuguese visitor reached the Bay of Canton in 1516 and reported that 'the Chinese wanted peace and friendship with the Portuguese'. In 1517 a fleet under Fernando Peres arrived at Canton and terrified the Chinese when it fired its guns in salute. The Governor-General of Canton reported the outrage, and other acts of presumed insolence, to the emperor, and when a delegation was permitted to travel to Peking in 1520, under Thomas Pires, its members were treated to a series of indignities: they were refused an audience with the emperor; a letter from the King of Portugal was burned; and their presents were rejected. From 1522 European seafarers were forbidden on pain of death to enter the coastal waters of China.

The Chinese were still prepared to lavish hospitality on visitors who did not offend them, to give expensive presents, and to insist on the use of sedan chairs, the best inns and other signs of munificence. But it was the generosity of the superior to the inferior, for the Chinese believed that their empire was the centre of civilisation, that all the peoples of the earth owed it tribute, and that it was the misfortune of the most remote lands to be unacquainted with the Heavenly Peace and Harmony it provided. A court official, one of the many mandarins who composed the elaborate Chinese civil

EYEWITNESS

THE MONGOL HORDES

THE MONGOLS were nomadic horsemen of Central Asia who, in the 13th century, won a vast empire stretching from Russia to China where they established a ruling dynasty under Kublai Khan. This description by an Englishman, Anthony Jenkinson, was written in 1557:

‘The Nagayans when they flourished, lived in this manner; they were divided into divers companies called Hordes, and every Horde had a ruler . . . called a Murse. Town or house they had none, but lived in the open fields, every Murse or King having his Hordes or people about him, with their wives, children, and cattle, who, having consumed the pasture in one place, removed unto another: and when they remove they have houses like tents set upon wagons or carts, which are drawn from place to place with camels, and therein their wives, children, and all their riches, which is very little, is carried about . . . They delight in no art nor science, except the wars, wherein they are expert, but for the most part they be pasturing people, and have great store of cattle, which is all their riches. They eat much flesh, and especially the horse, and they drink mare's milk, wherewith they be oftentimes drunk . . . Corn they sow not, neither do eat any bread, mocking the Christians for the same . . . allowing their great devouring of flesh, and drinking of milk, to be the increase of their strength.’

CHOPSTICKS AND MANNERS

THE EUROPEANS were gluttons – certainly by comparison with the fastidious Chinese and Japanese, for whom the presentation of food was an artform. The ceremony of eating was so important to the wealthier Oriental because it provided a delicate aesthetic experience involving taste; the quality of the plates, bowls and cups in which the meal was served; and the politeness, ritual and good manners with which it was accompanied.

The Chinese sat at a table for their food. They ate out of glazed bowls and carried their chopsticks in a special case, described by the 16th-century Dominican Gaspar da Cruz: 'And presently there were two small sticks, very fine and gilt, for to eat with, holding them between the fingers; they use them like a pair of pincers, so that they touch nothing of that which is on the board with their hand. Yea, though they eat a dish of rice, they do it with those sticks, without any grain of the rice falling.'

All these habits were part of a wider tradition of good manners. All strangers were acknowledged with a slight inclination of the head. There was the Chinese 'common courtesy': a form of greeting by which, wrote da Cruz, 'the left hand closed, they enclose it within the right hand, and they move their hands repeatedly up and down towards the breast, showing that they have one another enclosed in their heart; and to this motion of the hands, they join words of courtesy.'

Some of these oriental customs even rubbed off on European settlers. Nothing amazed visitors to Macao more than the sight of the Portuguese taking regular baths and wearing clean clothes.

TURNING JAPANESE Dutch merchants eat their food with chopsticks.

service, wrote: 'The *Feringhis* [European 'barbarians'] are most cruel and crafty . . . some years ago they came suddenly to the city of Canton, and the noise of their cannon shook the earth . . . Now if we allow them to come and go and carry on their trade, it will inevitably lead to fighting and bloodshed and the misfortune of our South may be boundless.' Therefore, until the trade ban was relaxed in 1554, and the Portuguese were allowed their own settlement on the peninsula of Macao three years later, European trade with China was confined to smuggling and the occasional visit to a provincial capital or to Peking.

In 1542, some years before the Portuguese were allowed to settle in Macao, three unknown Portuguese sailors had landed during a storm on the coast of what turned out to be Japan. Here again, Europeans found a largely incomprehensible lifestyle where attitudes to life

CHINA SEAS A Chinese junk from the 16th century.

CHINESE CONVERT The Annunciation depicted in a 'Chinese style' by a local artist in order to make it more acceptable to a Chinese audience.

and death, correct and incorrect behaviour were completely different from anything they had encountered before. The trading relationships that the Portuguese were eventually able to establish via Macao, Nagasaki and other settlements opened up these strange new worlds, but what was revealed?

Most obviously, it was a world of rice, which, in many areas, accounted for 90 per cent of the diet for 90 per cent of the population. That rice played such a central role in the lives of the people of China and 'Monsoon Asia' was partly a matter of habit, taste and ceremony but was far more to do with necessity, for only rice could support the enormous concentrations of population to be found throughout Asia. Fernand Braudel, the great French historian of everyday life, estimated that 1 hectare (2.4 acres) devoted to rice produced nearly 7.5 million calories, compared with less than 350 000 provided from the same area devoted to livestock reared for meat. Only in Japan and the coastal regions of south China was fish eaten on any scale.

Rice was not easy to cultivate and required more human effort than any other comparable crop. The paddy fields gave two, sometimes even three, crops in a year. In southern China, for example, sowing might begin in January. Men and women planted the seed by hand in rows spaced some 6 in (15 cm) apart, and the land had to be weeded constantly. When the crop was ready, the soil was drained and the rice harvested, threshed, stacked and transported by coolies. If all went well, the first five-month crop was harvested in June and the whole process repeated at breakneck speed for the second, November crop. Preparations would then have to begin immediately for the next January planting. Sometimes a third crop – perhaps wheat – could be grown between the two rice crops.

All aspects of eating and drinking were a constant source of amazement to visitors; this was particularly true of the tea-drinking ceremonies of both China and Japan. To drink tea properly, it was reckoned, you needed a teacher, just as you needed dancing lessons in Europe. For it was not just a matter of carefully stored green leaves being infused in boiling water; more important still were the furnishings, cutlery, sweetmeats and manners that accompanied the event. In China:

'There are very suitable implements for that purpose, such as a decorated table, with a small stove beside it, boxes with drawers, bowls, cups, saucers, spoons for jam, crystallised sugar in pieces shaped

OUT AND ABOUT A 'land ship', using wheel and sail, and a comfortable passenger in a palanquin, illustrated at the end of the 16th century.

POPULAR IMPORT **The Portuguese introduced Arab and Barbary horses into Japan, together with the sport of horse-racing.**

like nuts, to hold in the mouth whilst drinking the tea, for this has the least effect on its good taste, and uses up less sugar. All this is accompanied by various preserves, both dry and liquid, the Chinese having a much better understanding of how to make them dainty and attractive than European confectioners.'

The importance of ritual in both China and Japan stemmed from the very basis on which society was constructed, from the top downwards. For example, life in China was lived according to the wisdom of Confucius (551–479 BC), a sage whose teachings had, by the 15th century, been formalised into a code of behaviour through the writings of subsequent followers. The central features of Confucian thought were filial piety and ancestor-worship, which applied first and foremost to the obligations of the emperor himself. For the emperor was the Son of Heaven, ruler of 'all under Heaven' and the father-mother of the people. If the emperor's conduct as a dutiful son was inadequate, his mandate to rule might be withdrawn, and chaos and calamity would follow. This was simply the highest manifestation of rules that governed the whole of society. For all its apparent centralisation, life for most people in China revolved around their own families and their family class.

FAMILY RULES

In Chinese, *chia* means both a house and a family. An ideal family unit was that of a husband, his wife, their sons, the sons' families, and their livestock and possessions all in a single home. In such households the parents were all-powerful: a father could beat his son mercilessly, but striking your father carried the death penalty.

Marriage in these close-knit communities was a great event, often referred to as 'taking a daughter-in-law', and was invariably arranged by the parents through a go-between and after consulting the horoscope. There was a Chinese saying that 'a boy is born facing in; a girl is born facing out'; for as soon as was practical, a girl would leave her own family for her husband's and soon find herself worshipping another family's ancestors. A woman's life was regarded as one of three subordinations: first to her father before marriage; then to her husband; and finally to her eldest son after her husband's death.

Weddings were as lavish as the husband's family could afford. The bride would travel on a red bridal chair, so that her feet were undefiled by touching the ground from the moment she left her family home to when she set foot in her new one. Once together in their new home, husband and wife first paid homage to Heaven and Earth at the household

THE RULING CLASS **The Chinese mandarin, left, would have lived very comfortably in comparison with many Chinese. Right: A Chinese flower seller.**

The Great Wall of Macao

Walled In Europeans in Macao wishing to travel to the mainland had to pass through a great gate.

When the Portuguese were allowed to establish a settlement on the Macao peninsula in 1557, they were forbidden to carry arms or to fortify it in any way. They paid a heavy rent, as well as customs duties and harbour dues. However, in 1574, when the settlement had risen to over 10 000, the Chinese decided it was time to erect a wall, manned by guards, between the settlement and the mainland. Those Portuguese who wished to travel to the mainland had to do so with a pass.

The wall was generally opened only once a week, on market day, and since it provided the only access to the mainland for buying much-needed provisions, the potential threat from the Chinese was obvious. The predicament was described by a Dominican friar, Domingo Navarette, in 1670:

❛ At a quarter of a League distant from that city, where the narrow part of that neck of land is, the Chinese many years ago built a Wall from Sea to Sea, in the middle of it a Gate with a Tower over it, where there is always a Guard so that the People of Macao may not pass across, nor the Chinese to them . . . Of late Years the Gate was shut; at first they open'd it every five days, when the Portugueses bought Provisions; afterwards it grew stricter, and was only open'd twice a Month. Then the rich, which were but very few, could buy a Fortnight's Store; the Poor perish'd, and many have starv'd.❜

shrine; they also performed a ceremony before a set of tablets bearing the names of the husband's ancestors. The following day the bride's mother-in-law would begin instructing her in her new duties.

Funerals were elaborate affairs. The deceased was buried in fine clothes and with precious objects to accompany the spirit to the next world. This was followed by a mourning period – three years of wearing coarse clothes, eating coarse food and, for government officials, resignation from office. Further to emphasise the essential unity of the family in life and death, every home had a domestic shrine where a wooden tablet recorded the name of each newly deceased member. Here, incense was offered every day, with special sacrifices on the 1st and 15th of each month and on the death dates.

Ritual was very much a feature of everyday Japanese life as well. Worshipping at a shrine or removing your outdoor shoes in the home, making sacrifices to your ancestors or performing the tea ceremony: these were all parts of an overall unity in which everything had its proper place and function. And yet rites as brutal as suicide cults existed alongside the codes of exquisite politeness. According to Francesco Carletti, the 16th-century Florentine merchant, men 'often kill themselves in cold blood for different reasons and causes, slashing their bodies crosswise with a scimitar. Women also do that . . . And many others kill themselves at the command of the king or of their overlords. And women do that if the husbands tell them to.'

Formality extended to the dwellings, small houses as well as great palaces, in China and Japan, and homes were clean and tidy. Each room or area had its prescribed function: eating, sleeping and maintaining the family shrines. Francesco Carletti described the folding screens, which made the most of limited space: '. . . in the space of a single hall or room, they make

MASSACRE This illustration shows a massacre of Christians, one of many, at Nagasaki in 1622. Some were beheaded, others burnt at the stake.

other apartments by partitioning off and erecting a sort of large variety of pictures. Depicting various things, these open and shut like a fan . . . At the corners these stand up, making a most beautiful sight. And if there are several people in a room, they have the virtue that . . . they also keep you from being seen by the others, as the pictures rise to a man's height.'

Throughout the age of exploration, the mysteries of China and Japan remained closed to all but a few coastal traders and privileged travellers. There were, however, two exceptions: Nagasaki, where the Portuguese obtained permission to establish a trading settlement; and Macao on a peninsula of the Chinese coast some 90 miles (145 km) south of Canton. Built on the site of a run-down fishing village, Macao had grown, within 30 years of its beginnings in 1557, into a sumptuous town of some 20 000 inhabitants, with 500 Portuguese households living in luxury. It monopolised trade between China and Japan, so that only through its small fleet of galleons could Chinese silks and gold be exchanged for Japanese silver. Macao's merchants also brought silver from Persia and, via Manila, from Peru to China, while spices from India and prisms and lenses from Europe were also traded with the Chinese. In return, the luxuries of China – silks, carvings, lacquerwork and porcelain – were sold throughout markets in India, Malaya, Manila and Europe.

BOOM YEARS European merchants traded successfully in Japan until the early 17th century. They were the inspiration for many painted Japanese screens.

DARK CONTINENT AND SOUTHERN SEAS

Portuguese navigators explored the coasts of Africa; later generations of Europeans set up the infamous slave trade between Africa and the New World. Ferdinand Magellan opened up the possibilities of Pacific exploration when he crossed the unknown 'Southern Seas' through the strait that bears his name. Later, the English freebooter Francis Drake returned home with a ship full of spices after his own circumnavigation of the world. The explorers had united the globe.

ACROSS UNKNOWN OCEANS

A remarkable breed of Portuguese seamen travelled down Africa's western coast, rounded the Cape, and 'discovered' the highly developed civilisations along the coast of East Africa. Meanwhile, Magellan crossed the Pacific from the west . . .

ALTHOUGH THE discoverers did not believe the earth was flat, they had no idea of its size – and, in particular, of the sheer extent of the oceans. That was why Columbus thought he had reached Japan when he had only got to the West Indies; why Verrazzano thought he could see the Pacific across the sand bars off Carolina's coast; and why the first explorers of West Africa thought that the Niger River must be a tributary of the Nile.

The explorers were ignorant of much else besides. Legends told of boiling seas at the Equator; of an uninhabitable Torrid Zone; and of currents beyond the Tropic that swept any ship that passed it onwards forever. So the push down the African coast and round the Cape of Good Hope was a feat of extraordinary pioneering bravery as well as skill.

Portugal's drive along the West African coast is generally credited to Prince Henry the Navigator, who had a passionate interest both in exploration and in bringing Christianity to pagan people; he also believed the legend that somewhere in Africa, or perhaps Asia, there was a Christian kingdom ruled by Prester John. Under his initiative uninhabited Madeira was discovered in 1419. Fifteen years later his sailors passed Cape Bojador on the north-west coast of Africa – a 'point of no return' it was thought, because no

GOLD RUSH A detail of a map of West Africa shows a Portuguese fortress amid villages. It is a formidable statement of Portugal's intentions towards the West African territories it acquired.

GOD AND MAMMON **A 17th-century illustration of Elmina, a centre for the gold trade. The Portuguese spread Christianity, but took their reward in worldly goods.**

European vessels had yet been beyond it. Another landmark came in 1445 when Dinis Dias took an expedition past Cape Verde; and ten years later Alvise de Cadamosto sailed up the River Gambia.

OPENING UP THE EAST

Prince Henry's work was continued by Portugal's kings, in particular John II (1481-95), known as 'The Perfect', and Manuel I (1495-1521), whose nicknames, 'The Grocer King' and 'Pepperpot Potentate', reflected the increasing emphasis placed by Portugal on trade. In 1482 Diogo Cão reached the mouth of the Zaire, and two years later Cape Cross, displaying that mixture of piety and piracy that characterised Portuguese expansion. He erected stone crosses, called *padroes*, where he landed, but also took hostages and threatened force when he met with opposition.

On the whole, however, Portuguese activity on the West African coast was mild compared with their depredations along the East Coast and in Asia. A flourishing trade in slaves from West Africa developed, and also in gold, protected by the great fortress built at Elmina. Cão's voyages, which took him 1400 miles south of Cape St Catherine, opened the possibility of sailing the whole of the African coastline and finding a sea route to Asia beyond it. Accordingly, in 1487, King John ordered a unique double mission: one overland to Asia, and the other by sea under the command of Bartolomeu Dias.

The overland expedition was entrusted to Pedro de Covilhã and Affonso de Paiva. The latter died on the way, but de Covilhã, disguised as an Arab trader, travelled widely in India and Arabia, and then made his way to the court of the King of Ethiopia. It was some six years since de Covilhã had left Portugal, and in Ethiopia he was forced to remain. He made himself so indispensable that he stayed to serve four successive rulers over a period of 30 years, dying there in his 90s.

Bartolomeu Dias set sail in August 1487 with a fleet of two caravels and a storeship. His voyage charted a further 1400 miles of coast and took him far enough to prove that there was no land obstacle to the Indian Ocean. But it was a desperate journey lasting some 16 months. Round the southern shores of Africa the crews were so demoralised by hunger, scurvy and fear that they threatened mutiny, forcing Dias to turn back. He had discovered and named the Cape of Good Hope – good hope that a route to the Indies had been found – but failed to enter the Indian Ocean. That was left to Vasco da Gama, whose expedition sailed on July 8, 1497.

Da Gama had learned from the misfortunes of Dias. He sailed far to

FINE WORKMANSHIP **An example of African craft in ivory: a 16th-century saltcellar showing a Portuguese sea captain.**

the south-west before turning south-east, entailing over 90 days without sight of land, the longest yet experienced by European voyagers. On November 22 his fleet rounded the Cape and became the first expedition to enter the Indian Ocean by a route that would remain the main artery to the East until the opening of the Suez Canal in 1869. Once in the Indian Ocean, da Gama's expedition travelled up Africa's east coast, finding a world of city states ruled by sultans and dominated by Arab merchants, before continuing across the Indian Ocean to Calicut.

Uniting West and East

Some 20 years later, on September 20, 1519, Ferdinand Magellan set sail on a voyage that would take him to the same waters – but westwards via the Antarctic reaches of South America. In so doing, he would cross the Pacific, an ocean that occupies more than a third of the world's surface.

Magellan's fleet consisted of five small ships and a crew of only 240. Their journey to the southernmost tip of South America took a year and a month, during which time Magellan survived fierce storms, a mutiny, and a meeting with giant natives, whom he called *patagon* (big foot), from which Patagonia gets its name. On October 20, 1520, the fleet entered the long, treacherous passage now known as the Strait of Magellan, and the crews named the land to the south Tierra del Fuego – land of fire – because at night they could see fires glowing in the mountains of the region. And then, on November 28, in the words of Antonio Pigafetta, who chronicled the voyage, the three surviving ships 'debouched from that Strait, engulfing ourselves in the Pacific Sea'.

The Pacific involved hardships unknown even to those who had endured the heaving seas of Patagonia. For weeks the ships were blown north-west, with no land in sight. As Pigafetta described, the enemies now

Round the Horn
Ferdinand Magellan navigated the dangerous waters of Cape Horn to forge a new route to the Indies via the Pacific.

Devon Man
Sir Francis Drake was the first expedition leader to circumnavigate the world. His exploits as a privateer struck terror into the hearts of his enemies. Right: Prince Maurice, who helped the Netherlands secure independence from Spain, descends on the Philippine Islands.

Staking a Claim in America

In June 1579, Francis Drake took possession of the San Francisco area of California for Queen Elizabeth of England. Crew members of the *Golden Hind* recorded the event:

❛ The newes of our being there, being spread through the Countrey, the people that inhabited round about came downe, and amongst them the King himselfe . . . with many other tall and warlike men . . . In the fore front was a man of goodly personage, who bare the scepter, or mace before the King, whereupon hanged two crownes, a lesse and a bigger, with three chaines of a marvelous length . . .

In comming towards our bulwarks and tents, the scepter bearer began a song, observing his measures in a daunce . . . whom the King with his Garde, and every degree of persons following, did in like manner sing and daunce . . . They made signes to our General to sit downe, to whom the King, and divers others made several orations, or rather supplications, that he would take their province & kingdome into his hand, and became their King . . . which thing our General thought not meete to reject, because he knew not what honour and profite it might be to our Countrey. Wherefore in the name, and to the use of her Majestie, he tooke the scepter, crowne and dignitie of the said Countrey into his hands . . .

At our departure hence our General set up a monument of our being there . . . namely a plate, nailed upon a faire greate poste, whereupon was ingraven her Majesties name, the day and yeere of our arrivall there, with the free giving up of the province and people into her Majesties hands, together with her highness picture and armes, in a peece of sixe pence of current English money under the plate, where under was also written the name of our General . . . ❜

Staking a Claim
The 'brass plate' recording the English claim to territory in the San Francisco area is now known to be a forgery.

were insufferable heat, rotting provisions and scurvy:

'We were three months and twenty days without refreshments from any kind of fresh food. We ate biscuit, which was no longer biscuit but a powder of biscuits swarming with worms, for they had eaten the good. It stank strongly of the urine of rats. We drank yellow water that had been putrid for many days. We also ate some ox-hides that covered the top of the mainyard . . . Rats were sold for one half-ducado apiece, and even then we could not get them. But above all the other misfortunes the following was the worst. The gums of both the lower and upper teeth of some of our men swelled, so that they could not eat under any circumstances and therefore died.'

It was not until April 1521 that they reached the Philippines. But even here none of them realised how close they were to the Spice Islands and the safety of familiar waters. On Cebu, Magellan let his friendship with the local Sultan lead him into joining a raid on

Routes are plotted according to the best estimates of modern scholarship. In some cases, however, accurate information is available only for parts of a voyage.

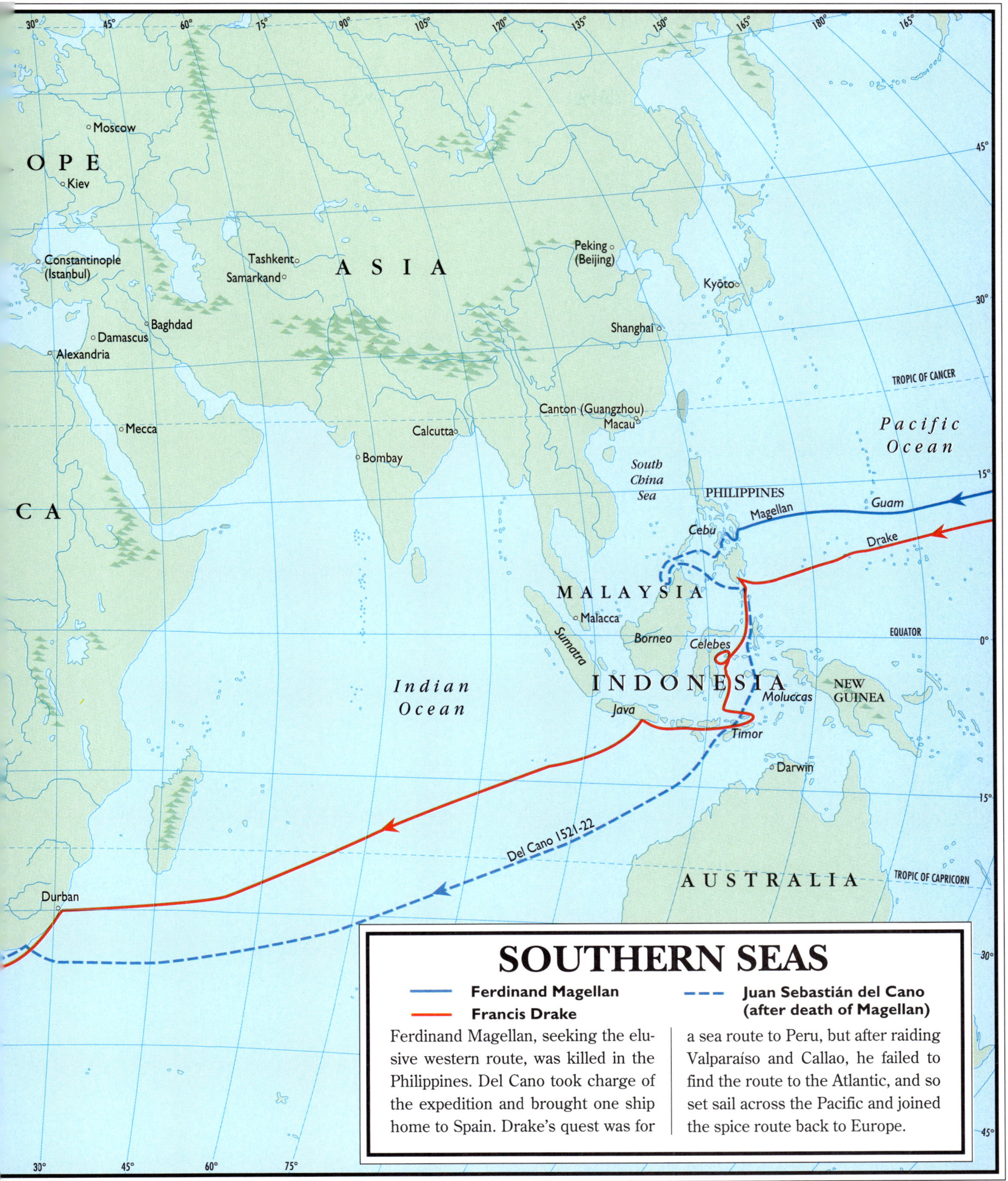

SOUTHERN SEAS

Ferdinand Magellan

Francis Drake

Juan Sebastián del Cano (after death of Magellan)

Ferdinand Magellan, seeking the elusive western route, was killed in the Philippines. Del Cano took charge of the expedition and brought one ship home to Spain. Drake's quest was for a sea route to Peru, but after raiding Valparaíso and Callao, he failed to find the route to the Atlantic, and so set sail across the Pacific and joined the spice route back to Europe.

EYEWITNESS

THEY CANNOT LIVE HERE WITHOUT GREAT PERIL

THE ARAB LEO Africanus, a Christian convert, was one of the great 16th-century travel writers. He crossed the Sahara twice to Timbuktu and was well aware of the importance of the salt trade of the mining regions. One of the great mining centres was Tegaza, a desolate place in the heart of the desert where even houses were built of salt:

❛ In this region is great store of salt digged, being whiter than any marble. This salt is taken out of certain caves or pits, at the entrance whereof stand their cottages that work in the salt-mines. And these workmen are all strangers, who sell the salt which they dig, unto certain merchants that carry the same upon camels to the kingdom of Timbuktu . . . Neither have the said diggers of salt any victuals but such as the merchants bring unto them: for they are distant from all inhabited places, almost twenty days' journey . . . Moreover the south-east wind doth so often blind them, that they cannot live here without great peril. I myself continued three days amongst them, all which time I was constrained to drink salt-water drawn from certain wells not far from the salt-pits. ❜

the Sultan's enemies on neighbouring Mactan, and on April 27, 1521, he was killed in battle. Only one of the original five ships, the *Victoria*, managed to get home to Portugal, with only 17 Europeans surviving the three-year epic.

The Spaniards mounted a series of Pacific voyages soon after Magellan, but it was not until 1564-5 that they met with any success. Miguel Lopez de Legaspi led an expedition from Mexico, establishing colonies at Manila and Cebu in the Philippines. By proving that the Pacific crossing could be made from Mexico, Legaspi inaugurated a new era of ocean trade based on the Pacific and centred on Manila.

RICH PICKINGS Spanish trading ports in the Caribbean were popular targets for pirates and privateers.

DID YOU KNOW?

The *Thousand and One Nights* were told over hundreds of years before being written down: recounted in Arab homes and marketplaces, and then passed down, re-told, embellished and developed over many generations, with settings that reflect the opulent worlds of their Asian and African origins. The tales include the stories of Ali Baba, Sinbad and Aladdin.

Spain's activities in the Pacific were interrupted by England's Francis Drake, who turned what should have been a voyage of discovery into the most profitable privateering expedition in history. Starting with five ships, and following Magellan's route into the Pacific, he was soon left with only his 100 ton flagship, which he re-named the *Golden Hind*. Drake ranged along the Pacific coast from Chile to Mexico, plundering ships and towns before reaching the area of San Francisco Bay, which he named New Albion and took possession of on behalf of Queen Elizabeth. Then he travelled to the Philippines and the Moluccas, loaded his ship with spices, and returned to England in triumph on September 26, 1580. His voyage had lasted three years and made him the first sea captain to take his ship around the world.

A LIFE OF SLAVERY

Slavery is as old as civilisation. The age of exploration gave the slave trade a new dimension, however, as black Africans were uprooted from their homelands to serve new colonial masters across the Atlantic in the New World.

MILLIONS OF people in the 16th century were somebody else's property, to be bought and sold like any other possession. Yet slavery was nothing new. In 1500 it was common to almost all societies, including those of the Mediterranean, where Christians and Moors had been enslaving each other for centuries. From the 1440s on, black slaves came to Portugal in increasing numbers, to work as household servants or to act as status symbols for the grandees; by the middle of the 16th century, they accounted for about 10 per cent of Lisbon's population. But the age of exploration did create something quite new in the story of the slaves: the black African, violently uprooted from his homeland and transported thousands of miles across the Atlantic to work for colonial masters in the New World. Africans went in vast numbers to overseas colonies where, in time, their lifestyles, identities and cultures would enrich the New World.

The traffic in human cargo began just a few years after Columbus's discoveries, when the first Spanish settlers found the native Indians unsatisfactory as a labour force. The Indians were weak, prone to disease,

IMAGINATION RUN RIOT On this 16th-century map of Africa the cartographer has filled the interior with weird men and animals and other ingenious creations.

and in any case lacked the farming and mining skills required by the new overlords. The west coast Africans, on the other hand, had just those skills: they had farmed tropical crops with iron tools, and had mined, processed and refined gold. In 1505 a ship from Seville took 17 Africans and mining equipment to the Indies; and in 1516 the first slave-grown sugar arrived in Spain from the Caribbean. Ten years later the Spaniards brought the first shipment of slaves direct from West Africa to America.

HUMAN AUCTION A slave is offered for sale in the marketplace in Algiers, one of the centres of the slave trade in the Muslim world.

What made the African so vulnerable to the fate he was to meet in this new age – encouraging John Hawkins, the English slave trader of the 1560s, to boast that a 'store of Negroes might easily be had upon the coast of Guinea'? The answer lies largely in the societies that had developed in Senegal, Gambia, Sierra Leone, the Ivory Coast, the Gold Coast and all the other regions of West Africa that had proved so lucrative for the traders. Here there were already servile classes, firmly under the control of local kings and chiefs. Therefore, for at least a century after Columbus, some of the slaves who crossed the Atlantic came not from free people hunted down by raiders, but from already servile populations sold into slavery by their own leaders.

SELLING THEIR OWN

Regular procedures were soon established. The African chiefs provided lodgings for the traders and guaranteed their safety, in return for which the traders paid an annual rent and a tax on each slave exported, and also provided the weapons for the slave-gathering expeditions. The traders were generally sea captains, sailing either on Crown service or, in the case of interlopers such as the English and French, with the backing of syndicates of wealthy merchants and courtiers. They would try to sell a slave in America for around £22 – with the purchase price in Africa, therefore, considerably lower. It is difficult to estimate the cost of a slave, however, since the transactions in Africa were not made in money. The captains would bargain and barter, generally valuing a male slave between the ages of 16 and 35 as a 'piece' – the price of a measurement of handwoven African or Indian cloth. Two women and a baby were also thought to be worth a piece, and there were other calculations that valued women and children of different ages in a similar way. In America the slaves were sold as pieces at an

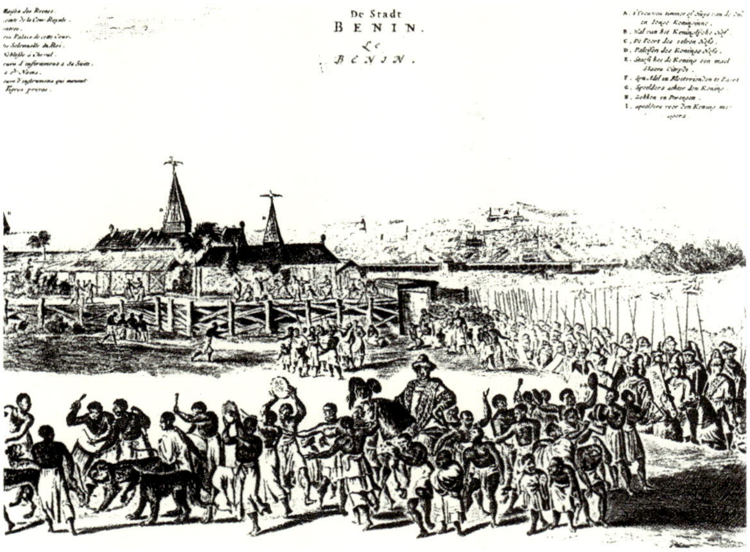

JUNGLE KINGDOM Benin, in the age of exploration, was the centre of a large empire stretching inland from the Niger delta to Lagos.

equivalent value in hides or other goods, which the traders then imported to Europe. Elsewhere there were equally degrading valuations. In North Africa, for example, 12 slaves from the Sudan were reckoned to be worth one Moroccan horse; in Goa a horse was the same as 40 African slaves.

Some of the African kings regretted the trade on which they had embarked. The Kongo king, christened Affonso I by the Portuguese, wrote to his 'royal brother' in Lisbon in 1526: 'We cannot reckon how great the damage is . . . and so great, Sire, is the corruption and licentiousness that our country is being completely depopulated.' Yet the African rulers had little choice in the matter. Slavery was a profitable business, and there were always powerful subjects ready to cooperate independently with the traders. Furthermore, firearms had become a principal European exchange for slaves, and any ruler who refused these could be sure his rivals would be quick to take advantage.

To imagine the plight of the slaves assembled for sale and then transported across the sea, let us picture them stored like cattle in the great cages built close to the beaches. There have been several deaths in the village as terrified men, women and children have been rounded up, beaten, tied and taken to the cages. Some yell defiance, others wail in terror, while

CRUEL TRADE A slave trader with two of his charges. The traders were often sea captains, and acquired their slaves with the help of local rulers.

EYEWITNESS

THE DEVIL SPEAKS OUT

AFRICAN KINGS claimed divine powers. In the 16th century Joao dos Santos, a Portuguese friar, visited Sofala and wrote about the King of Uteve, who ruled in the hinterland. Once a year the king went to the top of a mountain to commune with his dead ancestors. Santos's record is the nearest there is to an eyewitness account:

“When the king has feasted for eight days, he begins his lamentation for the dead who are buried there, and all join in continual lamentation for two or three days, until the devil enters into one of the Kaffirs of the assembly, saying that he is the soul of the dead king, the father of him who is engaged in these ceremonies, come to converse with his son. The demoniac becomes as one into whose body the devil has entered, stretched on the ground, disfigured, deformed, and out of his senses, and while he is in this state the devil speaks through his mouth in all the foreign tongues of other Kaffir nations, which are understood by many of those present. Besides this, he begins to cough and speak like the dead king whom he represents, in such a manner that it seems to be his very self, both in voice and movements, by which signs the Kaffirs recognise the soul of the dead king has come as they expected. The king who is performing the ceremonies, being informed of this, comes accompanied by all his nobles to the place where the demoniac is, and all prostrate themselves before him . . . Then all withdraw, leaving the king alone with the demoniac, with whom he converses amicably as if with his dead father, asking him if there will be war, and if he will triumph over his enemies, and if there will be famine or misfortunes in his kingdom, and everything else which he wishes to know. The devil answers all the questions, and counsels him as to what he is to do . . . After this conference the devil goes out of the man's body, leaving the negro very exhausted and broken down, and still disfigured.”

SLAVE HUNTER This bronze figure, dating from 1600, shows a Portuguese slave hunter arriving at Benin.

bewildered children hug their distraught mothers. Days, then weeks, will be spent in shackles in the cages, as the floors become filthier and the air fouler by the hour. The traders arrive, and the miserable, naked captives shuffle into line to be examined briefly by the ship's surgeon, who sorts the strongest and best-looking to one side and rejects the sick and elderly. Then the screams start again as red-hot branding irons are pressed onto the backs of men, women and children alike – to ensure that they can be identified as the property of the King of Spain, or of Portugal, or whoever now owns them.

Soon the slaves embark on an even more terrible ordeal: the infamous 'Middle Passage' that takes them to the New World. They are held below deck, shackled in pairs, left leg to right leg and left wrist to right wrist. Stifled by the blistering heat, and suffocating in the putrid air of the overcrowded holds, they toss and turn as the ship rolls and plunges in the high seas. Once a day they are allowed on deck for fresh air and forced under the whip to jump about for exercise, for those who survive the voyage have to be in reasonable shape to secure a good price. Twice a day, they are fed stale water, taken on board in Africa, and possibly rice with yams. A quarter of the slaves do not survive the journey, falling victim to fever, smallpox, scurvy, measles, malaria or ophthalmia which – although not a killer – blinds them, thereby making them unsaleable and liable to be thrown overboard. Some of the slaves even commit suicide by jumping over the side.

Unless the voyage was to supply a specific colony, the captain rarely knew the slaves' destination until he had completed his sale. This was certainly

INTERLOPER John Hawkins, the English slave-trader, intruded on the trade of other countries.

true of the interlopers in the Caribbean, where English, French, Portuguese and Canary Islands traders operated with or without licence in Spanish territories. When the English slave trader John Hawkins took a cargo of some 400 slaves to the Caribbean in 1564, conditions in the holds must have been insufferable because, while waiting for his licence, he had to get permission to off-load 30 'leane and sicke negros'. A follow-up voyage under John Lovell failed to get a licence at all, so 'ninety two pieces of Blacks, all old and very sick and thin' were simply dumped on shore.

Black slaves in the Caribbean ended up in a variety of places. Some went to the mines of Venezuela or as servants into the households of government officials in Santo Domingo. Others were sold as porters in

SLAVES ON THE SHORE Slaves wait for their 'examination' and branding before being transported.

Panama for the murderous coast-to-coast trek, carrying goods and bullion across the disease-ridden jungles. Equally terrible was the fate of those destined for the pearl fisheries where, by 1600, black divers had almost replaced the local Indians along the eastern Venezuelan coast. Around the middle of the 16th century, Vazquez de Espinosa wrote:

'Now each canoe master has in his house, or rancheria, a room . . . called the prison, where the Negroes have their beds and sleep under lock and key, for even in pearl fishing chastity is necessary, to such a degree that if anyone among them did otherwise, he would not be able to fish or dive under water, but would stay on the surface like a cork. Those who have disappointed their master in their catch of pearls, or who are contrary, they keep in these dormitories or prisons, grills and cells, and they punish them by beating and flogging them in a cruel and savage manner, a procedure quite alien to the profession of Christianity, except that in what concerns this traffic every possible means is required, for without it they would not do a thing.'

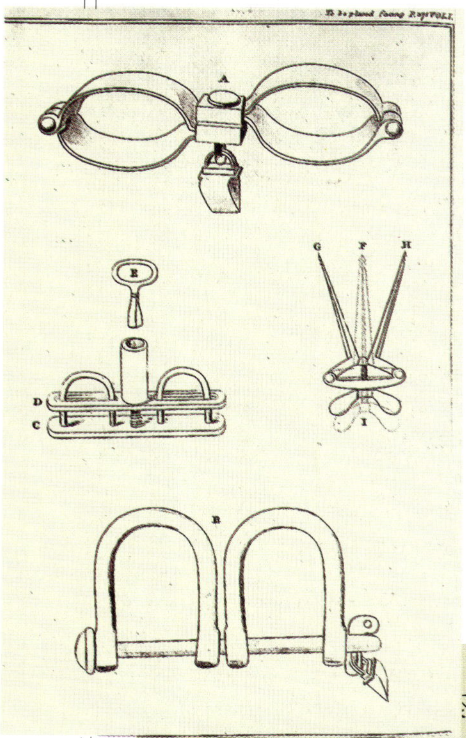

NO ESCAPE
Iron shackles were used on the slaves. Below: Overcrowding on slave ships was the rule, as this 18th-century plan shows.

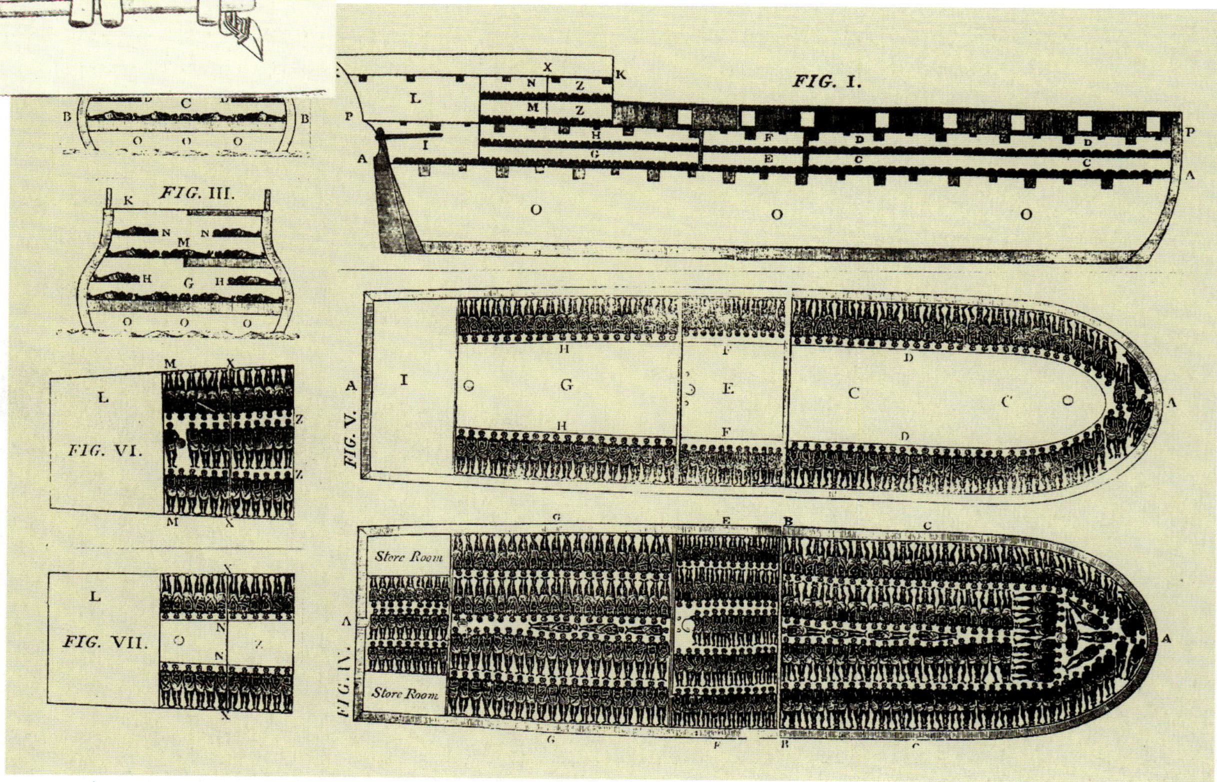

DID YOU KNOW?

The word 'slave' comes directly from the European word 'Slav'. This was because the Slav peoples, such as Russians, Ukrainians, Poles, Czechs, Slovaks, Serbs and Slovenes, were once conquered and 'enslaved' so regularly by powerful neighbours or invaders that the name became synonymous with all peoples who lost their liberty.

Traders of the Desert

In the 16th century, the trans-Saharan trade was a vital link between the lands of gold, ivory and slaves to the south and those of horses, books and metalwork to the north, and the desert was a way of life for the traders of the Sahara.

The Berber merchants of the desert depended on their camels much as seamen depended on their ships. Indeed, a caravan of 6000 camels, each carrying loads of up to 1500 lb (680 kg), could transport as much as half a dozen ships. The camel was far more than a beast of burden; it could also be used as a bride's dowry or as ransom.

When the caravan moved, it had the atmosphere of a religious as well as a commercial enterprise. Pilgrims accompanied the northbound trains, singing and reciting prayers as they went. Many hundreds of merchants and thousands of camels would make the journey, all under the direction of a leader, the Khabir. The responsibilities of the Khabir were as great as those of the captain of a fleet. He needed a full knowledge of the desert routes and the location of oases; the skills of a navigator, using sun and stars; and experience of hazards, such as scorpions, sandstorms, the intense heat of the day and the cold of the night. To help him, he had an array of special guides and officials, including the *Imam*, who led the prayers and buried the dead, and a scribe, who kept the accounts and dealt with matters such as the property of those who died en route.

CAMEL POWER Trade across the desert was a vital element of Arab commerce.

Typically, each merchant might have three camels for merchandise and one for provisions. The goods carried from north to south included manufactured goods from North Africa and Europe, and highly valued horses and sugar. Salt was moved in the opposite direction, from the mines of the desert regions to North and West Africa, along with precious metals, ivory, ostrich feathers and perfumes.

Whatever their work or whereabouts, the African slaves, according to a contemporary, Juan Echagoian, 'were not only corporeally maltreated, but have so much work that they do not sleep at night and likewise do not eat'. Most of them were to be found on the plantations of the Caribbean and Brazil, their lives controlled by a single crop – sugar.

A Life of Degradation

By 1600, 90 per cent of Brazil's exports consisted of sugar, and there were at least 30 000 black slaves among a population of some 100 000 colonists. The first European language learned by Africans en masse was Portuguese in Brazil, where climate, soil and the availability of slave labour made an irresistible combination. Sugar in Brazil revolved around the *engenho*, literally an 'engine' or production unit consisting of living quarters, cane fields and the mill. *Engenhos* – some with over 100 000 acres and many hundreds of slaves – did indeed resemble engines, throbbing with activity dictated by the needs of their product.

The cane fields produced a new crop every nine months. The harvest, or *safra*, which began in July,

SUGAR HELL The sugar mills and furnaces of the New World were the destination of many slaves in the 16th century.

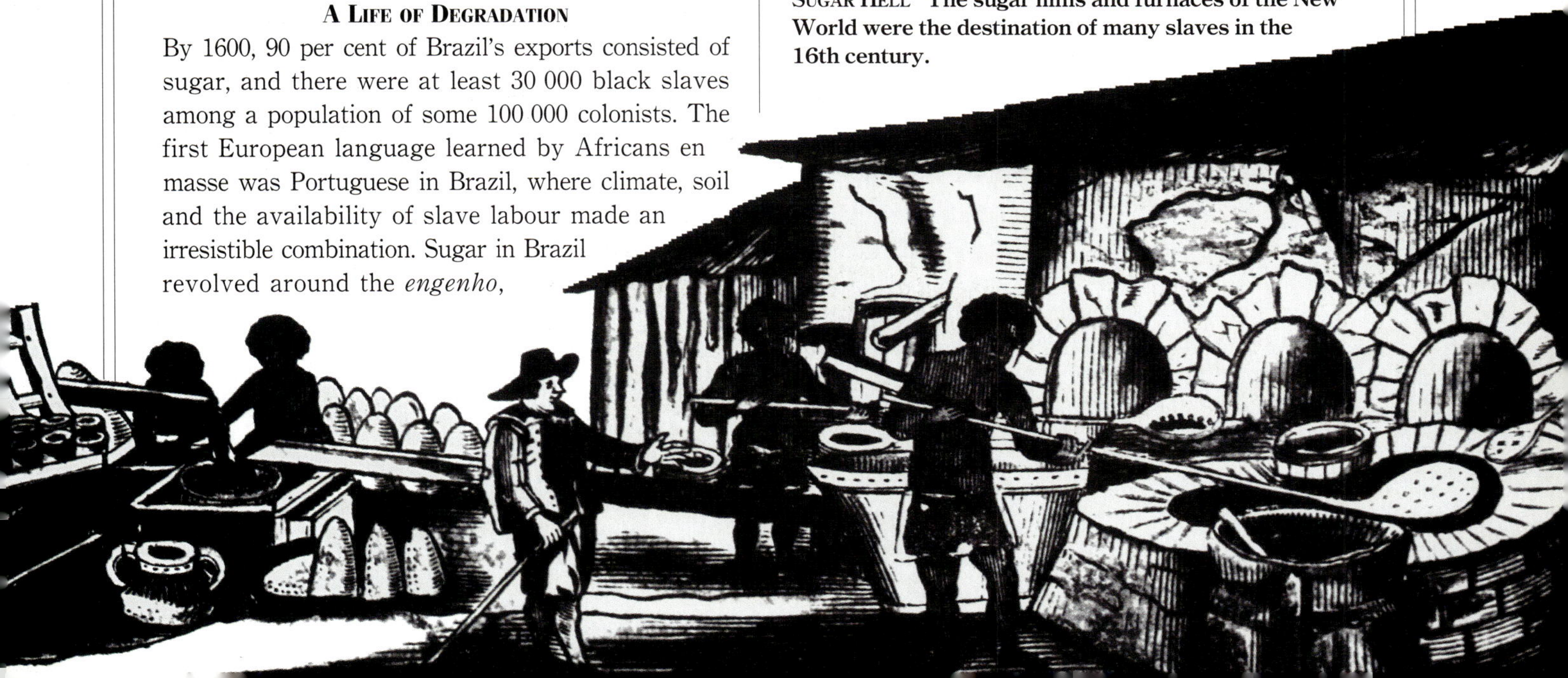

TIME OUT Africans brought their traditional dances to Brazil. The slave traders (right) destroyed a way of life on one continent and opened a new, desperate one on another.

was a time of nonstop labour. Slaves bent low in the fields as they hacked away at the huge stalks of cane, which they then piled into heavy bundles and loaded onto ox-carts bound for the mill. Here cane was crushed between vertical roller presses, powered by water or oxen, under the direction of overseers, some of whom might be slaves themselves. This produced a syrup that was then boiled in a series of cauldrons, and cleaned until it formed liquid sugar. Next, a team of slaves poured the liquid into conical moulds – the 'sugar loaf' shape – which they laid out in a drying shed. After a few weeks the moulds were opened and the crystallised loaf examined: the best, white, sugar was separated from the lower grades, which were used to make rum. Finally, the loaves were left to dry completely before being packed, crated and transported to the port for shipment.

The enterprise was everything implied by 'slave labour'. During the *safra* the mills worked 20 hours a day. And the back-breaking toil in the fields, where the slaves were whipped by their overseers, was only marginally better than the numbing work among the cauldrons. 'Sugar is the Hell of the slave' was a contemporary saying – and not necessarily a living hell either, since slave owners expected more than 10 per cent of their workforce to die each year.

Life, of course, held richer rewards for the owner. Few Brazilian slave owners came from titled families, but to be a *senhor de engenho* was to be a figure of some social standing. His

lifestyle set the tone for the upper reaches of local society and was imitated by many who could not afford it. His wines and clothes were all imported from Europe, and he cultivated an easy-going air of hospitality, leisure and good living. The owner's *casa grande*, or great house, and its various surrounding buildings housed the master and his family, relatives and servants, over whom the owner presided with an easy assurance. Some distance from the mansion lay the guarded sheds housing the slaves over whom the owner had an authority even more absolute.

How did these owners view their slaves? In many cases, they saw them quite simply as goods. Contemporary records give accounts of slave girls being bound and whipped because they would not sleep with an owner or overseer. Slaves were often inadequately fed and clothed; there was rarely any kind of medical treatment provided for them, except what fellow slaves could offer, using traditional remedies.

On the other hand, there were some incentives for treating slaves well. A slave produced about three-quarters of a ton of sugar each year and could therefore repay the initial investment made in him in two or three years. So if a slave had a working life of six years, the owner could then make a profit of double his original outlay and afford a strong, healthy replacement.

Profitable as it was, sugar-growing held plenty of risks, which a number of *senhors* attempted to spread by making contracts with *lavradores*, or share-croppers, who provided them with cane already cut for the mill. These small landowners employed possibly no more than a dozen slaves, whom they worked equally hard and for whom the mortality rates were equally high.

INTO BONDAGE Captives in Benin are rounded up by native slave-traders for transport to the coast.

But there was one major difference. With the *lavrador* the slave lived in much more intimate contact with the owner's family and his fellow slaves than on the *casa grande,* where slaves were spread over thousands of acres and regimented by overseers. The existence of small units made it possible for slaves to protect something of their African identities: a shared language, for example, and a belief in the spirit world. And just as the Africans adopted the dress, language and at least the outward forms of

THE BARBARY PIRATES

FOR THE SEAMEN of the Mediterranean, capture by pirates was a hazard of everyday life. The pirates operated with notorious ferocity from towns like Tunis and Tripoli on the Barbary Coast of North Africa, named after its Berber inhabitants. The coast had been a favourite haunt of pirates since Roman times, but the defeat of Granada, the last Moorish kingdom in Spain, in 1492 gave the pirates a new impetus. Many of the Muslims who fled from Spain with the return of Christian monarchs crossed the Mediterranean to the North African coast, and sought revenge for their defeat by plundering Christian ships, enslaving their crews and selling them to the hungry markets of Muslim Africa and Asia.

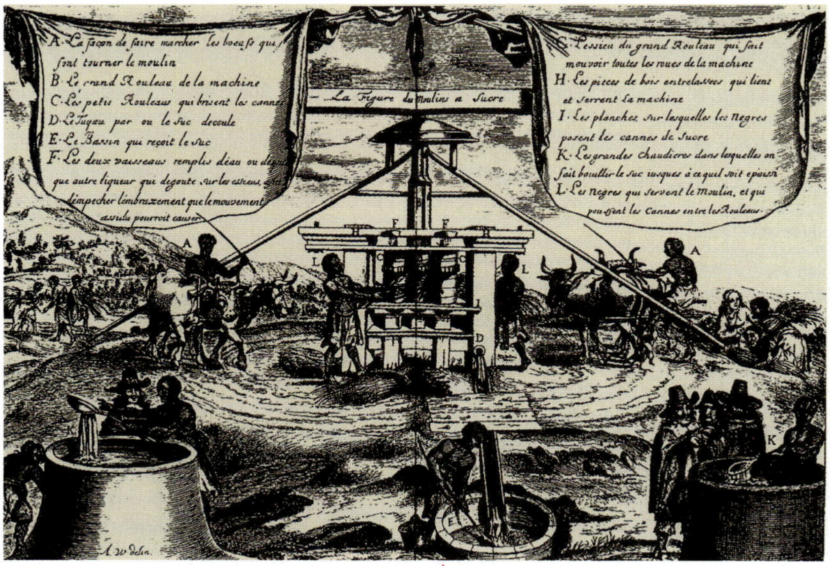

SWEET FOR SOME The sugar plantations created wealth for Brazil, but brought enslavement to countless Africans.

Christianity from the colonials, so the colonials absorbed African ways that eventually became features of the mixed society that emerged.

Nonetheless, the day-to-day reality of the average slave's life was one of degradation. Death rates were at first so high that, far from a distinctive 'black American' culture being able to develop, replacements kept arriving from Africa, with the result that the slaves remained 'African' with all the tribal differences that this implied. Men outnumbered women two to one, which made any normal evolution of family life impossible for them. Slave populations declined for other reasons, too: some slaves managed to buy their freedom, or were granted it by an owner's last will and testament, while others simply ran away.

Usually they were caught by professional slave catchers, mainly Indians, but sometimes they evaded capture, and sometimes even managed to set up their own townships, called *quilimbos*. One of these, Palmares, was set up in 1607 between Bahia and Pernambuco, and its population grew to several thousand. It was not overthrown until 1694: almost a century of existence for an African town in the New World.

ARTS AND ANCIENT CULTURES IN AFRICA

VASCO DA GAMA discovered several Muslim cities along the east coast of Africa and would have found others if he had penetrated inland. He would have seen towns where the mosque was the focus of the holy day, Friday; where people prayed facing Mecca and fasted from dawn to dusk during the month of Ramadan; and where the women were veiled.

As the age of exploration dawned, the achievements of Islamic civilisation far exceeded those of Christian Europe. Islamic literature, science, mathematics, medicine, philosophy and geography enjoyed a pre-eminence in which Africa played its part. Cairo was one of the world's great cities; so too was Timbuktu, south of the Sahara – a religious and scholarly capital in which life for a large community was dominated by learning. However, Islam did not obliterate traditional beliefs among the villagers, and there were areas untouched by the Muslim faith.

African kings were worshipped as divine. They had supernatural powers; they could make themselves invisible and communicate with their ancestors. Belief in the supernatural permeated the life of every village community. The villagers acknowledged the power of witch doctors. They believed in spells and sacrifices (human and animal), rainmaking and ancestor worship – all of which reinforced the divine authority of their kings.

There was an isolated group of Christians in Africa, surviving in the mountain kingdom of Ethiopia. Ethiopian Christians looked to the traditions of the Old Testament: they practised polygamy and circumcision; kept the Sabbath holy; and adopted ritual cleansing and dancing. Like the kings of the Old Testament, the king was spiritually all-powerful and lived in seclusion.

PEOPLE OF THE PACIFIC

The Pacific Ocean occupies over one-third of the surface of the earth. Yet it remained unknown to Europeans until the 16th century – as did its remarkable inhabitants, who had spread across many thousands of islands during previous centuries.

THE VOYAGES of Magellan through to those of the Dutch seamen of the 17th century linked the world in the waters of the Pacific. Yet most of the Pacific islands, such as Hawaii, Tahiti, New Guinea and Easter Island, remained unknown and unvisited. As late as the 1640s, the Dutchman Abel Janszoon Tasman could not adequately chart the Australian and New Zealand coasts he passed, or the Fiji and Tonga island groups he sighted. Overall, the South Sea Islanders left little impression on the discoverers, as indeed the discoverers made little impact on the islanders. In time – from the late 18th century onwards – the Pacific islanders would provide

SOUTHERN SEA A map dating from 1623 shows that much remained undiscovered after Magellan's voyage.

the most romantic image of native innocence for Europeans: that of grass-skirted Tahitian beauties splashing out to greet the crews of European ships. But during the 16th century the islands were, in the eyes of the authorities, populated by 'savages', and possessed none of the gold, silver and spices that justified the expense of exploration or colonisation.

Yet the islands' inhabitants were remarkable. Nobody knows for certain where they came from, or when. What is certain is that over thousands of years, generation after generation of what were to become known as Melanesians and Polynesians had spread thousands of miles across an ocean that occupies more than a third of the surface of the globe. Most of what they brought with them – their belief in gods and heroes, Stone Age tools and, in the case of the Polynesians, some skills in cultivation beyond hunting and gathering – had remained unchanged during the centuries before Magellan and would survive until more modern times. Of course they had to adapt to their island environments, developing navigational and fishing skills and creating a lifestyle of relatively untroubled self-sufficiency.

A mixture of enchantment and contempt emerges from European comments about the islanders whom

DID YOU KNOW?

The coconut is one of the world's most versatile plants. The islanders of Indonesia and the Pacific ate the kernel, drank the milk and made palm wine from it; they used the fibre from the husks for making rope and rigging for boats. Palm leaves became sails and roofs, and palm oil was used for cooking.

NEW GUINEA HUNTERS A rare 16th-century picture of a group of New Guineans.

CANNIBAL? A Papuan belonging to a tribe described by one of the European discoverers as 'cannibals with frizzled hair'.

they encountered. To the Spaniard Saavreda, who reached the Moluccas from Mexico in 1528, the Papuans were merely 'cannibals with frizzled hair'. On the Marshalls he was greeted by swarms of body-painted natives, singing and dancing with delight as they ran riot over the ships and clambered up the rigging.

When Alvaro de Mendaña reached the Solomons from Peru in the late 1560s, he was welcomed equally enthusiastically, though his crew was disgusted by a present they were offered of a child's arm and leg. Members of the crew then decided to punish 'the infidels', putting many of the islanders to death and destroying their homes. This was a pattern repeated almost everywhere, from Malaita to Guadalcanal: an initial welcome followed by some supposed outrage and an outbreak of brutality.

AN ANCIENT ISLAND RACE

Of the inhabitants of the Pacific Islands, it was the Polynesians who were the most advanced. Their methods of cultivation succeeded on the richer volcanic soils of many of their islands. They ate coconuts, bananas, pineapples, rice – and brought with them the sweet potato. Their lives were deeply affected by gods whom they worshipped at large stone altars and to whom they sacrificed animals, and sometimes humans, before each significant enterprise or voyage. The Polynesians gave the Europeans the word 'tabu', or taboo, meaning to isolate a person or object too sacred or unclean for contact. One of their great heroes, about whom they told elaborate stories, was Con Tiki, who sent his people on voyages across great expanses of sea.

In most of their settlements the Polynesians retained their ancient skills, carving decorative wood and making clever use of animal skins and vegetable fibres for clothing. The picture of the trusting, joyous Polynesians paddling their canoes towards the ships of the explorers seems to reflect the untroubled lives of a people who knew nothing of private property, who lived and worked in a communal society, and who had enough to satisfy every material need.

It was the sea, of course, that dominated the lives of the Polynesians and their island neighbours. They were expert fishermen, navigators and boat-builders, using small dugout canoes for short-distance trading and coastal fishing, and much larger ones for ocean voyages. These canoes were usually made from hollowed-out single trunks and could be up to 100 ft (30 m) in length with room for 100 people, together with food, water, anchors and bailers, for crossings lasting several weeks.

The Polynesians built their boats with tools made from stone, coral and fishbone; sewed together the planking for the sides with vegetable – usually coconut – fibre; caulked the boats with earth and

MACTAN MASSACRE A woodcut of 1575 shows the battle between Magellan and the natives of Mactan in which the explorer died a hero's death.

New Tastes from the Tropics

In the days of slow travel, and before refrigeration, few tropical plants, fruits or vegetables were widely available in Europe. Some tropical products, such as spices, travelled well, but these were expensive luxuries. And even sugar, which could be grown in Mediterranean countries, and was popular in England, was rare throughout most of the continent. Yet the age of exploration did provide opportunities for explorers and settlers to appreciate them overseas; and, as a result, some of the plants were deliberately spread, through seeds and cuttings, to and from tropical Asia, Africa and America.

Bananas, which probably originated in South-east Asia, spread via Madagascar to Africa, and then to the Mediterranean, where they became popular. The Portuguese and Spaniards then introduced them to South America and the West Indies, where they became a feature of both daily life and the landscape. Much the same happened to the coconut, which was encountered by the Portuguese in East Africa and taken to Brazil and the Caribbean. By the 1580s travellers were noting the abundance of palm trees along the Caribbean shores of South America. The Italian Francesco Carletti tasted both fruits on his travels in South-east Asia. He found the banana 'one of the most delicious fruits to be found anywhere in the world'; coconut milk 'of great substance and nourishment'; breadfruit 'a little hard'; mangosteen 'admirable'; and pineapple strong and 'corrosive'.

The colonial authorities introduced Asian spices, such as cinnamon, nutmeg, mace, cloves, ginger and pepper, to Brazil and Spanish America. They were never a commercial success, however, and the fastidious tastes of the colonists ensured that the main supplies continued to come directly from India, Ceylon and Indonesia.

Most of the tropical fruits and vegetables went from the Old World to the New, and few went the other way. The New World got plantains, mangoes, taro, yams and African peppers: yams from the Pacific and Indian Ocean were particularly successful as slave foods in West Africa, Brazil and the West Indies. But the New World gave the peanut to the Old, as well as Brazil nuts, cashews and the pineapple, which is native to Brazil, or possibly the Caribbean.

A look at the products of hot climates gives only a fraction of the overall picture, which is one of developing movement across the globe. Whether we talk about coffee drunk in New York, bananas eaten in the West Indies or chips eaten almost everywhere, the transport of tastes encouraged by the age of exploration became a central contributor to today's 'global village'.

Pure Pleasure The pineapple travelled from New World to Old.

vegetable gum; and painted them in a variety of colours. The boats were stabilised, too, by connecting a long plank of wood to the hull or, even more effectively, by adding an outrigger – a second canoe lashed to the first – a device recorded by the early explorers. In shallow waters and calms the Polynesians paddled their canoes, but in the open ocean they used the lateen sails with which the boats were fitted and a wide paddle as a stern rudder. Magellan was so taken by the sight of the fast, manoeuvrable canoes of a fishing fleet off Guam that he named it and its neighbour, Rota, 'Isles of Lateen Sails'. That was before he re-named them 'Isles of Thieves' after experiencing the activities of a people innocent of any concept of private property. The Polynesians were natural and expert sailors, navigating by the sun, moon and stars; by the directions of the waves, winds and currents; and from any information they could glean from the flight of the birds.

Such tales of the South Sea Islanders did not impress the European authorities at home, however. They wanted something more tangible, in the form of gold and spices. There was one exception to this: the

BODY PAINTING Europeans found Pacific Islanders covered with elaborate designs.

Philippines, whose eastern coasts fronted the Pacific and where, ironically, the first European to explore the ocean, Ferdinand Magellan, had lost his life. The Philippines lacked spices, and they had very litte gold; but for strategic reasons in a Portuguese-dominated sea the northern islands became the site of Spanish settlements, where they became 'absolute masters of the lands, of the men, and also of the women, all of whom pay them tribute'.

AN EMPIRE IS FOUNDED

The Italian traveller Francesco Carletti visited the Philippines in 1596 and was able to record something of the lives of the Filipinos, as well as those of the colonists. His picture of the Filipinos is a glowing one; he described their 'beautiful bodies, robust and virile', and how, to appear 'more comely' to their wives, they tattooed themselves all over with iron implements 'in a style of bizarre workmanship and lineaments as well executed as could be done by a skilled and dexterous mathematician'. The men dyed their tattoos blue with herb juices and went about naked, while the women wore clothes and covered their arms and legs with metal bracelets and rings. Both men and women wore metal earrings, so heavy that their ears were stretched 'to such length that they reach to their shoulders'; they also tinted their teeth red, and kept them highly polished.

Carletti described the Filipinos' houses: built on poles with woven reeds for the floors and walls, and roofed with palm leaves. They were high enough to need ladders to get in and out, and underneath the islanders kept their pigs and poultry. He recorded their food; rice cooked with water and salt was the main dish, but they also made a bread from fish and another from thick palms. He also described their cockfights, and the careful way in which they kept the cocks away from hens before the fight because the battle would be fought to get possession of the hen. Cockfights were clearly bloody affairs and occasions for heavy gambling. Carletti concluded that 'everything good is in those islands'.

But Carletti also noted that 'whatever those islands lack is brought in from outside'. These imports were not for the Filipinos but for the Spaniards, and included wheat from Japan and silks, satins, sugar

LOOKING FOR SPICES Hernando de Grijalva leaves Mexico in 1537 on his unsuccessful attempt to reach the Spice Islands from the west.

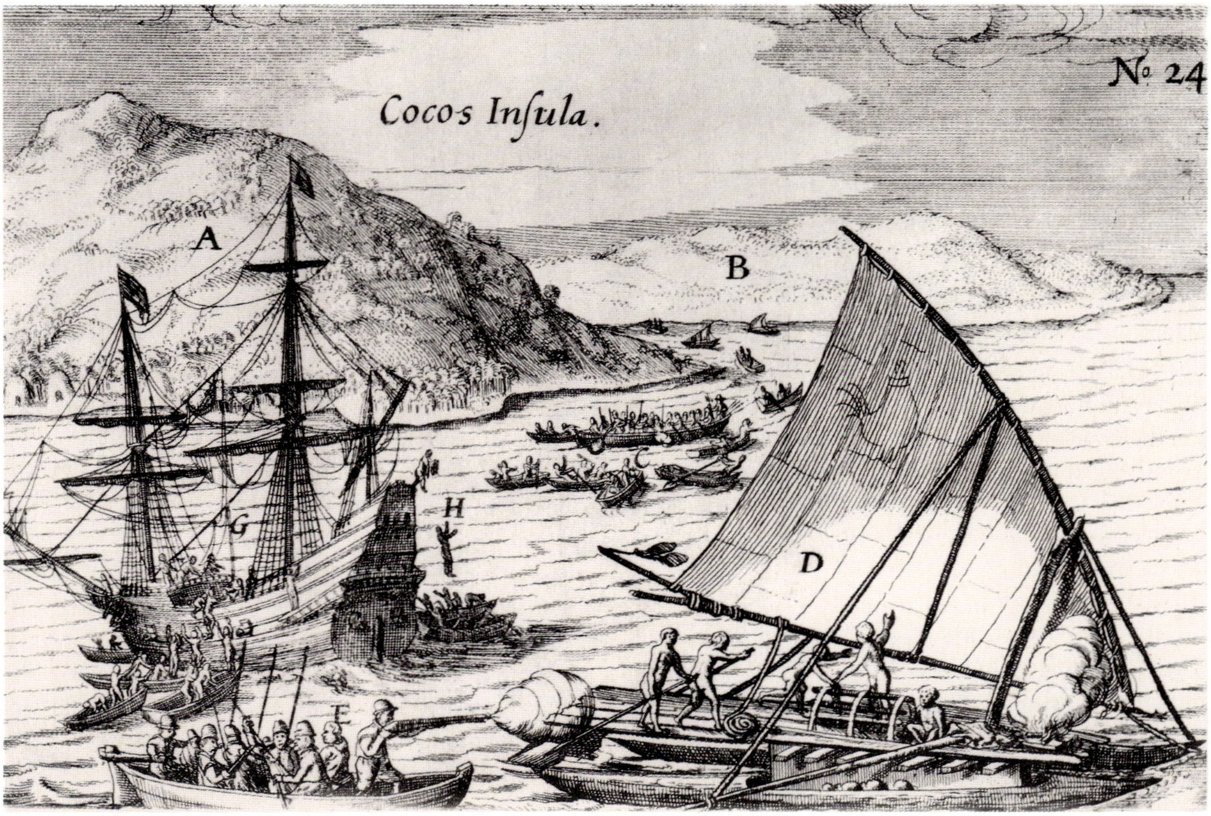

THE EXPERTS Pacific Island canoes were used for local fishing and for long, ocean-going voyages.
Right: Polynesian navigators used stick charts made from palm sticks tied together with coconut fibre.

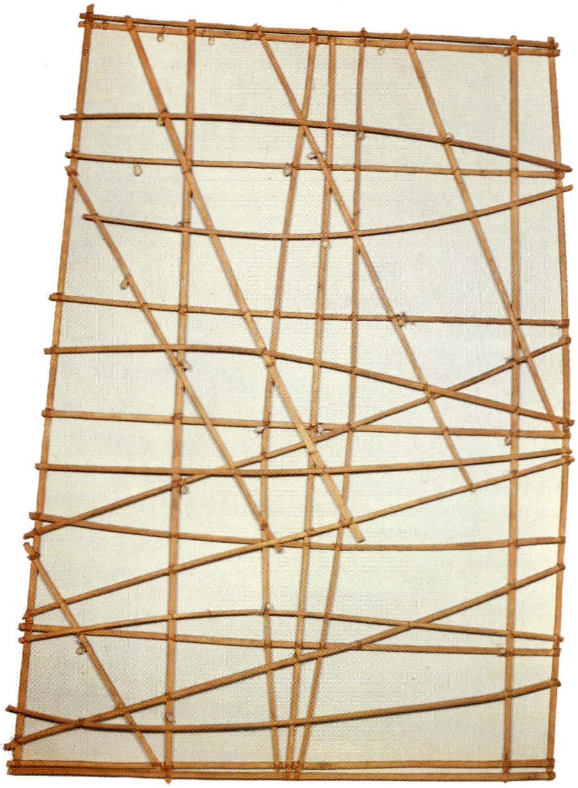

and musk from China. By the end of the 16th century Manila had become one of the great cosmopolitan ports of the world. Traders from China, Japan, Thailand, Cambodia and the Spice Islands sold luxury goods to Spanish merchants who arrived on 'Manila galleons' from Acapulco bringing with them bullion from the New World.

In Manila, sizable communities, such as the Chinese and Japanese, lived in their own separate quarters, while the rich houses and palaces of the centre provided the Spaniards with grand dwellings whose opulence astounded visitors. The Spaniards built, as Carletti noted, 'a city in the manner of the City of Mexico in New Spain', surrounded by 'a thick wall with good fortresses'.

No luxury was lacking. Native produce, fruit, fish and game were cheap and abundant; from Mexico, or indeed Seville, came fine wines and the latest European fashions; from the Orient came all the

EYEWITNESS

The Death of Magellan

Magellan died on Mactan Island in the Philippines on April 27, 1521. His death was witnessed by Antonio Pigafetta:

‘The natives continued to pursue us . . . Recognising the captain, so many turned upon him that they knocked his helmet off his head twice . . .

Thus did we fight for more than one hour, refusing to retire further. An Indian hurled a bamboo spear into the captain's face, but the latter immediately killed him with his lance, which he left in the Indian's body. Then, trying to lay hand on sword, he could draw it out but halfway, because he had been wounded in the arm with a bamboo spear. When the natives saw that, they all hurled themselves upon him. One of them wounded him on the left leg with a large cutlass, which resembles a scimitar, only being larger. That caused the captain to fall face downward, when immediately they rushed upon him with iron and bamboo spears and with their cutlasses, until they killed our mirror, our light, our comfort, and our true guide . . . Among the other virtues which he possessed, he was more constant than ever anyone else in the greatest of adversity. He endured hunger better than all the others, and more accurately than any man in the world did he understand sea charts and navigation . . . no other had had so much natural talent nor the boldness to learn how to circumnavigate the world, as he had almost done.’

spices, silks and fine craftsmanship that would eventually find their way to the New World and Europe at astronomical prices.

With their retinues of servants and slaves, the Spaniards moved in elaborate carriages and sedan chairs. They did no manual work themselves, of course, but after a late afternoon dinner would emerge to parade in their fine clothes and indulge in those innumerable assignations that scandalised the Church but gave Manila a reputation for colonial high life reminiscent of that of Golden Goa in its heyday.

Just as the colonists built a life of luxury for themselves, so they transformed the lives of the Filipinos. Before the arrival of the Spaniards, the Filipinos had no concept of private property, but lived in territorial kinship units called *barangays*. The Spaniards commandeered these, giving some to the Church, keeping some for the colonists and giving the bulk of the land to chieftains whose cooperation they needed. Spanish land was organised into *encomiendas*, as in Spanish America, and each *encomendero* was allotted between 500 and 1000 Filipinos who had to pay tribute to the state, usually in the form of labour. At times this system was supplemented by the pool system, whereby all males except the chiefs and their eldest sons were forced to join the labour pool, or by the *vandala*, which compelled the labourer to sell all his produce in return for promissory notes, which were rarely honoured. Not surprisingly, demands for more produce to supply the colonists led to shortages, famine and disease. Some people even think today that the social turbulence in the modern Philippines originated in the appropriation of the *barangays* and the installation of local chiefs as a new class of landowner.

For most Filipinos, conversion to Roman Catholicism brought about an abrupt change in their daily lives. Yet it seems that they were genuine converts, some 90 per cent of the population eventually coming to embrace the new faith, and the old practices of magic and nature worship that they had accepted for centuries were replaced by the rituals of the Church.

Mixed Blood
Above left: A group of *mestizos*, of mixed Spanish and Filipino blood. Right: A Spice Islands ‘Mardica’, and next to him a Japanese.

Time Chart

1490 – 1509

Politics and Religion

1492: Granada, the last Muslim foothold in Spain, falls to the 'Catholic Kings', Ferdinand and Isabella. In the same year, the Jews are expelled from Spain.

1492-3: On his first voyage to the New World, Christopher Columbus makes a landfall on an island of the Bahamas while searching for a westward route to Asia; he names it San Salvador and takes possession in the name of Spain.

1493: Pope Alexander VI issues a Papal Bull granting to Spain all undiscovered lands beyond a line running north to south 100 leagues (about 250 miles) west of the Cape Verde Islands, and all those to the east to Portugal. In the following year this is revised by the Treaty of Tordesillas between Spain and Portugal, which moves the line of demarkation to 370 leagues west of the Cape Verdes, and which later enables Portugal to claim Brazil (see **1500**).

Fortune Seekers Spanish adventurers en route from their homeland.

1493-6: Columbus makes his second voyage, discovering Puerto Rico and Jamaica, and founds Santo Domingo, the first European city in the New World.

1497: In the service of Henry VII, John Cabot discovers Newfoundland, thinking he has reached China.

1498: The Portuguese explorer Vasco da Gama is the first European to reach India by going round the Cape of Good Hope, establishing a sea route to the east and laying the foundation for Portugal's commercial domination in India and the Far East.

1500: Pedro Cabral discovers Brazil, after being blown off course from Africa, and claims it for Portugal.

Reminder A tile commemorates the discovery of America.

1498-1501: Columbus makes his third voyage, during which he explores Trinidad and Venezuela. He fails to contain a rebellion against Spanish rule on Hispaniola and returns to Spain in disgrace.

1501: Amerigo Vespucci explores the east coast of South America and establishes that it is a separate continent, not an island off Asia. He describes it as a New World.

1502-4: Columbus makes his last voyage, to Honduras and Panama. He dies in Spain in 1506.

1509: Henry VIII becomes king of England. His reign will see the break with Rome and the foundations laid for the Protestant Reformation in England.

Culture and Society

1490: The Aldine Press, established by Aldus Minutius in Venice, begins to publish the high-quality, low-priced editions of classical texts for which it will become famous.

1492: Over the next three years, Pinturicchio decorates the Borgia apartments in the Vatican.

1493: Hartmann Schedel's *Nuremberg Chronicle*, an illustrated history of the world from the Creation to the present, is published in Latin and German.

1499: Oxford University, England, introduces degrees in music.

1503: The construction of Canterbury Cathedral, England, started in 1070, is completed.

1503: The pocket handkerchief comes into use in Europe.

1505: The trade in black slaves between Africa and North America begins.

1506: The *Laocoon*, one of the few documented sculptures from ancient Greece, is unearthed in the ruins of Nero's villa in Rome.

1507: Leonardo da Vinci completes the *Mona Lisa*, on which he began work in 1503.

1508: Michelangelo begins work on the Sistine Chapel ceiling in Rome. He takes four years to complete it.

New World Illustration from Amerigo Vespucci's writings.

Invention and Technology

1492: Martin Behaim, of Nuremberg, constructs the first terrestrial globe.

1492: Leonardo produces drawings for a flying machine.

1500: The first book on herbal medicine, *Liber de arti distillandi*, is published.

1500: The first recorded Caesarean operation on a living woman is performed.

Herbs for Health Herbal books become increasingly popular.

1500: Two types of colourful pottery, *faience* (from Italy) and *maiolica* (from Majorca), are produced.

1500: Black lead pencils are used in England for the first time.

1502: Clockmaker Peter Henlein of Nuremberg constructs the first watch, known at the time as the 'Nuremberg Egg'.

1507: German geographer Martin Waldseemuhler produces a world map that for the first time refers to the New World as America, named after Amerigo Vespucci.

1509: For the first time attempts are made to limit the right to practise medicine to trained and licensed doctors.

1510 – 1530

Politics and Religion

1510: The Portuguese seize Goa on the west coast of India, gaining a naval base for the protection of their trading posts in the Indian Ocean and Far East.

1512: Francisco Serrao reaches the Spice Islands and claims them for Portugal.

1513: Vasco Nunez da Balboa crosses Panama and is the first European to see the Pacific Ocean.

1514: The Portuguese are the first Europeans to enter Chinese waters, near the South China coast (modern Hong Kong). In 1517 they reach Canton, where they terrify the Chinese with a gun salute.

1516: Archduke Charles of Austria, grandson of Ferdinand of Spain, is proclaimed King of Spain on Ferdinand's death. In 1519 he is also elected Holy Roman Emperor.

1517: In Wittenberg, Germany, Martin Luther nails his 95 theses, attacking the Church practice of selling indulgences, to a church door – heralding the Protestant Reformation in Europe.

IMMORTAL The *Victoria*, made famous as Magellan's flagship.

1519: Ferdinand Magellan sets off to circumnavigate the world and claim the Spice Islands for Spain. He is killed in the Philippines in 1521, but in 1522 one ship from the expedition reaches Spain.

1519: The Spaniard Hernán Cortés embarks on an expedition to destroy the Aztec Empire in Mexico. In 1521 the capital, Tenochtitlán, surrenders to him.

1520: Suleiman the Magnificent becomes Ottoman Emperor. During his rule Ottoman power greatly increases in Europe and the eastern Mediterranean.

1526: The Mogul Babur, a descendant of Genghis Khan, defeats the Sultan of Delhi in northern India. This enables him to create the Mogul Empire, with boundaries stretching from Bakul to Bengal.

1529: The Ottoman army reaches the outskirts of Vienna, but is decisively defeated.

CONQUEST The Aztec capital under siege by Hernán Cortés.

Culture and Society

1510: The most famous of all Morality Plays, *Everyman*, which is already popular in Europe, is first performed in England.

1513: Niccolo Machiavelli writes *The Prince*, which is published posthumously in 1532. Purporting to be a manual of advice to a ruler who wants success, it advocates lying, deception and the use of force. It removes any ideas of morality from statecraft and gives the word 'Machiavellian' to the language.

1515: The painter Raphael is appointed chief architect of St Peter's, Rome.

UTOPIA The first edition of Thomas More's famous work.

1515: Thomas More writes *Utopia,* a picture of an 'ideal' American island where property is held in common.

1516: The palace of Hampton Court, England, is completed for Cardinal Wolsey. At his fall from power it is taken over by Henry VIII.

1520: Michelangelo works on the Medici Chapel, Florence.

1520: Chocolate comes to Europe from Mexico. Like tea and coffee, it does not become popular until the late 17th century.

1523: Publication of the first manual on lute-playing, by Hans Judenkunig of Vienna.

NEW TASTE Grinding cocoa beans.

Invention and Technology

1510: Leonardo da Vinci designs a horizontal water wheel.

1514: Nicolaus Copernicus circulates his *Commentariolus* among his friends. In it he first asserts that the Earth revolves around its axis and moves around the Sun with the other planets. He eventually publishes these theories in *De Revolutionibus Orbium Coelestium* (On the Revolutions of the Celestial Spheres) in 1543.

HORSE CARE The loading of horses is a delicate job.

1518: In Europe, spectacles come into use for shortsightedness.

1519: Horses, sheep and cattle become established in the New World. They will transform the lives of the Plains Indians and give the colonists new oportunities.

1522: The artist Albrecht Dürer designs a flying machine.

1523: Publication of the first English textbook on farming, *The Book of Husbandry* by Anthony Fitzherbert.

1528: Paracelsus revolutionises medical thought and practice by challenging the medieval theory that bodily health is dictated by four 'humours' – blood, phlegm, choler and melancholy. He introduces the idea that disease is carried into the body by outside agencies.

1530 – 1549

Politics and Religion

1530: Charles V is crowned Holy Roman Emperor and King of Naples by Pope Clement VII.

1532: Francisco Pizarro's Spanish expedition sets off from Tumbes in northern Peru to conquer the Inca Empire. In 1533 the Spaniards execute the Inca ruler, Atahualpa, and take the Inca capital, Cuzco.

1533: Henry VIII of England marries Anne Boleyn, having divorced his first, Catholic, wife Catherine of Aragon. The following year, the Act of Supremacy proclaims the King Head of the Church in England.

1535: Jacques Cartier discovers the St Lawrence River, providing the basis for the French claim to Canada.

1536: In England, the Dissolution of the Monasteries begins.

1541: The Jesuit Order is approved by the Pope, and its founder, Ignatius Loyola, becomes the first general.

1545: The Council of Trent opens and over the next 18 years directs the Catholic fight-back against Protestantism – the Counter-Reformation.

France Explores Jacques Cartier encounters Indians in Canada.

Ruler of Russia In 1547 Ivan IV (the Terrible) is crowned tsar.

1542: The Jesuit Francis Xavier begins his missionary work.

1546: Civil war breaks out in the German states between Charles V and the Protestant princes.

1547: The Portuguese establish a settlement on the island of Macao.

1547: Ivan the Terrible, the first Tsar of all the Russias, comes to power. He inaugurates a reign of terror at home, but he also defeats the Tatars and conquers Siberia.

Culture and Society

1530s: Syphilis, called *bubas* by the Spanish, spreads rapidly throughout Europe. The first signs of it appeared almost immediately after Columbus's return from his first voyage. However, the vast majority of transported diseases, such as smallpox, measles, typhoid and tuberculosis, go the other way – from Old World to New.

1530s: A new collar style, the 'ruff', finds its way to England from France. Other popular fashions of the time include Spanish-style padding for knees and shoulders, and hats adorned with feathers.

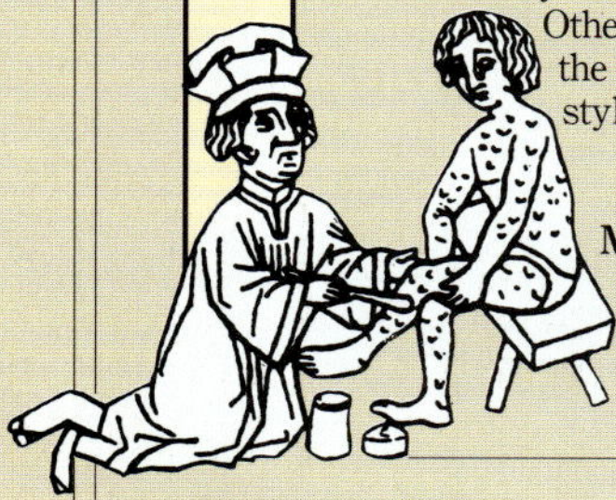

Medical Help A doctor treats a sufferer from syphilis.

1536: Michelangelo begins work on the *Last Judgment* on the altar wall of the Sistine Chapel. He completes it in 1541.

1536: Hans Holbein the Younger, who moved to England in 1532, is made Court painter to Henry VIII.

1530: Maize is introduced into China around this date. Like so many New World crops, it meets considerable resistance and never becomes a regular part of the diet.

1537: In Italy the first music conservatories are founded for training young musicians.

1546: Michelangelo takes over as architect of St Peter's, Rome, to design the dome and see through completion of the building work.

1546: Construction of the Louvre, Paris, begins for Francis I, under the supervision of architect Pierre Lescot.

1549: Jesters make their first appearance in the courts of Europe.

Style The 'Spanish ruff' becomes fashionable across Europe.

Invention and Technology

1530s: Andreas Vesalius, Professor of Anatomy at Padua University, begins his (forbidden) dissections on human corpses. His work vastly improves anatomical knowledge.

1535: Diving bells are used for the first time for underwater exploration.

1539: Antonio de Mendoza, the first Viceroy of New Spain, introduces the first printing press in the New World, in Mexico City.

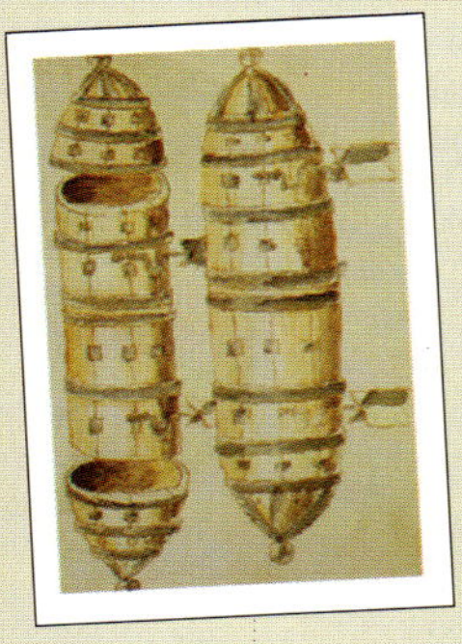

Underwater A contemporary design for a diving bell.

1540: Ether, later to be used as a painkiller and an anaesthetic, is produced from alcohol and sulphuric acid.

1543: Oil is discovered in Texas, North America. Of little immediate impact, it will create unimaginable wealth for future generations.

1543: Blasco da Garay submits a design for a steamboat to Charles V.

1545: The discovery of silver mines at Potosi, Peru, and Zacatecas, Mexico, in 1546, provides Spain with much-needed wealth.

1546: Flemish geographer and map-maker Gerardus Mercator announces that there is a magnetic pole.

1550 – 1569

Politics and Religion

1553: Mary becomes Queen of England and re-establishes the Roman Catholic faith. In 1554 she marries Philip of Spain, son of Emperor Charles V.

1555: At the Peace of Augsburg Charles V concedes the right of the German Protestant states to enjoy equal status with Catholic ones.

1556: Charles V abdicates and is succeeded by Philip II in Spain and the Netherlands. Charles's other son, Ferdinand, who is already King of Hungary and Bohemia, and Archduke of Austria, becomes Holy Roman Emperor Ferdinand I.

1556: Akbar the Great, grandson of Babur, becomes Mogul Emperor of India.

VIRGIN QUEEN Elizabeth I sponsors some of England's explorers.

1558: Elizabeth I becomes Queen of England and re-introduces the Protestant faith.

1560: The Inquisition arrives in Goa, and many Jews are burnt.

1562: Ferdinand I signs an eight-year truce with Suleiman I. Later in the year, Ferdinand dies and is succeeded as Emperor by Maximilian II.

1566: A rebellion against Philip II's rule begins in the Netherlands.

1567: The first Huguenot War begins in France between Roman Catholics and Protestants. Intermittent fighting between the two sides continues until 1628, when the last Huguenot stronghold, La Rochelle, is taken by Cardinal Richelieu for Louis XIII.

1568: Jesuit missionaries are welcomed in Japan.

TITLE DEED The patent giving land to the *Mayflower* Pilgrims.

Culture and Society

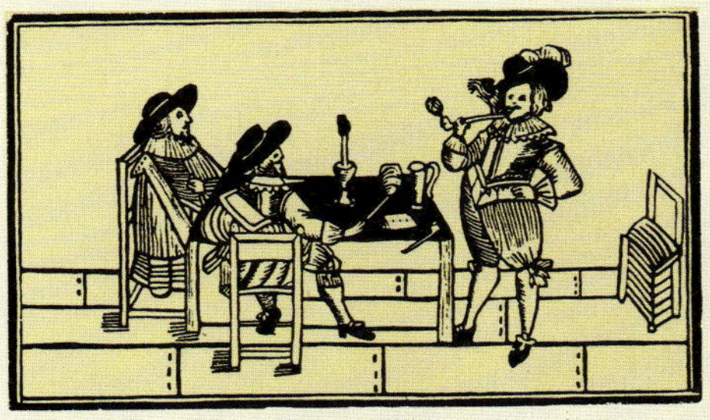

SPREADING POPULARITY Smokers enjoy the New World import.

1550: Publication of Giorgio Vasari's *Lives of the Artists*, in which he provides an account of the lives and work of the artists of the Renaissance.

1550s: The Church of St Basil, Moscow, is built by Ivan the Terrible.

1550s: There is an outpouring of writings in Nahuatl, the language of the native Indian populations of Central America. They include administrative records and legends and histories of the Indian peoples.

1555: Nostradamus publishes his *Centuries*, a phenomenal bestseller claiming to predict the future for the next 500 years.

1560: The tobacco plant is imported into Europe from America by Jean Nicot, French ambassador to Lisbon.

1563: An outbreak of the plague in England kills more than 20 000. It remains the scourge of Europe and is among the diseases transported to the New World.

1564: The horse-drawn coach, introduced from the Netherlands, makes its first appearance in England.

1560s: The sweet potato makes its appearance in China, though no import ever challenged the supremacy of rice.

CASH CROP The tobacco plant was the basis of Virginia's prosperity.

Invention and Technology

FIRE POWER The harquebus is in use in Europe in the early 1500s.

1550s: The first long-barrelled cannon appears on European and Japanese warships. The cannon is to become increasingly popular, not least to meet the challenge of pirates and privateers. Expert gunners are required on ships, and the old methods of grappling and boarding are gradually replaced by artillery duels at sea.

1550s: A Fellow of All Souls' College, Oxford, introduces algebra to England and invents the = sign as a mathematical notation.

1556: Georg Agricola publishes his study of mineralogy, *De Re Metallica*, the first book to appear on the subject.

1560: The *camera obscura*, the forerunner of the camera, is invented by Battista Porta.

1561: Gabriele Fallopius, in his *Observationes Anatomicae*, describes the female reproductive system.

1569: The cartographer Gerardus Mercator produces a map of the world that for the first time shows all the lines of latitude and longitude as parallel. It becomes indispensable to navigators and remains the most popular projection for producing flat maps of the world.

1570 – 1589

Politics and Religion

1570: The Ottoman Empire declares war on Venice. The next year the Pope, Venice and Spain form an alliance against the Ottomans, and Don John of Austria, half-brother of Spains' Philip II, destroys the Ottoman fleet at Lepanto.

1572: Following several years of unrest, the Dutch War of Independence begins. Holland and three other provinces support William of Orange against the Spanish Governor.

In France, 2000 Huguenots (Protestants) are murdered in a massacre in Paris on St Bartholomew's Day.

1573: The Peace of Constantinople ends war between Turkey and Venice.

1576: Englishman Martin Frobisher discovers Frobisher Bay in northern Canada while searching for the North-west Passage.

SEA DOG Martin Frobisher, an English master mariner.

1577-80: Sir Francis Drake makes the second circumnavigation of the world.

1579: In the Netherlands, the Union of Utrecht unites the rebel provinces against Philip II of Spain.

1580: Philip II invades Portugal and claims the Portuguese throne. The two countries remain united until 1640.

1584: Sir Waler Raleigh founds the British colony of Virginia on the eastern seaboard of North America. Supplies from England cannot be maintained and it fails in 1587.

1588: Philip II of Spain launches the Armada against England, but it is broken up in the English Channel and destroyed by storms off the Scottish and Irish coasts.

DRAMA Scenes from the life of Queen Elizabeth I.

Culture and Society

1570: The Italian architect Andrea Palladio publishes his *I Quattri Libri dell'Architettura* (On Architecture). The classical style that he favours influences building in many countries, but first and most significantly in northern Italy.

1577: Richard Burbage opens London's first theatre, called The Theatre, in Shoreditch.

1577: Holinshed's *Chronicles* is published. A history of the British Isles, it is used as source material by William Shakespeare for his historical plays.

TRIUMPH The potato transforms Europe's diet.

1580: The essay form is created by Michel de Montaigne with the publication of the first two volumes of his *Essays*. In them he explores questions of ambition, death and the limits of human knowledge. His work has a lasting influence on writers and thinkers.

1580: The first mention is made of the English folk tune *Greensleeves*.

1581: Sedan chairs come into general use in England.

1582: The emergence of classical ballet is signalled by the performance at the French court of *Balet de la Reyne* and by the publication of *Il Ballarino*, a treatise on dance technique.

1582: Pope Gregory XIII replaces the Julian calendar with the Gregorian, which entails eliminating ten days – October 5-15. Protestant countries do not make the change until the 18th century.

1584: The potato is introduced into Europe from South America.

1587: Christopher Marlowe's first play, *Tamburlaine*, is performed. It is the first true tragedy to be written in the English language.

1587: Monteverdi's first book of Madrigals is published.

1589: Forks are used at the French court.

Invention and Technology

1570: Abraham Ortelius of Antwerp publishes the first atlas of the world, containing 53 maps, under the title *Theatrum orbis terrarum*.

1572: Tycho Brahe, the Danish astronomer, observes a 'new star' in Cassiopeia, challenging the belief that the stars are fixed and unchanging. In the following year he publishes his observations in *De Nova Stella*.

1575: Imitations of Chinese porcelain begin to appear, produced in Florence and Venice.

1581: In Italy, Galileo observes the regular interval of the movement of the pendulum.

1587: The Rialto Bridge in Venice is constructed by Antonio da Ponte.

1588: A clergyman, Timothy Bright, publishes *Characterie*, the first English system of shorthand.

1589: An early version of the knitting machine is invented by the Rev William Lee of Cambridge, England.

FILLING IN THE GAPS Ortelius's map of 1570 shows recent discoveries.

1590 – 1620

Politics and Religion

1594: Henry of Navarre, Protestant claimant to the French throne, converts to Roman Catholicism, commenting that 'Paris is worth a mass'. His reign is marked by war with Spain.

1605: In England, a Roman Catholic plot to blow up the Houses of Parliament with King James I present is uncovered when Guy Fawkes is found in the cellars with 2 tons of gunpowder.

Arctic Tragedy The journeys of Willem Barents end in disaster.

1607: The English settlement of Jamestown, Virginia, is established by the Virginia Company with 100 colonists.

1608: Samuel de Champlain founds the French colony of Quebec in Canada.

1610: Henry Hudson discovers Hudson Bay and the Hudson River on behalf of the Dutch.

1618: The Thirty Years War breaks out between the German Protestant princes, supported by France, and the Habsburg Emperor. It will establish French supremacy at the expense of Spain.

Atrocities The Dutch torture an English captive in the East Indies.

The Dutch begin an assault on Portuguese colonies in the Far East. In 1619 they establish a new capital in the East Indies, at Jakarta.

1620: The Pilgrim Fathers establish their New World colony at New Plymouth in order to start a new life away from the oppressive religious regulations in England.

Culture and Society

1590: Edmund Spenser publishes the first three volumes of *The Faerie Queene*, an allegorical poem glorifying England and describing the eternal war between good and evil. The second three volumes are published in 1596.

1591: Trinity College, Dublin, is founded by Elizabeth I. Entrance is restricted to Protestant students until 1873.

1592: The ruined Roman city of Pompeii, which had lain buried under volcanic debris since the eruption of Vesuvius in AD 79, is discovered.

1599: The Globe Theatre, with room for an audience of 1200, is built in London for the Lord Chamberlain's Company (later called the King's Men). The company has writing for it the best dramatist of the day – William Shakespeare.

1600: Caravaggio introduces a fashion for chiaroscuro (the use of dramatic light and dark contrasts) in painting with his *Crucifixion of St Peter and Conversion of St Paul.*

1604: James I of England publishes his *Counterblast to Tobacco*, in which he describes football as a 'bloody and murdering practice' and a Maypole as a 'stinking idol' where 'heathens leap and dance'.

1605: Cervantes's *Don Quixote* is published.

1605: In India, the Golden Temple of Amritsar is completed, and becomes the holiest Sikh shrine. Its enormous dome, cupolas and spectacular walls are covered with gold leaf.

1609: In Constantinople, building work begins on the Blue Mosque. It is completed in 1616.

Man of La Mancha The first edition of *Don Quixote*.

1610: The Italian composer Monteverdi writes his *Vespers* at the court of Mantua.

1611: In England, the King James, or 'Authorised', version of the Bible is published. Fifty-four scholars took part in the translation and it remains one of the great masterpieces of English literature.

Invention and Technology

1596: Galileo invents the thermometer.

1604: Johannes Kepler publishes *Optics*, in which he explains human vision.

1605: Francis Bacon publishes *The Advancement of Learning*, in which he asserts that knowledge comes from experiment, not from divine revelation.

1608: Dutch lens maker Hans Lippershey invents the telescope. Lenses prove to be among the few European products sought by the Chinese.

1609: Kepler publishes *Astronomia Nova*, in which he demonstrates that Mars's orbit round the Sun follows an ellipse, not a circle as previously believed.

Seeing Stars Galileo's telescope enables him to add substantially to knowledge of the stars.

1610: Galileo uses an astronomical telescope of his own construction to study the motions of the stars and planets, and publishes his observations in *Sidereus Nuncius.*

1611: Mario de Dominis provides a scientific explanation for the phenomenon of the rainbow.

1619: William Harvey discovers the circulation of the blood. This has little immediate impact on medical practice, which continues to depend on bleeding the patient with leeches.

INDEX

NOTE: References in italics denote illustrations; there may also be textual references on these pages.

Acapulco 148
Acosta, Joseph de 53
Aden *97*, 102
Affonso I, Kongo King 135
Africa
  depopulation *10*, 135
  legends *133*
  monarchs 135, 136, 142
  Muslims 142
  Portuguese exploration 9, *100-1*, 104, 126-7
  religion 142
  trans-Saharan trade 139
  see also individual places and commodities and under slaves
Agra 116
agriculture
  Americas 57-58, 63
  Europe 14-15, 76-77, 151
  Far East 121
  Polynesia 144, 145
Akbar, Mogul ruler *105*, 116, 153
Alaric; sack of Rome 110, 117
Albuquerque, Alfonso de 98-99, 102
alcohol 11, 72, 78-79, 82, 89, 93
aldeas (mission villages) 67-68
Alexander VI, Pope 150
Algiers *134*
Almagro, Diego de 44, 45
Almeida, Francisco de 98
Amazon River 45, 58
ambergris 18
Amboina 115
America, Latin 8, 10, 41-68
  agriculture 57-58
  animal husbandry 12, 58, 59, 66
  cities 54, 55, 56, 58, 59
  colonists' lifestyle 54, 55, 58-59
  native lifestyles 10, 51-52, 53-58
  settlement pattern *60*
  see also individual countries and places, encomienda system; plantations; *and under* slaves
America, North 69-94
  conquest of south 45
  English colonisation 85-94
  firearms 72, 88
  horses 11, 151
  Indians 8, 72, 87, 88, 94;
    Plains 11, 151;
    villages 80, *88*, 93, *94*;
    see also Huron Indians
  internal exploration 10
  voyages of exploration 70-75
  see also Pilgrims; Puritanism; United States; Virginia
Amritsar, Golden Temple of 155
Amsterdam 110, 113
Andreoni, John 66, 141
animals, exotic 18
Antwerp 17, *115*
Arabia 104
  horses 110, 111, *122*
Arabs, *see* Muslims
architecture; Western influence *12*, 65
arrows, Brazilian Indians' 62-63
artillery 26, 102, 153
Asia, South-east 18, 103, 104, 108
astrolabe 7, *35*
astronomy 151, 154, *155*
Atahualpa 30, 44, *45*, 152
Australia 12
Aztecs 10, *44*, *46-47*, 151
  society 51-52

Babur, Mogul ruler 105, 151
Bahia 64
Balboa, Vasco Nunez de 43, 151
bananas 145, 146
Banda Islands 110, 114, 117
Bantam, Java *117*
barabgays (Filipino social units) 149
Barbary
  horses *122*
  pirates 141
barbers 40, 52
Barents, Willem *74-75*, *83*, *155*
Batavia (Jakarta) 103, 115, *116*
beacons, navigational 22
beaver pelts 82
beer 31
Benin *136*
Berbers 139, 141
Bilbao 17, 26
biscuit, ship's 31, 129
Boston 88, 94
Bradford, William 88, 93
Braithwait, Richard 32
brandy 78-79
Braudel, Fernand 121
Brazil 8, 11, 60-68
  Cabral's discovery 43, 98, 150
  cannibalism *61*, 63-64, 66
  crops 18, 60, 64, 139-42, 146
  missionaries 67-68
  native society 60-64, 66
  Portuguese interest *68*, 150
  slaves 18, 65, 139-40
  sugar plantations 139-42
Brazil nuts 146
brazilwood 18, 60, 64
Brewster, William 87
Bristol 16, 21, 26, 70
Brittany 16
Bruegel, Pieter the Elder *6*
Bruges; crane *31*
Brulé, Etienne 72
Buddhism 107-9
Burma 111

caballeros 49
Cabeza de Vaca, Alvar Núñez 45
Cabot, John 16, 70-71, 118, 150
Cabral, Pedro Alvares 43, 60, 98, 150
Cadamosto, Alvise de 127
Cairo 142
Cajamarca 44
calendar
  French Catholic 78
  International Dateline 98
  Julian and Gregorian 72, 154
Calicut 96, 97, *98-99*, 107, 128
California *129*, 132
camara (town council) 113
Cambodia 148
Cambridge, Massachusetts 89
Canada
  'diamonds' 79
  fisheries 76
  French colonisation 71-72, 76-83, 152
  fur trade 76, 82
  Hudson's exploration 155
  missionaries 82-83
  St Lawrence river 71, 76, 152
  see also Champlain, Samuel de
Canary Island slave traders 137
cannibalism *61*, 63-64, 66, 71
cannon 102, 153
Cano, Juan Sebastian del *130-1*
canoes 87, 145, *148*
Canton 102, 119, 120, 151
Cão, Diogo *100-1*, 127
Cape Horn *128*
Cape of Good Hope 8, 9, 110, 126, 127-8, 150
caravans, trans-Saharan 139
caravels *23*, 24, 25-26, *28*
Cardim, Fernando 66
Caribbean 9, *50-51*, 57, 146, 150
  slaves 137, 139
Caribs 71
Carletti, Francesco 54, 98, 113, 123-4, 146, 147-8
carracks 18, *21*, *25*
Cartier, Jacques 79, 84
  and Indians 62, 80, 81, *152*
  voyage 17, *71*, *78*, 118, 152
cartography
  ancient and medieval *7*
  imaginary creatures *33*, *133*
  Mercator 153
  Ortelius *154*
  Seville school 35
  Smith's map of Virginia *87*
  Speed *118*
  Vespucci's name given to Americas 43, 150
  see also charts
caste system 109
cat-o'-nine-tails 20
cattle 11, 49, 57, 58, 66, 151
caulking 24, 30, *29*, 37
Cebu 129, 132, 149
Cervantes Saavedra, Miguel de *155*
Ceylon
  Christian converts 109
  cinnamon 18, 96, 110, 111, 117
  elephants 110, 111
  Kandy, King of *103*
  Portuguese colonies 102, 103, 104
Champlain, Samuel de 37, *71*, 72, *79*, 118, 155
charts, maritime 35, *36*, *50-51*, *60*, 71
China 118-24
  Christianity 103, 108, 109, *121*
  cultural impact on West 8, 10-11, 118, 119-20
  family unit 122-3
  gold 124
  land transport *121*
  porcelain *10*, 111, 124
  Portuguese contacts 18, 103, 118-20, 151
  silks 59, 110, 111, 124, 147-8
  silver currency 99
  Speed's map *118*
  tea ceremony 84, *120*, 121-2
  trade 9, 59, 111, 112, 124, 147-8, 155
  walls *123*
  women 122
chocolate 53, 84, 151
Christianity
  encomienda promotes 54, 56
  Ethiopian 142
  fish days 26, 31
  in France 76, 77-78
  and Hinduism 96-97, 107
  and Islam 107
  in Japan 103, 109
  in Philippines 149
  sailors' piety *8*, 22, 29, *34*, *38*, 39
  see also Inquisition; Jesuits; missionaries; morality; Puritanism; *and under* China
Christmas 72, 88, 89
Cibola, Seven Cities of 7
cinnamon 96, 110, 111, 117
circumnavigation of world *130-1*, 132, 154
cities, American 49, 54, *55*, 56, 58, 59
class, social 12, 20, 33, 94
  Aztec 52
  Latin America 49, 59
cloves 110, *117*
Cochin 109, *111*
cochineal 57
cocoa 53, 84, *151*
coconut 144, 145, 146
coffee 84, 146
coins from *Mary Rose 33*
Cologne 84
'colonies' of foreign merchants 21, 148
colonisation 8, 9-10, 11-12
  life-style 66, 111, *112*
Columbus, Christopher 22, 24, 30-31, 38-39, 84
  navigation 36, 126
  voyages; first 10, 17, 37, 42-3, 62, 118, 150; subsequent 43, *56*, 150
Columbus, Ferdinand 31
compass *5*, *35*, 92
Con Tiki 145
Confucius 122
Congo River 127
conquistadores 10, 43-45, 48-59
  social class 12, 20, 49
convicts 12, 33
Copernicus, Nicolaus 151
Coronado, Francisco de 45
Corte Real, Gaspar and Miguel 71
Cortés, Hernán 43, *44*, 49, 51, 62, 151
cotton 12, 66
Covilhã, Pedro de 127
cranes *31*
Creoles 59
Cruz, Gaspar da 120
Cuba 42, 43, *46-47*, 84
cultural impact
  Chinese on West 8, 10-11, 118, 119-20
  Western on native 10-11, 105-6, 118
currency *33*, 99
Cuzco *12*, 52, 152

Dateline, International 98
Dauphine, La (Verrazzano's ship) 71
Davis, John 72
depopulation
  Africa *10*, 135
  Latin America 48-49, 57-58, 65
  see also mortality
Descaliers Planisphere *78*
diamonds 18, 105
  'Canadian' 79
Dias, Bartolomeu *100-1*, 127

Dias, Dinis 127
Diego, Don (Indian) 62
Dieppe 16, 22, 71
diet
Aztec 51
Far Eastern 121
fish 26, 121
French 77, 78-79
New England 86, 93
Polynesian 145
on ship 30-31, 38, 40, 129
slaves' 20-21, 58, 146
discipline 20, 37, 87-88, 114
disease 40, 111, 136
spread from Old World to New 10, 48, 57, 68, 152, 153
Diu *98*, 102
diving bell *152*
Donnaconna (Huron chief) 62
dos Santos, Joao 136
Doughty, Thomas 37
Drake, Sir Francis 37, 73, *128*, 129, 154
circumnavigation *130-1*, 132, 154
dress
Aztec 51
European 11, 54, 55, 59, *66*, 111, 141, 148, *152*
Inca *65*
Indian 54, *106-7*, *110*
Dürer, Albrecht *113*
Dutch East Indies Company 103, *114-15*
dyestuffs 18, 57, 60, 64, 110

East 95-124
Cape route 8, 9, 110, 126, 127-8, 150
Dutch supersede Portuguese 113-16, 155
voyages 96-103
see also individual countries
East India Company, English *96*, *112*
East Indies 8-9
East Indies Company, Dutch 103, *114-15*
Easter Island 143
ebony 18
Echagoian, Juan 139
economy, exchange and wage 51-52, 57
Edo (Tokyo) 109
El Dorado 7
elephants 110, 111
Elizabeth I of England 62, 73, *153*, *154*, 155
Elmina *127*
encomienda system *9*, 54, 56, 57, 149
engheros (sugar plantations) 139
England
East India Company *96*, *112*
fisheries 16
and India 12, *113*
language 11
and North America *74-75*, 85-94
North-west Passage 70, 72
and Portuguese decline in east 103
slave trade 134, *136*, 137
Statute of Artificers (1563) 15
see also individual rulers
Equator 126
Eskimos 10, 62, *72*, 83
Espinosa, Vazquez de 138
Ethiopia 127, 142
exchange economies 51-52, 57
executions 37

factories (trading posts) 105
factors (middlemen) 16
family unit
Chinese 122-23
Puritan *86*
Fancui (Europeans) 103
Far East 95-24
see also individual countries
fast days 78, 79
Fatehpur Sikri 116
Fells, Mr (New Englander) 88
Ferdinand and Isabella, sovereigns of Spain 42, 43, 62, 150
Feringhis (Europeans) 120
figurines, Peruvian ceramic *58*
Fiji 143
finance; impact of American gold 11
firearms 72, 82, 88, 135, *153*
see also artillery
fish consumption 26, 31, 78, 79, 121
fishing industry *15*, 16, 26, 33, 70-71, 76, 93
Fitch, Ralph 105, 116
Florida 8, 45, *77*
Folangchi (Europeans) 103
food and drink,
see diet; table manners
forests 27, 86
forks, table 79, 154
France
aristocracy 78-79, 81
and Canada 71-72, 76-83, 152
Church 76, 77-78
colonises Cochin 111
exploration of North America *74-75*
fisheries 16
and Indochina 12
Portuguese rivalry 64, *65*
Revolution 12
rural conditions 76-78, 81
search for 'Indies' 8
shipbuilding 26
slave trade 134, 137
trade with Brazil *64*
Francis I of France 62, 71, 152
Franklin, Benjamin 12
Frobisher, Martin 31, 62, *72*, *154*
fruit *52*, 93, 145, 146
funerals 123
fur trade 72, 76, 82, 110
furniture
Aztec 51
Chinese 110, 111
New England *86*

Gage, Thomas 55
Galileo Galilei *155*
galleasses 26
galleons 18, 26
galleys 20, 26
Gama, Vasco da 18, 96-98, *100-1*, 107, 127-8, 142, 150
Gambia River 127
gambling 55, 57, 80, 147
García, Andrés 65
Gardiner, Sir Christopher 88
Genoa 17, 20-21, 70
Gilbert, Humphrey 72
glass, Venetian 20, 111
Goa 99, 103, 104, *106*, *108-9*, 151
Inquisition 108, 153
life in 109, 111-12
slave valuations 135
gold
African 96, *126*, 127, 134
American 11, *57*
from east 17, 18, 97, 111, 124
Portuguese trade 18, 105, 111, *126*
Golden Hind (Drake's ship) 129, 132
Granada, kingdom of 141, 150
Grenville, Sir Richard 73
Grijalva, Hernando de *147*
Guadeloupe 71
Guam 146
guns 72, 82, 88
see also cannon
gypsies 15

haciendas 58
Hamburg 17
hammocks 38-39, 63
Hanseatic League 17
harquebus 153
Harvard College, Cambridge, Mass 89
Hawkins, Sir John 134, *136*, 137
Hawkins, William 62
Henry IV of France 110, 155
Henry VII of England 70, 150
Henry VIII of England 62, 150, 151, 152
Henry the Navigator, Prince of Portugal 126
Hiawatha 92
hickory 87
hides 58
hidalgos 49
Hinduism 96-97, 107-9, 112
Hispaniola 10, 42-43, *46-47*, 48-49, 150
Hochelaga (Montreal) *78*, *80*
Hooghly River, Bengal *114-15*
Hooke, David 86
Hormuz 99, 102, 104, 105
horses
in Americas 11, *30*, 54, *56*, 57, 58, 89, 151
Arab and Persian 105, 110, 111, *122*, 139
housing
interiors 51, *54*
Japan 123-4
merchants', in Europe 16, 18
North America 86, *90-91*, 94
Huascar (Inca leader) 44
Hudson Bay and River 155
Huitzilopochtli (Aztec sun god) 52
hunter-gatherers 62, 64
Huron Indians 11, 62, 80, 81, 82
Hy-Brasil, Island of 8
hygiene 38, *40*, 120

Iceland; fisheries 16
Incas *12*, 30, 44-45, *46-47*, *65*, 152
society 52-53
India 8
British in 12, *113*
dress *106-7*, *110*
Indian Ocean trade 9, 96
Lisbon trade with 18
map *104*
missionaries *105*, 108
Mogul Empire *105*, 107, 116, 151, 153
pepper 96, 110, 117
Portuguese in 18, *98-99*, 102, 104; *see also* Goa
shipping *111*
tea 12, *112*
Indian languages 56, 67, 87, 153
Indian Ocean trade 9, 104, 128
'Indies', 'Indians' 8-9
indigo 18
Indochina 12, 109
Indonesia 9, 96, 103, 104, 109, 114
Industrial Revolution 12
industry
in colonies 12, 58, 59
Venetian Arsenal 20
inns 21-22
Inquisition 108, 153
institutions, government 12, 93-94, 112-13
Iroquois Indians 81, 83, 92
Isabella, Hispaniola 43
Islam, *see* Muslims
Ivan IV (the Terrible), Tsar *152*
ivory 18, 96, 97, 105, 110, *127*, 139

Jakarta (Batavia) 103, 115, *116*
Jamestown, Virginia 73, *89*, 92, 155
Japan 118-24
Chinese trade 112, 124
horses *122*
housing 123-4
Jesuits *100-1*, 103, 108, 109, 153
Lisbon trade with 18
and Philippines 147, 148
Portuguese contacts 102, 103, 118-19, 120-1, 124
shogunate 109
silver 99, 124
tea ceremony 121-2, 123
Jenkinson, Anthony 119
Jeréz, Francisco de 30
Jesuits 8, 11, 67, 152
in Americas 67-68, 82-83
in east *100-1*, *103*, *105*, 108, 109, 153
Jews 20, 108, 150
John II of Portugal 127
John III of Portugal 64
Juggernaut ceremony *107*

Kandy, King of *103*
keel-hauling *37*, 114
Kepler, Johannes 155
Koh-i-Nor diamond 105
Kongo King, Affonso I 135
Korea *118*
kow-tow 8
Krishna (Hindu god) *107*
Kyoto 109

La Rochelle 16, 21, 78, 153
labour, forced 10, 33, 43, 48, 57-58
see also *encomienda* system
lacquer 18, 110, 124
lacrosse 81
Lagos, Portugal 26
Lakes, Great 71, 72
land allocation *9*, 54, 94
languages, spread of European 11, 12
Las Cortes, Father de 99
lavradores (share-croppers) 141
law and order 12, 15
legends 7-8, 33, 62, 126, *133*, 145, 153
Le Havre 26
Le Jeune, Fr, SJ 81, 82
lenses 124, 155
Leo Africanus 132
Levant 17, 96
Leyden, Pilgrims in 85, 87
Lima 54
Lippershey, Hans 155

Lisbon 11, 17, 18, *19*, 133
  trade 11, 18, 110, 148
llamas *52*, *53*
London; population 17
Lopez de Legaspi, Miguel 132
Lovell, John 137
Lübeck 17

Macao 102, 103, 118-19, 120, *123*, 124, 152
  monopoly of China-Japan trade 112, 124
mace 117
Mactan 132, *145*
Madagascar 9
Madeira 126
Magellan, Ferdinand 17, 128-9, *130-1*, 132, 143, 151
  death *145*, 147, 149, 151
  ship's company 21, 33, 37, 39
maize 93, 152
Malabar coast 96, 110
Malacca 99, 104, 109, 111, 112
Malaysia 12, 103, 104, 124
Malindi 104, *100-1*
Mamelukes 65, *66*
mangosteen 146
Manila 59, 124, 132, 148
Manuel I of Portugal 62, 98, 127
maps, *see* cartography
Mardica, Spice Islands *149*
Marina, Doña (Cortés' wife) *44*
marriage
  China 122-3
  mixed race 59, *65*, 105, 111, 112
  North American colonists 89, 94
  North American Indians 80, 82
Marshall Islands 145
Mary Rose (vessel) *33*, *39*
mask of Quetzalcoatl *49*
Massachusetts Bay 72, 94
master, ship's 33, 35
Mathew (Cabot's ship) 70
Maurice of Nassau, Prince *128-9*
Mayflower Pilgrims 73, 85-94, *153*, 155
Maypole 88, 155
meat 12, 58, 110, 117
medicine 18, 150, 151, 152, 153, 155
  on shipboard 37, *40*
medicine-men 80
Melanesia 144
Mendana, Alvaro de 145
Mendoza, Antonio de 152
Mendoza, Luis de 37
Mercator, Gerardus 152, 153
merchants *5*, 14, *16*, 18
  'colonies' of foreign 21, 148
mestizos 59, 112, *149*
metals, precious 8, 139
  New World 18, 45, 53, 59, 148
  see also gold; silver
mets (course of meal) 79
Mexico
  chocolate 53, 84
  city life 44, *55*, 59
  mines 53, *57*, 152
  missionaries *9*
  Pacific trade 132, 148
  turkeys 79
Mexico City 44, *55*, 152
Middle Eastern town life 106-7
militias, North American 89
mineralogy 153
misericordia (lay brotherhood) 113
missionaries 8, *9*, 11, 64, 103, 107-9, 126
  see also Jesuits
Mississippi River 45, 71
mobility 15
moccasins 87
Mogul Empire *105*, 107, 116, 151, 153
Moluccas 102, 110, 117, 132
Mongol Hordes 119
monopolies
  Macao, of China-Japan trade 112, 124
  royal 64
monsters, legendary *6*, 7, 33
Montezuma 44
Montreal *80*
morality
  imposition of Christian 56, 66, 67
  New England Puritans 86, 87
  North American Indian 80, 82
More, Sir Thomas *151*
Morison, Samuel Eliot 42
mortality
  child, Latin America 57-58
  at sea 114, 135, 136
  slaves 135, 136, 140, 141, 142
Morton, Thomas 88
Mozambique 105, 111-12
mulattos 59
mule trains 56, 59
music
  Huron Indians 83
  on ship 34, 38, *39*, 60
musk 147-8
Muslims
  in Africa 142
  Arab trader *21*
  coffee 84
  Granada 141, 150
  Indian Ocean traders 9, 96, *99*, 103, 104, 128
  in Levant 17
  monotheism 107
  pirates 141
  Portuguese contacts 98, 105-6, 112
  ships *99*
  storytelling 107, 132
  town life 106-7
  Venetian trade 20

Nagasaki 119, 124
Nagayans 119
Nahuatl language 56, 153
naos *23*, 24, 25-26, 27, 28
Naples *15*, 84
Narváez, Pánfilo de 44, 45
Navarette, Domingo 123
Navidad, Hispaniola 43
navigation 7, 22, 26, 34, 35-36
  dead reckoning 35-36
  instruments *5*, 7, *35*, 92
  land, in Sahara 139
  Polynesian 145, 146, *148*
Netherlands
  and East 8, 9, 68, *103*, 113-16, 155
  East Indies Company 103, *114-15*
  and New Amsterdam 72, 73, 89
  rebellion against Spain 153, 154
  ships 113-14
  and South Africa 12
New Amsterdam (New York) 72, *73*, 89
New England 85-94, 155
  see also Pilgrims; Puritanism
New France, Company of 82
New Guinea 143, *144*
New Plymouth 73, 85, 86, 90, 94, 155
New York (New Amsterdam) 72, 73, 89
Newetowne, Massachusetts 89
Newfoundland 16, 70-71, *83*, 150
Nicolet, Jean 72
Nicot, Jean 153
Niña (Columbus's ship) 42, *43*
Nobili, Fr Roberto de, SJ 108
Nobrega, Manuel da 67
nocturnal *36*
Nombre Dios 56
North Sea 16
North-east Passage *74-75*, 83
North-west Passage 70, 72, *74-75*, 110, 118
Nova Scotia 71
Novaya Zemlya 83
nutmeg 110, 117

oakum 29
officials, government 16, 18, 36-37
  Chinese *122*, 123
  Portuguese 112-13
opossums 89
Orellana, Francisco de 45
Ortelius, Abraham *154*
ostrich feathers 139
Ottoman Empire 84, 151, 153, 154
overland journeys 10, 127
  see also transport

Pacific Ocean
  discoveries 8, 43, 128-9, *130-1*, 132, 143-9, 151
  trade 59, 124, 132, 148
padroes (stone crosses) 127
Paiva, Affonso de 127
Palmares 142
Palos 17
Panama 43, 44, 56, 137-8, 150, 151
Panama City 56
Papuans *145*
Parkman, Francis 81
Patagonia 128
Paulistas 65
pearls 57, 105, 138
Pegu 110
Peking 119
penal colonies 105
pepper 96, 110, *117*
Peres, Fernando 119, 120
perfumes 18, 110, 139
Pernambuco 64-65, 66
Persia
  horses 105, 110, 111
  silver 124
Persian Gulf 99, 102
persimmon 87
Peru
  city life *11*, 59
  precious metals 45, 53, 124
  mule trains 59
  trade via Manila 124
  see also Incas
Philippine Islands *128-9*, 132, 147-9, 151
Pigafetta, Antonio 128-9, 149
pigs 57, 93
pilgrims 20, 139
Pilgrims, *Mayflower* 73, 85-94, *153*, 155
pineapple 145, *146*
Pinta (Columbus's ship) 42, *43*
piracy 56, *99*, 141, *132*, 153
piranhas 58
Pires, Thomas 119
Pizarro, Francisco 30, 44-45, 49, 51, 152
Pizarro, Gonzalo 45
plague, bubonic 153
Planisphere, Descaliers *78*
Plymouth 17
Pocahontas *92*
pole, magnetic 152
Polynesia 8, 10, 144, 145-6, *148*
pool system 149
porcelain *10*, 18, 110, 124, 154
Portobello 56
portolans *36*
ports 11, 14-22
  colonies of foreigners 21, 148
Portugal 104-13
  and Aden *97*
  and Africa 9, *100-1*, 104, 126-7
  in Asia 103, 104, 127
  black slaves in 133
  Brazil important to 64, *68*
  and Ceylon 102, 103, 104
  colonies 104-13
  cultural impact 105-6
  decline of empire 68, *103*, 113-16, 155
  fisheries 16
  French rivalry 64, *65*
  language spread to colonies 11
  missionaries 64, 67-68, 103, 108, 126, 152
  and Muslims 98, 105-6, 112
  navigation 26
  racial mix 65, 142
  shipbuilding 26, 28
  slave trade 137
  trade, emphasis on 127
  Treaty of Tordesillas 150
  union with Spain 154
  voyages of exploration 8, 96-103, 151
  see also individual places and explorers, and under China; India; Japan
postal service, Inca 53
potato 93, 146, 154
potato, sweet 145, 153
Potosi silver mines 57, *58*, 152
Powhatan Indians 92
press gangs 21, 33
Prester John 7-8, 126
privateering 128, *132*, 153
punishments 20, *37*, 114
Puritanism *85*, 86, 87-89

quadrants 7, 35
Quebec 71, 72, *79*, 81, 155
Quetzalcoatl (Aztec god) 44, *49*, *54*
quilimbos (slave townships) 142

raccoons 87, 89
races, mixture of 59, 65, 105, 111, 112, *149*
Raleigh, Sir Walter 72, *73*, 154
ranches 49, 58
raquettes (snowshoes) 81
record-keeping 56
Red Sea 97
religion
  African 142
  Aztec *51*, 52
  Brazilian shamanism 61-62, 67
  Huron Indian 83
  see also Christianity; Muslims
rhinoceros *113*
rice 120, 121, 145, 147, 153
Richelieu, Cardinal de 81-82
rituals, Far Eastern 120, 121-3
roads 22, 53, 56
Roanoke Island, Virginia 73

Rolfe, John 92
Rome, sack of (AD 410) 110, 117
Rouen Pageant (1550) *61*
rubber 12
rubies 18
rum 140
rummaging of ship 38
rural life, European 14-15
Russia 84, 152

Sa, Mem de 66
Saavreda 145
sacrifice
  African beliefs 142
  Aztec human *51*, 52
Sagne, legend of *78*
Saguenay, legend of 62, 78
Sahara Desert 132, 139
sails 29-30, *32*
  'bonaventure' 30
  lateen *23*, 25-26, 97, 146
  square 25-26
St Lawrence River 71, 76, 152
St Malo 17
salt 132, 139
salt-cellar, ivory *127*
Salvador, Bahia 65-66
Salve Regina (hymn) 29, 34, *38*
San Francisco Bay *129*, 132
sandalwood 110
sandglasses 34, *35*, 36, 38
Santa Maria (Columbus's ship) 42, *43*
Sao Jorge da Mina *126*
Sao Vicente, Brazil 64
'savage, noble' 61, 62
sawyers *27*
scurvy 40, 127, 129
Secota, Virginia *94*
Senegal River 126
Serrao, Francisco 151
Seven Cities, Kingdom of the 7, 45
Seville 17, 21, 26, 35, *57*, 134
'shake a leg' 38
shamanism 61-62, 67
share-croppers (*lavradores*) 141
sheep 11, 59, 151
shipbuilding 23-24, 26-30
  Polynesian 145-6, *148*
  see also caulking; sails
ships and shipping 13-40, 23-31, *97*
  artillery 153
  captains 24, 37, 134
  captains-general 32-33
  Chinese 9
  conditions 6-7
  cookbox *40*
  crews 32-40
  design of ships 24-26
  discipline 20, 37, 114
  disease 40
  'gentleman travellers' 37
  hygiene 38, *40*
  Indian coastal *111*
  mariners' day 33
  medicine 37, *40*
  music 34, 38, *39*, 60
  navigation 35-36
  Netherlands 113-14
  piety *8*, 22, *34*, *38*, 39
  piracy *99*
  provisions 30-31, *37*, 38, 40, 129
  recruitment 33
  sandglasses 38
  slave ships 135-7, *138*
  treasure fleets 53
  women on 38
  see also sails; shipbuilding *and individual types of ship*
shogunate, Japanese 109
Siam 148
silks 17, 59, 110, 124, 147-8
  Portuguese trade 18, 105, 111
silver
  Americas 53, 54, 57, *58*, 124, 152
  Far East 99, 124
Sitting Bull 92
skunks 87
slash-and-burn cultivation 62, 64
Slavs 138
slaves
  aldeas raided for 68
  conditions 20-21, 66, 135-9, 140, 141, 142
  diet 58, 146, 20-21
  dress 55
  gold miners *57*
  Jesuits' attitude to 67
  mortality 40, 66, 136, 140, 141, 142
  official sanction in Brazil 64
  origin of word 'slave' 138
  ships 40, 135-7, *138*
  slave owners' lifestyle 140-2
  on sugar plantations 134, 139-42
  trade across Indian Ocean 111-12
  trade between Africa and America 10, 11, 18, 49, 54, 59, 65, 127, 133-42, 150
  valuations 134-5
  in Venice 20, 21
smallpox *68*, 92
Smith, John *73*, *87*, 92
snowshoes, Huron 81
Solomon Islands 145
Soto, Hernando de *45*
Sousa, Thomas de 65
South Africa 12
southern hemisphere 125-49
  voyages 126-32
  see also individual countries and continents
Spain 10, 48-59
  atrocities 43, *45*, *59*
  class of conquistadores 12, 20, 49
  colonial lifestyle *11*, 49, 149
  Dutch war of independence 153, 154
  exploration 8, 12, 42-47,
  see also individual explorers
  language spread to colonies 11
  shipbuilding 26, 26
  Treaty of Tordesillas 150
  treasure fleets 53, 56, *59*
  union with Portugal 154
Speed, John *118*
Spice Islands *100-1*
  Portugese colonies 102, 104, 151
  trade 9, 18, 59, 99, 148
spices 8, 11, *12*, 96, 97, 146
  Dutch trade 110, 113, 115
  Indian trade with China 124
  Portuguese trade 18, 96, 97, 110, 111, 112
  trade to Latin America 59
  use 79, 117
  Venetian trade 17, 110
Spitzbergen, West 83
Squanto (Wampanoag Indian) 93
squash 87
Sri Lanka, *see* Ceylon
Statute of Artificers (1563) 15
stones, precious 18, 55, 97, 110, 111, 116
  see also diamonds
storytelling, eastern 107, 132
Suez Canal 128
sugar
  American plantations 11, 49, 58, 64-5, 66, 134, 139-42
  trade 18, 139, 147-8
suicide 58, 65, 66, 136
suttee (widow-burning) 109
Swally Hole *102*
Sweden 84
syphilis *152*

Tabascan tribe 44
table manners 79, 81, 120, 154
'tabu' 145
Tahiti 143, 144
Taino people 48-49
tallow 29, 37, 58
Tampa Bay 45
Tasman, Abel Janszoon 143
Tatars 119
taxation *54*, 84
tea 12, 84, *112*
  ceremonies *120*, 121-2, 123
technology 11-12, 151-5 *passim*
  Aztec 51
  cannon; penalties for divulging 102
  Inca 52, 53
  slash-and-burn 62, 64
Tegaza 132
Tenochtitlán *44*, *49*, 51, 52, *151*
Texas 152
Thanksgiving Day *89*, 94
Thousand and One Nights, A 107, 132
Tierra del Fuego 128
Timbuktu 132, 142
time, measurement of
  church bells mark rural 78
  International Dateline 98
  seven-day week 56
  watch 150
  see also sandglasses
Timor 110
tithingman (Puritan official) 87-88
Tlaxcalan tribe 44
tobacco 11, 12, 18, 66, 84, *153*, 155
  Virginia 73, 89, 92
toboggans 81
Tokyo (Edo) 109
Tonga 143
Tordesillas, Treaty of 150
Torre, Tomás de la 40
Torrid Zone 126
towns
  Chinese walled *123*
  Middle Eastern 106-7
  see also cities
trade 11
  luxuries 110
  middlemen 16
  as motive for exploration 8
  Pacific route 59, 124, 132, 148
  in ports 14, 16, 18
  Portuguese emphasis 127
  regulation 16, 18, 36-37, 84
  see also monopolies *and individual commodities*
transport, land 22, 153, 154
  Chinese *121*
  pack animals *53*, 56, 59
  porters 137-8
  see also roads
transportation of undesirables 12, 33
treadmill *31*
treasure
  Crown's share 36-37
  fleets 53, 56, *59*
Tripoli, Libya 141
triumph of the West 8-9
Tunis 141
Tupi-speaking tribes 60-64, 67
turkey 79, 86, 93

United Provinces 116, 154
United States of America
  independence 12
  technology and institutions 12
  Thanksgiving Day *89*, 94
  see also America, North; New England; Virginia
Uteve, King of 136

vagabonds 12, *14*
vandala (compulsory sale of produce) 149
Varthema, Ludovico di 102
Velasquez, Diego 43
Venezuela 137, 138, 150
Venice *17*, 18, 20, 21, 154
  Arsenal 20, *30*
  glass 20, 111
  spice trade 110
venison 86, 93
Vera Cruz 56
Verrazzano, Giovanni da 71, 118, 126
Vespucci, Amerigo *43*, 150
Victoria (Magellan's ship) 132, *151*
Virginia 72, *73*, 85, 88-89, 154, 155
  tobacco 73, 89, 92, 153
  see also Jamestown

wages 15, 33, 57
Waldseemuhler, Martin 150
walls, Chinese town *123*
walrus *79*
Wampanoag Indians 93
wars
  Aztec raids 52
  Brazilian inter-tribal 62, *63*, 64, 66
  European; recruitment 21
  Indian, in North America 92
Washington, George 12
West Indies 9, 42
whale hunting *83*
wheel 51
White, John *94*
widow-burning (*suttee*) 109
wine 78, *111*, 141, 148
Winslow, Edward 73
women
  Brazilian 45, 63
  Chinese 122
  North American Indian 80
  in ports 16
  separation from children 57-58
  on shipboard 38
wool *52*, 59
work ethic 86, 88, 94
world, knowledge of *7*, *33*, 98, 126, 132
  magnetic pole 152
  see also astronomy; cartography

Xavier, St Francis *100-1*, 103, 152

Zacatecas silver mines, Mexico 152
zambos 59

ACKNOWLEDGMENTS

ABBREVIATIONS T = Top; M = Middle; B = Bottom; R = Right; L = Left.

A.K.G. = Archiv für Kunst und Geschichte, Berlin.
B.A.L. = Bridgeman Art Library, London.
BrL. = British Library, London.
BrM. = British Museum, London.
E.T.A. = E.T. Archive, London.
F.I. = Fotomas Index, London.
M.A.S. = MAS, Barcelona.
M.S.I. = Mirror Syndication International, London.
N.M.M. = National Maritime Museum, London.
T.B.A. = Toucan Books Archive.
V & A = Victoria and Albert Museum, London.
W.F.A. = Werner Forman Archive, London.

1 *Flying Fish* by T. de Bry, New York Public Library/E.T. A. 2-3 *The Story of Odysseus* by Pintoricchio, National Gallery, London. 4 *Merchant of Meissen*, 1577, T.B.A., BL; *Farming in the Philippines*, from the map by Murillo Verde, Map Room, BrL., T; *Magnetic compass*, c 1580, N.M.M., (A1763), BR. 5 *Spaniards helped by Tlaxcoltecs* by Lienzo de Tlaxcala, 1541, Nuno de Guzman/E.T. A. 6 *Scene from the Life of Alexander the Great*, Bibliothèque Nationale, Paris/T.B.A.; *The Storm* by Pieter Brueghel, A.K.G., B. 7 *Ptolemaic map of the world*, 1486, Michael Holford; 8 *Virgen de los Navegantes* by Alejo Fernández, Alcázar, Seville/M.A.S. 9 *Spanish and Mexicans at Mass* by Lienzo de Tlaxacala, E.T.A., T; *Indian drawing of encomienda system*, Kingsborough Codex, BrM./M.S.I., B. 10 *Deserted African Village* , 1643, T.B.A., T; *Chinese porcelain* , 16th century, B.A.L., B; 11 *Spanish in Peru*, Francesco Venturi, Lima. 12 *Cayenne pepper plant* , M.S.I., T; *Cuzco doorway*, Hutchison Library, London/Photography H.R.Dörig, B. 13 *The Ship* by Hans Holbein the Younger, c 1532, Städel Institute, Frankfurt; 14 *Detail of beggars,* Egerton MS 1065 f. 116v BrL., T; *Shearing sheep*, Benninck Book of Hours, Add 18855 f. 109v, BrL., B. 15 *Detail of fish sellers from Winter* by Van Valkenborgh, Giraudon, Paris, T; *Detail from View of the Port of Naples* by Tavolo Strozzi, Museum of San Martino, Naples/Scala, B. 16 *Merchants* by Jean Fouquet, Bibliothèque Nationale, Paris/R.M.N., T; *Coopers*, Yates Thompson MS30, f.8, BrL., B. 17 *Map of Venice*, Museo Correr, Venice/B.A.L. 18, 19 (Detail from) *Port of Lisbon* by T. de Bry, Giraudon. 20 *Detail of Scene in Venice* by Bassano, Museo Real Academia de Bellas Artes, Madrid/B.A.L. 21 *German carrack* c 1490, Osterreichische Nationalbibliothek, Vienna, L; *Woodcut of women in port*, T.B.A., R. 22 *Detail from The Port of Seville* by A. Coello, Museo de America, Madrid/Giraudon, T; *Ships*, from M.775 f.130v, Pierpoint Morgan Library, New York, B. 23 Illustration by Kate Simunek, T; *Detail from Atlantic Chart*, 1513, by Piri Re'is, (facsimile) James Ford Bell Library, University of Minnesota, B. 24 - 25 Illustration by Peter Morter. 26 *Master shipwrights*, Magdalene College, Cambridge. 27 Illustration by Gill Tomblin. 28 *Caulking a Dutch East Indiaman*, N.M.M. (B726), T; *Building a caravel* by T. de Bry, N.M.M. (D 5269-25), B. 29 *Caulking a galley*, detail from the Basilica di S. Marco, Venice/Alinari, T; *Detail from The Oakmakers*, Museo Correr, Venice/B.A.L., B. 30 *Detail from shipyard scene*, Museo di Storia Veneziano, Venice/Scala, T; *Detail of an anonymous painting of the Spanish landing at Veracruz*, 1519, E.T.A., B. 31 *Crane in Bruges*, Bayerische Museum, Munich. 32 Illustration by Michael Shoebridge. 33 *Drawing showing curvature of earth*, Biblioteca Palatina, Parma/Agenzia Luisa Ricciarini, T; *Spanish Coins*, BrM., M; *Engraving of sea monster*, T.B.A., B. 34 Illustration by Gill Tomblin. 35 *Navigation at Sea*, Fr 2810 f. 188r, Bibliothèque Nationale Paris/B.A.L., T; *Astrolabe*, N.M.M. (8450), BL; *Hourglass*, N.M.M./Mike Holford, BR. 36 *Portolan chart of Atlantic*, BrL./M.S.I., T; *Nocturne*, Aspect Picture Library, BL; *Trying to find longitude by magnetic variation*, N.M.M. (2330), BR. 37 *Keel-hauling*, T.B.A., TR; Illustration by Paul Wright, B. 38 *Detail from Salve Regina*, MS Norton, Houghton Library, Harvard/T.B.A. 39 *Wooden plates from the Mary Rose*, Mary Rose Trust, Portsmouth, T; Illustration by Paul Wright, B. 40 *Instruments from The Surgeon's Mate* by John Woodhall, 1617, T.B.A., T; Illustration by Kate Simunek, B. 41 *Spanish ships unloading in the New World from the Florentine Codex*, Med. Palat. 220, c. 406, Biblioteca Medicea Laurenziana, Florence. 42 *Portrait of Columbus* by Sebastiano de Piombo, 1519, Metropolitan Museum of Art, New York/T.B.A., T; 42-43 Illustration by Paul Wright, B; 43 *Portrait of Vespucci*, Gallerie Nazionali di Capodimonte, Naples/Mansell Collection, TL; *Page from early edition of Vespucci's Mundus Novus*, 1505, /A.K.G., text T.B.A., TR. 44 *Dona Marina and Cortes*, /M.A.S., T; *Cortes*, Museo Nationale de Historico, Mexico/Giraudon, M; *The Fall of Tenochtilan*, Aspect Picture Library, B. 45 *Pizarro meeting Atahualpa from the eye-witness account by Francisco de Xerez*, BrL., M.S.I., T; *De Soto atrocities* by T. de Bry, T.B.A., B. 46 - 47 Map by Swanston Publishing Ltd. 48 *Detail of Hispaniola from the Monrates Map*, 1519, Biblioteca Universitaria, Bologna, Photography , Roncaglia, T; *Indian Women*, T.B.A., B. 49 *Turquoise mask of Quetzacoatl*, BrM./Michael Holford, T; *Map of Tenochtitlan*, T.B.A., B. 50-51 *Map of the Caribbean* c 1540, MS129 A24 fol 23v and 24v, Koninklijke Bibliotheek, The Hague. 51 *Aztec Sacrifice*, Museo de America, Madrid/M.A.S. 52 *Indio Yumbo*, M.A.S., T; *Llama*, Hulton-Deutsch, B. 53 *Indian with Cacao*, T.B.A., T; *Llamas used for carrying*, by T. de Bry, T.B.A., B. 54 *Aztec Symbols*. MS Arch. Seld. A. 1 fol 46r, Bodleian Library, Oxford, T; *Quetzacoatl* from Codex Maglia Bachiano, Florence/M.S.I., M; *Facade of Mexico Cathedral*, Wim Swaan, New York, B. 55 *Mexico City* by C. de Villapando, Corsham Court, Wiltshire/B.A.L. 56 *Spanish treasure fleet*, T.B.A., T; *Santiago overcoming the Indians*, Peru, Hutchison Picture Library/Photography H.R.Dörig, B. 57 *Gold Mine from the Drake Mss.*, MA 3900, f.100, Pierpoint Morgan Library, New York, L; *Gold facade of Seville Cathedral*, Oronoz Madrid, R. 58 *Potosi mine*, T.B.A., T; *Peruvian figurines*, American Museum of Natural History/Photography John Bigelow Taylor, B. 59 *The Return of the Spanish Expedition* by A. Van Eertvect, N.M.M. (BNC 0746), T; *Two scenes from an account of Spanish brutality in Mexico* by Bartolomé de la Casas, William Clements Library, Ann Arbor, Michigan, B. 60 *French map of South America*, 1550, BrM./M.S.I. 61 *Brazilian Indians in Rouen*, 1550, T.B.A., T; *Oldest known woodcut of Cannibal Indians*, from Vespucci's voyage, T.B.A., B. 62 *Watercolour of Indian*, Germanisches Nationalmuseum, Nuremberg/E.T.A. 63 *Map of Brazil* from the Miller Atlas, 1519, BrL., T; *Tapuya men*, by A. van der Eeckhout, Nationalmuseet, Copenhagen /B.A.L., B. 64 *Detail of map of Brazil*, 1542, Royal MS 20 E. ix, fol. 28, BrM., T; *Wood panel showing the shipping of timber*, Musée de la Seine Maritime, Rouen/Giraudon, B. 65 *Detail of a marriage of Inca princess to a Spanish nobleman*, Peru, Hutchison Picture Library/Photography H.R.Dörig, T; *Battle scene* by T. de Bry, T.B.A., B. 66 *Dutch settlement in Brazil*, A.K.G. 67 French missionaries, John Carter Brown Library, Brown University, T; *Trading with natives* by T. de Bry, T.B.A., B. 68 *Indian smallpox victim*, Biblioteca del Palacio Real, Madrid/A.K.G., T; *Brazilian scene* by FJ Post, Harold Samuel Collection, Corporation of London/B.A.L., B. 69 *Detail of the French at Port Royal* by T. de Bry, New York Public Library/ E.T.A.; 70 *Map of Labrador*, John Rylands Library, University of Manchester, T; *Portrait of Cabot*, Bristol Museum and Art Gallery/B.A.L., B; 71 *Portrait of Cartier*, BrL./B.A.L, T; *Portrait of Champlain*, Hulton Deutsch, London, M; *Hurons and French attacking Onondaga village*, M.S.I., B. 72 Drawing of Frobisher's second voyage, 1577, BrM./B.A.L, T; *Drawing of Indian woman* by John White, 1906-5-9-1 (30), BrM., B; 73 *Miniature of Walter Raleigh* by N. Hilliard, 1618, National Portrait Gallery, London, TL; *Title page of John Smith's account*, F.I., TL; *New Amsterdam*, Algemeen Rijksarchief, The Hague, B. 74-75 Map by Swanston Publications Ltd.. 76 *Engraving of French nobleman and peasant*, T.B.A., T; *Detail of engraving showing beggar*, B. 77 *Indian hunters* by T. de Bry, T.B.A, T; *Indians with column*, M.S.I., B. 78 *Detail of Canada from Descalier's World Map*, BrL. 79 *Quebec*, Add, 24065, Dorka, Paris, T; *Walrus and calf*, T.B.A., B. 80 *Hochelaga*, T.B.A. 81 *Huron Indian*, T.B.A. 82-83 *Whale hunting*, detail from Nova Francia, map by Cornelius Claesz, 1594, MAPS 144 c. 25, BrL. 83 *Barents' ship* by T. de Bry, New York Public Library, E.T.A. 84 *Dutch smoking club*, Mary Evans Picture Library. 85 *Persecuted Christians*, T.B.A., T; *Puritans*, T.B.A., B. 86 *Puritan family*, T.B.A., T; *Standish Chair*, Plymouth Pilgrim Society, Massachusetts, B. 87 From *John Smith's General History of Virginia*, 1624, Hulton Deutsch, London. 88 *Pomeiouc* by John White, BrM. 89 *Sport in Virginia* by T. de Bry/S.I., T; *The First Thanksgiving* by Jennie Brownscombe, Pilgrim Society, Massachusetts, B. 90-91 Illustration by Malcolm McGregor. 92 *Portrait of Pocohontas*, Dorka, Paris, T; *John Smith's illustration of Pocohontas saving his life*, M.S.I., B. 93 *Map of Virginia* by John White, T.B.A., T; *Barbecue* by John White, BrM., B. 94 *Engraving of the village of Secota* after the drawing by John White, E.T.A. 95 *Japanese screen of Portuguese merchant ship*, The Avery Brundage Collection, Asian Art Museum, San Francisco. 96 *Vasco de Gama*, M.A.S., T; *Map of Southern Africa*, T.B.A., B. 97 *Aden*, F.I., T; *Ships in the Indian Ocean,* from the *Livro das Armadas*, Academia das Ciencias, Lisbon/M.S.I., B. 98 *Port of Diu (Badur)*, N.M.M. (A 385). 99 *Pirates*, Biblioteca Casanatense, Rome/Photography Studio Serra, Rome, T; *Calicut*, M.S.I., B. 100-101 Map by Swanston Publications Ltd. 102 *Portuguese ships*, M.S.I. 103 *King of Kandy* by T. de Bry, BrL., T; *Bantam*, N.M.M. (369), B. 104 *Map of Asia from Miller Atlas*, 1519, Bulloz, Paris. 105 *Map of Arabia*, M.S.I., T; *Akbar giving an audience*, c1590, V & A/B.A.L., B. 106 *Goa market place* by T. de Bry, F. I., T. 106-107 *Indian wedding*, Biblioteca Casanatense/Photography Studio Serra, Rome. 107 *Juggernaut*, 1575, Newberry Library, Chicago. 108-109 *Map of Goa*, M.S.I. 110 *Fabric from Madras depicting European merchants*, V & A. 111 *King of Cochin*, T.B.A., T; *Chinese wine ewer*, B.A.L., M; *Indian boats*, by T. de Bry, BrL., B. 112 *Fidalgo*, Pierpont Morgan Library, New York/M.S.I., T. *Tea planting*, V & A/ W.F.A., London, B. 113 *Rhinoceros* by Albrecht Dürer, B.A.L., T. *English traveller in India*, V & A/B.A.L., B. 114-115 *Dutch East India Company*, Rijksmuseum, Amsterdam/M.S.I. 115 *Antwerp marketplace*, Musées Royaux des Beaux Arts de Belgique, Brussels. 116 *Batavia*, M.S.I. 117 *Cinnamon cultivation*, 1575, Newberry Library, Chicago, TL; *Clove branch*, Natural History Museum, London/M.S.I., TR; *Marketplace at Bantam*, M.S.I., B. 118 *Map of China* by William Blaeu, 1623, M.S.I. 119 *Macao* by T. de Bry, BrL., L; *Detail of Blaeu's map showing natives of Asia*, M.S.I., R. 120 *Dutch merchants using chopsticks* from a Japanese scroll, B.A.L., T; *Chinese Galley*, by T. de Bry, N.M.M. (442), B. 121 *Chinese Annunciation*, BrL., (or 59b 19/2), T; *Landship and palanquin*, by T. de Bry, Newberry Library, Chicago, B. 122 *Portuguese and horses* from a Japanese screen, Kobe City Art Museum, Japan, T; *Chinese mandarin*, BrL., BL; *Chinese flower seller* by T. de Bry, BrL., BR. 123 *Macao*, by T. de Bry, F.I., London. 124 *Massacre of Christians*, Chiesa del Gesu, Rome/Scala, T; *Portuguese merchants*, detail from a Japanese screen, The Avery Brundage Collection, Asian Art Museum, San Francisco, B. 125 *Slave market in Brazil*, A.K.G. 126 *Map of West Africa*, M.S.I. 127 *Elmina*, West Africa, M.S.I., T; *Benin ivory*, BrM./Aspect Picture Library, London, B. 128 *Magellan*, M.A.S., T; *Francis Drake*, National Portrait Gallery, London, M. 128-129 *Prince Maurice in the Philippines*, N.M.M. (5096) B. 129 *Drake's brass plate*, found near San Francisco, M.S.I. 130-131 Map by Swanston Publications Ltd. 132 *Drake in Santa Domingo*, New York Public Library, B.A.L. 133 *Map of Africa* by Descalier, Robert Harding Photo Library, London. 134 *Algerian slave market* by T. de Bry, F.I. 135 *Benin city*, M.S.I., T; *Slave and traders*, BrL., B. 136 *Slave hunter* , W.F.A., L; *John Hawkins*, Plymouth City Museum, Plymouth, R. 137 Illustration by Gill Tomblin. 138 *Iron shackles*, from an 18th century engraving, F.I., T; *Slave ship* from an 18th-century engraving F.I., B. 139 *Arab caravan*, M.S.I., T; *Sugar mill*, M.S.I., B. 140 *Slaves dancing*, A.K.G., T; *Portuguese hunter*, Palace of Obas, Benin, W.F.A., B. 141 *Capturing slaves in Benin*, by T. de Bry, M.S.I. 142 *Sugar mill*, T.B.A. 143 *Map of Pacific*, N.M.M./M.S.I. 144 *New Guinea hunters*, from a contemporary Spanish illustration, Archivo di Simancas, Valladolid. 145 *Papuan*, Dagli Orti, Paris, T; *Death of Magellan* , Newberry Library, Chicago, B. 146 *Pineapple* by John White, BrM. 147 *Body painting in the Philippines*, Boxer Codex, University of Indiana/Newberry Library, Chicago, T; *Hernando de Grijalva*, 1537, M.A.S., B. 148 *Pacific canoes*, N.M.M. (740) /M.S.I., T; *Polynesian stick chart*, M.S.I., B. 149 *Drawings by Francesco Suarez to illustrate Murillo Velarde's map of the Philippines: a Spanish mestizo's family*, L; *a Moluccan and a Japanese*, R. 150 *Commemorative tile*, T.B.A., T; *Spanish adventurers*, M.S.I., ML; *Vespucci woodcut*, B.A.L., MR; *Herbal*, T.B.A., B; 151 *Victoria*, T.B.A., TM; *Tenochtitlan*, E.T.A., TR; *Utopia*, Hulton Deutsch, MM; *Grinding cocoa*, T.B.A., MR; *Loading horses*, Bancroft Library, University of California, BL. 152 *Cartier in Canada*, M.S.I., TL; *Ivan the Terrible*, T.B.A., TR; *Treating syphilis*, T.B.A., ML; *Spanish ruff*, E.T.A., MR; *Diving bell*, Dagli Orti, Paris, B. 153 *Elizabeth I*, National Portrait Gallery, London, TL; *Pilgrim's patent*, M.S.I., TR;. *Smokers*, T.B.A., ML; *Tobacco plant*, T.B.A., MR; *Arquebus*, Wim Swaan, New York, BL. 154 *Frobisher*, Bodleian Library, Oxford, T; *Potato plant*, T.B.A., ML; *Scenes from Elizabeth I's reign*, T.B.A., MR; *Ortelius' World Map*, Michael Holford, B. 155 *William Barents' Journey*, E.T.A., TL; *Dutch atrocities*, B.A.L., TR; *Don Quixote*, T.B.A., M; *Galileo's telescope*, Scala, B.

The publishers thank the following for their kind permission to quote passages from the publications below:
Cambridge University Press. *The Petty Dealer, a letter from Andrea Garcia: Letters and People of the Spanish Indies, Sixteenth Century*, edited by James Lockhart and Enrique Otte, 1976; *The Travels and Controversies of Friar Domingo Navarette, 1618-1686*, edited by J.S. Cummins, 1962.
Oxford University Press. *The Oxford Book of Exploration* edited by Robin Hanbury-Tenison 1993; the extracts quoted are from *The Voyages of Jacques Cartier (Publications of the Public Archive of Canada, no. 11)* translated by H.P. Biggar, Ottawa, 1924.
Oxford University Press, New York. *The Great Explorers: The European Discovery of America*, by Samuel Eliot Morison, 1978.
Random House. *My Voyage Around the World* , by Francesco Carletti, translated by Hubert Weinstock, 1964.
Weidenfeld and Nicolson. *Africa: History of a Continent* , by Basil Davidson, 1966.
Westview Press. *Latin American Civilisation, History and Society 1492 to the Present* , edited by Benjamin Keen, 1991.

Front cover: *Vasco da Gama*, M.A.S., TL; illustration by Paul Wright, ML; *Spanish coins*, Coin Department, BrM., MR; *Peruvian figure*, American Museum of Natural History/Photography John Bigelow Taylor, BL; *Fish sellers from Winter* by Van Valkenborgh, Giraudon, Paris, BC; *watercolour of Indian*, Germanisches National museum, Nuremburg BR.

Back cover: *Engraving of a sea monster*, T.B.A., TL; *Astrolabe*, N.M.M. (8450), TC; *Detail of scene in Venice by Bassano*, Museo Real Academia de Bellas Artes, Madrid, B.A.L., TR; *Map of the Caribbean*, c. 1540, MS129 A24 fol 23v and 24r, Koninklijke Bibliotheek, The Hague, M; *Indian with cacao utensils*, T.B.A., BL; *Wooden bowls from the Mary Rose*, Mary Rose Trust, Portsmouth, BR.

59-006-4